DO WORLD BANK AND IMF POLICIES WORK?

Also by Shahrukh Rafi Khan

HANDING BACK RURAL WATER SUPPLY SCHEMES TO COMMUNITIES: A Case for Collective Action

JUST DEVELOPMENT: Beyond Adjustment with a Human Face

FIFTY YEARS OF PAKISTAN'S ECONOMY: Traditional Issues and New Concerns

Do World Bank and IMF Policies Work?

Shahrukh Rafi Khan
Executive Director
Sustainable Development Policy Institute
Islamabad
Pakistan

palgrave

Published by PALGRAVE
Houndmills, Basingstoke, Hampshire RG21 6XS and
175 Fifth Avenue, New York, N. Y. 10010
Companies and representatives throughout the world

PALGRAVE is the new global academic imprint of
St. Martin's Press LLC Scholarly and Reference Division and
Palgrave Publishers Ltd (formerly Macmillan Press Ltd).

Outside North America
ISBN 0–333–73361–4

In North America
ISBN 0–312–21704–8

This book is printed on paper suitable for recycling and made from fully managed and sustained forest sources.

A catalogue record for this book is available from the British Library.

Library of Congress Cataloging-in-Publication Data
Khan, Shahrukh Rafi.
Do World Bank and IMF policies work? / Shahrukh Rafi Khan.
p. cm.
Includes bibliographical references and index.
ISBN 0–312–21704–8 (cloth)
1. World Bank. 2. International Monetary Fund. 3. Banks and banking, International. I. Title.
HG3881.5.W57K48 1998
332.1'5—dc21 98–27631
CIP

10 9 8 7 6 5 4 3 2
08 07 06 05 04 03 02 01

Printed and bound in Great Britain by
Antony Rowe Ltd, Chippenham, Wiltshire

For Stephanie, Sophia and Lila

Contents

List of Tables

Introduction

Do World Bank and IMF policies work? The idea of writing or editing a book on this topic first came to mind when I was teaching a course in development economics at Vassar College. Teaching structural adjustment (SA) as the central element of a development economics course is unavoidable, since it represents the most predominant set of economic policies confronting poor countries. Also, it can provide a logical and coherent way of structuring a course since its scope is vast and it provides an entry point to most sectoral issues and to the debate on various schools of thought in development economics, both on a broad level and on a sectoral level. The difficulty I confronted in teaching such a course was finding evidence to report. Much of the evidence was of a cross-country nature, which many scholars found unsatisfactory. Country case studies were available, but they rarely used time series data in a systematic way.

When I joined the Sustainable Development Policy Institute (SDPI) in Pakistan over four years ago, a research programme on SA was already underway, inspired by the UNICEF sponsored book titled *Adjustment With a Human Face* by Cornia, Jolly and Stewart (1987). The research at SDPI resulted in the publication of *Just Development: Beyond Adjustment with a Human Face*.[1] This book is intended to be an empirical complement to *Just Development* and it shares the latter's concern for the poor and the vulnerable.

To find out whether structural adjustment works, it is necessary to establish how SA is to be assessed and then to conduct the necessary empirical exercises. From the perspective of the Bretton Woods Institutions, success or failure can be defined by looking at whether 'conditionalities' for specific loans are being met. Such conditions vary a great deal and could include, for example, requiring a government to conform to macro-targets such as deficit and money supply reductions, liberalizing the interest rate and the exchange rate, reducing tariffs and eliminating subsidies.

These prescriptions emerge from an economic philosophy now commonly referred to as neo-liberalism which focuses mainly on efficiency and market production. Thus the goal of the prescribed conditions can be viewed as economic efficiency and growth.[2] Ideally, then, the researcher needs to identify the mechanisms that link particular policies to particular effects and then engage in empirical measurement.

Not all agree that the neo-liberal paradigm offers the best set of economic policies. We briefly cite alternative critiques here to set the debate in perspective and to introduce the approach to assessing SA adopted in this book. These critiques of neo-liberalism can be bifurcated into external and internal critiques. The external critique rejects the neo-liberal paradigm altogether, setting the problem and its solution in different domains. The prominent alternative critiques include neo-Marxism (perhaps temporarily in retreat), neo-structuralism (could be viewed as a version of institutional economics), grassroots development (an alternative version of institutional economics focusing on rural development and particularly on collective action issues), and the property rights and public choice perspective, which can incorporate governance issues.

The internal critique stays on neo-liberal ground and argues that specific remedies may not work and or that a particularly kind of sequencing may be called for. This critique represents 'friendly fire' in that it is market friendly or does not reject the paradigm but looks for more effective remedies. However, there are also alternative internal critiques from national and political economic perspectives.

The focus of the national perspective is to look at specific policies from the point of view of the country undergoing structural reform. A national perspective would recognize that there may be at least a long-term conflict of interest between the interests of lenders who require being paid back and that of the borrowing country. For example, a devaluation may improve the balance of payments of a reforming country in the short run and hence prevent default. However, whether it helps in the long run is a more complicated question, and the answer is likely to differ for each country. Among other things, the outcome depends on the relative demand and supply elasticities of imports and exports. Also, production costs go up due to more expensive imports in local currency terms and these higher costs could lead to one-time higher price increases. There is of course a danger that inflationary expectations might be fanned by this one-time price increase. If so, the result would be ongoing inflation. Persistent higher costs of production could also hurt exports. Hence there is a real danger confronting poor economies of a vicious cycle of devaluation, inflation, and balance of payment disequilibrium resulting in pressures for further devaluation. This is particularly so when the country suffers from a fiscal imbalance which also feeds into the inflationary cycle.

Consider the case of liberalizing foreign direct investment (FDI). There is no question that poor countries can benefit from access to technologies, marketing and managerial skills that can accompany FDI. However, a nationalistic fear is often expressed that the price of welcoming FDI could be that of wiping out domestic industry. If local industries lack competition, foreign investment may be one welcome antidote. If that is not the issue, a hard-nosed and selective attitude towards foreign investment may be warranted. Once again, there is no substitute for a case by case empirical examination if a reasonably honest administrative capacity exists. If it does not, many have rightly recognized that improved management, rather than liberalization, should be first on the reform agenda.

While one of our approaches to assessing SA is that of adopting a national perspective, our insistence is that evidence rather than rhetoric or ideology should guide national policy. Those reforms which are in the national interest should be implemented anyway. However, until LDCs get their fiscal house in order, they can use these reforms as leverage for loans. Those not in the national interest should be resisted. A solid foundation of empirical evidence would help in the negotiation process.

There is an important qualification to what is stated in the paragraph above. On many issues, it is not at all clear what the national interest means. In fact, since structural reforms usually have a varying impact by social class, one invariably needs to go beyond thinking in broad categories such as the national interest. Thus, apart from a national perspective on assessing structural adjustment, we also adopt a political economic perspective. Here the focus is on identifying the gainers and losers resulting from specific structural adjustment policies such as financial sector reform, privatization or trade liberalization. In addition, we also assess the overall impact of structural adjustment on labour and the poor as well as its gender, health, environmental and food security impact.

Pakistan is a poor country. Its per capita GNP of $460 in 1995 ranked it among the lowest-income countries according to World Bank categorization.[3] It also ranked among the least developed countries on the UNDP human development scale.[4] It is thus clear that the country needs to adopt sensible economic policies. In most of this book, our analysis begins in the early seventies, after the splitting up of the country, since consistent time series are available only from then onwards. Prior to that, aggregate data include both West Pakistan (now Pakistan) and East Pakistan (now Bangladesh). We have divided this period into three sub-periods which represent significant shifts in policy or changes in administration. The first sub-period from 1971 to 1977 represents the populist administration of Zulfiqar Ali Bhutto.[5]

Bhutto's populism was a response to the 'crony capitalism'-driven inequalities of the Ayub Khan decade of 1958–68. The radical ideas of the 1960s found expression in nationalization and extensive state intervention. However, the perceived failure of a direct interventionist approach, which came to be known as 'dirigism' in the literature, via planning, controls, regulation and nationalization brought the market approach back into ascendancy in the 1980s. This change in economic philosophy was mirrored in Pakistan. Reforms suggested by the market approach included privatization, deregulation and market determination of key macro prices such as the interest rate and the exchange rate. External competition was encouraged by liberalizing foreign trade.

The military regime of Zia-ul-Haque (1977–88) began the era of liberalization. However, the intensive phase of structural adjustment began with the first Benazir Bhutto administration following the Zia period and has continued since. While all democratic regimes since 1988 have identified with the basic neo-liberal ideology and substantive sectoral structural adjustments have occurred, the IMF has complained about the violation of conditionalities, as will be explained in the next section.

In the next section we piece together an account of structural adjustment policies in Pakistan, in the third section we review method, in the fourth section we present a brief outline of the book, and in the final section we summarize the objectives of the book.

STRUCTURAL ADJUSTMENT PROGRAMMES IN PAKISTAN

Pakistan's first agreement with the IMF dates back to 1958. This was a stand-by loan for SDR 25 million, but it was not utilized. ('SDR' means 'Special Drawing Rights', an IMF accounting created for settling debts. It started out as equal to $1, but is now more than that.) Since the first plea to the IMF for assistance in 1978–9 by the Zia regime, some form of conditionality in return for loans has become a permanent feature in the economic landscape of the country.[6] Pakistan and the IMF signed a Trust Fund Loan for 1979–80. In the following year, Pakistan negotiated a three-year Extended Fund Facility (EFF) for 1980–1 to 1982–3. In 1983–4 the IMF offered another Structural Adjustment Loan (SAL) which the government refused, presumably to avoid conditionality, but also because its foreign exchange reserves had recovered to over $2 billion mainly due to large remittances from overseas workers. As an alternative, a series of sectoral loans – for agriculture, industry, energy and the financial sector – were negotiated with the World Bank. Each loan was conditional upon reforms in the specific sector, with no cross-conditionality across sectors.

As earlier mentioned, the Zia-ul-Haq regime began the process of liberalization. However, after Zia's death, towards the end of the 1987–8 fiscal year when elections were pending, the more concerted period of adjustment began. A surge in imports, coupled with a sharp reduction in workers' remittances, drove the current account deficit up to 4.4 per cent of the GDP.

The budget deficit in the same year shot to a record level of 8.5 per cent of the GDP.[7] The government was not equipped to deal with these persistent macroeconomic imbalances and began to negotiate with the IMF and the World Bank for the disbursement of a series of loans under the Structural Adjustment Facility (SAF).[8] This was to be accompanied by a package of structural reforms. The assistance was to be divided between the IMF's general purpose loan, the WB's sectoral loans and the ADB's sectoral loans.

The first three-year Structural Adjustment Facility for $2.1 billion was ratified and signed on December 28, 1988. Besides other conditionalities, this called for a substantial reduction in the budgetary deficit from 8.5 to 4.8 per cent of GDP over the 1988–9 to 1990–1 period. To meet these objectives, the revenue–GDP ratio was to be raised to 20 per cent by 1990–1 through a series of measures which included the extension of the general sales tax to cover at least 30 per cent of domestic industrial production, and reforms in the tax collection and assessment systems. The expenditure–GDP ratio was to be contained to less than 25 per cent of the GDP, largely through reductions in subsidies. The resource mobilization measures proposed by the programme included the withdrawal of exemptions from custom duties, imposition of user charges and improvement in tax administration. The conditionalities also included ensuring controls on credit expansion and instituting a series of financial and exchange-rate reforms.

The government responded to these conditionalities immediately and did institute a series of reforms, but these remained largely unsuccessful in achieving the performance criteria set by the donor agencies. The government subsequently renegotiated for a one-year extension for meeting specified targets.

The objectives of the 1991–4 structural adjustment programme were set down in a memorandum at the time of the agreement. The broad objectives to be achieved over a three-year period largely remained consistent with the earlier agreement. They were an annual growth rate of GDP of at least 5.5 per cent of GDP, increase in foreign exchange reserves to at least 4 weeks of imports, decrease in the external debt ratio from 31 to 25 per cent of GDP, decrease in fiscal deficit eventually from 8.5 to 4.5 per cent of GDP, increase in domestic savings from 9 to 10 per cent of GDP, increase in gross investment from 16 to 19 per cent of GDP, reduction in domestic borrowing for budgetary support to 4 per cent of GDP, bank borrowing of no more than 1 per cent of GDP, decreased reliance on taxes on international trade, especially import duties, and an expansion of the tax base.

In August 1993, the interim government set about negotiating a stand-by agreement with the Bank and the Fund, and announced a set of economic reforms that essentially set the guidelines for the economic policies of the next government. In December 1993, the newly elected government formalized the agreement with these agencies by submitting a request for another three-year Structural Adjustment Facility loan of SDR 606.6 million.[9] This proposal was approved in February 1994, and carried with it an even more stringent set of conditionalities. This time the emphasis was on trade reforms including the elimination of multiple exchange-rate practices, full convertibility of the rupee and stringent tariff reduction over a three-year period. Taxation reforms suggested included the extension of the general sales tax to cover almost all items on the free list and all businesses in the trading and services sectors as well as the imposition of further excise duties on utilities. The government was also bound to eliminate all subsidies on fertilizers within three years, as well as to the reduction or elimination of subsidies on other agricultural inputs. The prices of output in this sector were also to be liberalized. Other conditionalities related to further financial liberalization, the continuation of the privatization programme and sustained expenditure on the social sectors through the Social Action Plan (SAP).

However, the situation in 1994–5 was more difficult than that in 1988–9. The Gulf war led to a drop in remittances. Added to this was the disruption of trade with Middle Eastern countries which jacked up the total loss in foreign exchange earnings to approximately $2 billion. Finally, political differences led to the winding down and termination of bilateral aid from the USA, which made generating additional revenues more necessary.

The performance criteria of the 1994 extended SAF agreement required the budget deficit to be restricted to 4 per cent of GDP, inflation contained to 7 per cent and the highest import tariff reduced to 70 per cent in 1994–5, 45 per cent in 1995–6 and 35 per cent in 1996–7. However, due to political compulsions and adverse financial considerations, described in the paragraph above, in framing the 1994–5 budget, Pakistan reneged on the revenue and tariff targets. This lead to the angry cancellation by the IMF of the Structural Adjustment Facility. The government of Pakistan subsequently became suitably contrite, made all the proper noises about keeping within specified targets, and hoped for a resumption of the SAF. While an SAF was not granted by the IMF, a stand-by loan for balance of payments support was agreed to.

Negotiations were impeded by Pakistan's loss of credibility with the IMF. This occurred both because performance criteria were viewed as being wilfully ignored and because the government was viewed as doctoring the books. Economic mismanagement, as indicated by the rapid decline in the foreign exchange reserves and the stock-market index, by the likelihood of default on international debt obligations, and by the downgrading of Pakistan's international credit rating was cited as one of the main reasons for constitutionally terminating Benazir Bhutto's government in October 1996. The care-taker government had extensive discussions with the Bretton Woods Institutions to continue the reform process and to find ways of ensuring its continuity. The second tranche of the stand-by agreement was released at the end of January 1997, shortly before the elections scheduled for early February 1997. This appears to have been done because the conditions of reducing expenditure by Rs 11 billion, enhancing taxes and reducing borrowing by Rs 12 billion were met by the caretakers.[10]

The newly elected Nawaz Sharif government (1997–) decided to cancel the expensive stand-by agreement and instead initiated further structural adjustment reforms as a prelude to seeking an agreement with the IMF on an ESAF. These reforms include basic tax reforms (reducing the rates and enhancing the base) and the reduction of import duties (maximum statutory duty reduced from 65 per cent to 45 per cent). The IMF in principle expressed support for these reforms and on 21 October 1997 the IMF approved a three-year ESAF/EFF loan package for Pakistan worth $1.56 billion. The conditions the government made a commitment to implement include good governance and civil service reforms, a value added tax at the retail stage, an income based, rather than the current land based, agricultural tax, tax administration reform, enhanced privatization, financial sector reforms and capital market reforms, 8.7 per cent devaluation and large-scale downsizing in the public sector. The government also made commitments to give priority to the social sectors and the environment. The performance criteria included achieving by end of programme, compared to 1996–7, an average growth rate of real GDP of 5–6 per cent, progressively reducing inflation from 11.7 per cent to 7 per cent, reducing the current account deficit from 6.4 to between 4 and 4.5 per cent, reducing the budget deficit from 6.1 to 4 per cent and increasing the national saving rate from 12 to 15 per cent.

Concentrating solely on performance criteria is misleading. While the violation of such criteria has provoked the IMF's ire, this does not mean that fundamental structural adjustment policies have not been instituted in the various sectors. We will indicate in the present book that far-reaching structural reforms have been undertaken in almost all sectors and that these reforms have had significant impact. Cross-conditionality also ensures implementation of sector loan conditionalities. For example, the Pakistani press speculated that the second tranche ($76.32 million) of the stand-by agreement with the IMF in February 1997 was being withheld until the Banking Sector Reform conditionalities (privatization, more autonomy for the State Bank) for a $300 million World Bank loan were met. The cross-conditionalities were written into the IMF stand-by agreement.

In Pakistan, as elsewhere, structural adjustment has come under sharp criticism for a single-minded focus on economic growth and neglect of the social sectors. Probably the most influential of such criticisms was the earlier mentioned UNICEF sponsored book titled *Adjustment With a Human Face*. Policies to give adjustment in Pakistan a human face have emerged, based essentially on the old basic needs approach, but now referred to as human development. In Pakistan it has taken the shape of a World Bank endorsed and partially World Bank funded Social Action Plan, which we will review in the second part of the book. There is a more explicit focus now on making the poor better market players by ensuring investment in their education and health. In this regard, the two SAPs (the Structural Adjustment Programme and the Social Action Plan) are complementary.

METHOD

Testing hypotheses using Pakistani time series data is methodologically the most straight-forward of our tasks. However, even here there is much ground for quibbling. For example, consider testing hypotheses concerning interest rate liberalization. When looking at historic data, one certainly finds enough variation in the interest rate. However, inferring from the past into the future era of structural adjustment, when the policy and economic environment have changed, remains problematic. The same criticism would apply to testing the impact of the depreciation of the real effective exchange rate on the balance of trade. Further criticism could be levelled at the partial nature of such analyses and the limited number of observations available.

Assessing the overall social impact of structural adjustment in the second part of the book is even more methodologically problematic. Most empirical work on the impact of structural adjustment confronts the problem of establishing causality, since it is impossible to replay history to see what the condition of the relevant social group would have been without structural adjustment. Simulation, using computable general equilibrium models or social accounting matrices, could provide a way around this. While making defensible assumptions when using such methods is certainly a challenge, the paucity of relevant observations is a more serious constraint in this case.

The lack of counterfactuals deters only the purist, while the rest pursue other lines of inquiry making the relevant qualifications.[11] One such qualified line of inquiry is 'before–after' studies. Here one has to make the assumption that the change observed by such studies can be attributed predominantly to the impact of structural adjustment. Since many other social and economic trends could be operating independently of structural adjustment, such evidence is at best viewed as suspect.

At times it is possible to go beyond this. Consider the impact of structural adjustment on women. While investigating the role of women as producers in the agricultural sector, it is possible to identify how price liberalization affected the agricultural goods price structure and subsequently how the cropping pattern changed. Given independent information on female labour intensity by cropping pattern, it would be possible to infer how structural adjustment is likely to have affected agricultural employment of women.

Again, it is possible to see how reform-induced subsidy cuts changed prices of essentials and how this altered consumption patterns and nutritional intake over time. Thus, women may change consumption patterns by switching to cheaper foods, economizing on fuel, cutting expenditures on consumer durables and attempting communal buying. As mothers, women may have to confront cuts in basic social services like health, education and water supply or deal with new user charges for such services. Cuts in social sector expenditures may raise morbidity rates, decrease life expectancy and reduce educational attainment. Thus, it may be possible in some cases to isolate specific structural adjustment polices and investigate their impact using a 'before–after' scenario. Since the intensive period of structural adjustment reform in Pakistan started after 1988, we compare the period following 1987/8 to earlier periods when using this method.

Such analyses are done here with caution and when it appears that teasing out the relevant impact may be possible. However, we do so with many qualifications and state *ad nauseam* that the results should be viewed as suggestive. Even so, this method is preferred to the cross-country approaches that have often been used to establish a case for particular structural reforms or for the set of policies as a whole. Thus while our findings are not conclusive, as social science evidence rarely is, we also feel that the burden of proof should be on those who advocate particular policies.

OUTLINE

This book has two parts. The first part of the book tests hypotheses that are embodied in a structural adjustment package, such as the expected positive impact of interest rate liberalization on financial deepening and savings, or the expected positive impact of exchange-rate liberalization on the balance of trade. The second part of the book focuses on assessing the overall social impact of structural adjustment policies.

Part I begins with an overview chapter in which we explore the aggregate impact of aid, the vehicle introducing structural adjustment, on economic growth. This is followed by various chapters that investigate structural adjustment hypotheses at the sectoral level. These include hypotheses pertaining to financial sector reform, exchange-rate liberalization, privatization, industrialization and export promotion. In Part II, the overall impact of structural adjustment on labour and the poor, women, health, environment and food security are explored.

The findings in Part I are mixed. In some cases there is support for SA prescriptions. Thus privatization is consistent with higher productivity and trade liberalization is consistent with successful export promotion in the consumer goods sector. In other cases, such as those of financial sector reform and exchange-rate liberalization, we find little support for the SA hypotheses. The findings in Part II are more overwhelmingly negative to date, except in the health sector. During the intensive phase of structural adjustment, poverty increased and income distribution worsened. There is little positive to report about the changing social and economic status of women, and it appears that conditions worsened for them in their productive and reproductive roles during the structural adjustment period. The liberali-zation in the agricultural sector seems to be accompanied by severe adverse effects on the environment and increasing concentration of land ownership.

We invite the reader to turn to Chapters 1–5 for a more detailed evaluation of the hypotheses outlined above, and Chapters 6–10 for the overall social impact of structural adjustment in Pakistan. We turn now briefly to summarizing the book's objectives.

OBJECTIVES AND ACKNOWLEDGEMENTS

Our assessment of SA in Pakistan is not exhaustive. For the most part, we picked hypotheses for testing where it appeared that, methodologically, a reasonable assessment was possible. In assessing overall impact, we chose issues and topics we believed to be of policy significance. Our purpose was to conduct empirical analysis to show how the national interest and the poor and vulnerable fare under SA.

As earlier indicated, our results are mixed. These results show that while some policies like trade reform and privatization have clear national benefits as suggested by maintained SA hypotheses, other policies like financial liberalization and devaluation have more ambiguous effects that call into question the maintained hypotheses. Also, during the last and most intense bout of structural adjustment in Pakistan, the social and economic condition of the poor has worsened. Our reaction to this is not to reject market economics but to emphasize that multilateral and bilateral agencies should be more sensitive to what we refer to as national and political economic perspectives when framing SA policies.

To summarize, this book has four objectives. The first is to establish a case for assessing SA from a national and political economic perspective. We demonstrate this by using the case of Pakistan and, in so doing, address important policy issues for Pakistan. The second is to emphasize the importance of relying on evidence rather than ideology, rhetoric or anecdotes. In so doing, we contribute to the body of evidence on structural adjustment for enabling sensible discourse. The third is to address economists and other scholars who are interested in Pakistan in particular and South Asia in general. Finally, this book is intended to provide resource material for theses and papers in development economics courses. The chapters in this book demonstrate how specific hypotheses in a different context could be tested using standard tools of economic analysis and how secondary data can be marshalled to identify the social impact of specific policies or a set of policies.

This book has been written as a series of papers, mostly in response to conference invitations. Several have been co-authored with Safiya Aftab and others written with her assistance, and therefore I owe her the utmost thanks. Other co-authorships and acknowledgements are mentioned in the first note of each chapter. Thanks are also due in particular to Tariq Banuri for helpful suggestions on the introduction and on most of the other chapters. Sajid Kazmi provided valuable assistance in updating the chapters and co-authored a chapter. Arshad Khursheed and M. D. Malik provided invaluable help in getting the manuscript into shape for publication. Since I was so busy with other responsibilities at this point, without their patient help, I might have given up and certainly not met the deadline. Thanks are also due to many individuals at the Sustainable Development Policy Institute (SDPI), including, in particular, Iftikhar Ahmad, Kaiser Bengali, Saba Khattak, Zia Mian and Tariq Rehman, for creating an atmosphere that encouraged me to pursue this work, and to SDPI where, between other tasks, this research was conducted. Finally, many thanks are due to my editor, Cameron Laux.

NOTES

1. Eds Banuri, Khan and Mahmood (1997).
2. Broader social indicators such as the Human Development Indicators have become more important in assessing performance. This is partly because the linkage of social development and economic growth has been acknowledged.
3. *World Development Report 1997* (1997, p. 214). Its purchasing power parity GNP per capita is $2,230.
4. *Human Development Report 1997* (p. 148). Ranked 139th out of 175 countries, it ranked highest among the low human development group of countries.
5. Each of these sub-periods is referred to as a period in the rest of the book.
6. The following description of structural adjustment agreements is partly based on sections of chapter 5 of *Just Development*, eds Banuri, Khan and Mahmood (1997) and partly on press reports. Press reports have to be relied on since most World Bank and IMF documents are confidential and selectively released to the press. Unfortunately, it is difficult to piece together a story from these clippings. There are numerous inconsistencies in numbers and, in a highly charged political atmosphere, many journalists assume partisan positions.
7. *Economic Survey 1995–96*, Statistical Appendix (1996, p. 138, p. 160).
8. SAF loans are designed to address immediate balance of payments (BOP) crises. They may provide general import financing or may be used to finance the import needs of a particular sector. Although the loans are almost always meant to correct BOP difficulties, there is a string of conditionalities attached to them which relate to all sectors of the economy and which are aimed at bringing about fundamental changes in the macroeconomic structure of the economy.
9. This was the biggest ever loan request received by the Fund under the SAF, according to *Dawn* (Pakistan), 21 Jan. 1994.
10. On 1 January 1998 the Pakistan rupee (which is on a managed float) for dollar exchange rate was Rs 46.27 for one dollar.
11. Toye, 1995, pp. 13–18.

REFERENCES

Banuri, T., S. R. Khan and M. Mahmood (eds), 1997, *Just Development: Beyond Adjustment with a Human Face* (Karachi: Oxford University Press).

Cornia, G. A., R. Jolly and F. Stewart, 1987, *Adjustment with a Human Face: Protecting the Vulnerable and Promoting Growth*. (New York: Oxford University Press).

Toye, J., 1995, *Structural Adjustment and Employment Policies: Issues and Experience* (Geneva: International Labour Organization).

UNDP, 1997, *Human Development Report 1997* (New York: Oxford University Press).

World Bank, 1997, *World Development Report 1997* (New York: Oxford University Press).

Part I Testing Hypotheses

1 Structural Adjustment, Aid, Debt and Growth[1]

INTRODUCTION[2]

Aid theory in the early period of thinking in economic development was straightforward. The developing countries were perceived to be in need of substantial investments in infrastructure and capital which could not be financed internally. According to the traditional two-gap theory, aid was necessary to bridge both the savings–investment gap and the trade gap in developing countries, and was thus considered indispensable. Aid was advocated for establishing the preconditions for growth by strengthening institutions and building infrastructure and for enhancing growth via resources for investment. The increase in economic activity generated by aid-supported investments was expected to increase output growth, eventually generating enough income to render aid superfluous.

Ridell (1987) and White (1992) present rich reviews of the long and as yet unresolved debates. For applied economists, the message is that most attempts at assessing the impact of aid on saving, investment and growth suffer from various flaws. These include unresolved theoretical issues, faulty data, particularly for cross-country analysis, specification errors that call into question the scientific rigour of the findings and the difficulty in modelling the mechanisms via which aid actually impacts various macroeconomic variables including growth.[3]

These reviews and the conclusions they reach would give pause to applied economists seeking to empirically test the aid–growth association as we do in this chapter. We proceed because our contention is that causality and sensitivity tests that have been used elsewhere can make a contribution to the empirical debate on the association of aid with economic growth by identifying empirical regularities. The method used in this chapter is straightforward, and time series data for other countries are readily available in the sources cited; thus the research done for this chapter could easily be replicated for other countries, given the availability of specific country knowledge.

In the next section, we review how the terms of aid have been changing over time in Pakistan. Later we describe the method and data sources and present the findings. We end with a discussion of the findings.

AID TERMS AND THE STRUCTURE OF DEBT

While Pakistan's foreign debt is large ($20.4 billion in 1993 in nominal terms), and has been growing rapidly (at an annual average rate of 7.8 per cent between 1972 to 1993), in a cross-country perspective it is still modest. Pakistan's total long-term debt in 1992 was 57 per cent below what one might expect it to be given its per capita GDP (in purchasing power parity terms) and population.[4] However, other than this, there is little encouraging that can be said about the current change in Pakistan's debt situation and about how the terms on which Pakistan receives aid over time have changed.

Concessional aid as a percentage of the total has declined, the average interest rate has increased, the maturity period has decreased, the net transfer has decreased and the grant element has decreased. Thus Pakistan's debt, the debt/GDP ratio, debt/export ratio and debt/service ratio have increased, particularly since 1987/8 when the more intensive phase of the structural adjustment period started. In the summary tables below, we present evidence to back these statements. Our analysis here covers the period 1972–3 to 1992–3.[5]

As mentioned above, Table 1.1 shows that the terms on which Pakistan has received aid over time have worsened across the board. The average maturity period of loans, grant element in loans and concessional aid as a percentage of the total have all declined. The average interest rate on which loans were contracted increased by one percentage point at a time when market interest rates were declining. Thus in the 1988–9 to 1992–3 period, the loans were contracted at only 2 per cent below the market interest rate, down from 6 per cent below in the 1977–8 to 1987–8 period.

Table 1.1 Terms of debt

Years	Average interest rate	Average market interest rate@	Average maturity period years	Average grant element	Concessional aid as a % of total
1972–3/ 1976–7	4	na	28	48	73
1976–8/ 1987–8	5	11.2	27	42	69
1988–9/ 1992–3	5	6.7	22	37	56

Source: *World Debt Tables*, World Bank
Notes: @ = LIBOR for one year $ deposits (*International Financial Statistics Yearbook* 1994, IMF, Washington, DC, p. 96)

Table 1.2 Debt ratios and debt indicators

Period	Average debt–GNP ratio	Average debt service export ratio	Average transfer (billion $)	Average net transfer as a % of GNP	Nominal end period debt (billion $s)
1972–3/ 1976–7	57	0.21	0.51	5.08	6.8
1977–8/ 1987–8	42	0.20	0.16	0.87	13.9
1988–9/ 1992–3	48	0.24	0.14	0.30	20.4

Source: *World Debt Tables*, World Bank

With the worsening of the terms of the debt, one would expect the debt ratios to rise and debt indicators to worsen, particularly when the debt stock was increasing. This is evident from Table 1.2.

The debt–GNP ratio was exceptionally high in the 1970s, partly due to lower GNP growth rates. It rose 6 per cent since 1988–9, which represents the start of the intensive bouts of structural adjustment, compared to the earlier period. While debt has been steadily mounting (from $6.8 billion in 1977 to $20.4 billion in 1993), the net transfer (gross inflows minus principal and interest payments) has rapidly declined. Thus, it declined from a substantive 5.1 per cent of GNP in 1972–3/1976–7 to 0.3 of one per cent in 1988–9/1992–3.

Sustainable debt management is possible if the likely trajectory of resource inflows will exceed or at least converge on the likely trajectory of resource outflows. The important outflows are imports and debt servicing and the important inflows are exports and remittances. Based on these flows, we compared debt servicing with the sum of remittances and export revenues minus the import bill. As a percentage of the GNP, this sum amounted to a negative 32.9 per cent in the first period (1972–3/1976–7), improved to 3.10 per cent (due to remittances) in the second period (1977–8/1987–8), but worsened again to 24.9 per cent in the third period (1978–9/1992–3). The worsening of this inflow/outflow balance resulted from both a decline in remittances and the worsening of the balance of trade. The result is that Pakistan is now in a non-sustainable situation with regards to managing its debt comfortably.

Given this analysis and the changing terms under which Pakistan is receiving aid, there is every likelihood that the debt/GDP ratio will continue to rise. Pakistan is in an all too familiar situation – as the country's dependence on foreign aid increases, the terms and conditions of aid inflows are becoming all the more stringent. Not only does debt repayment threaten to become 'an exchange-rate drag' in perpetuity,[6] the conditionality under which aid has been received since the later 1980s have also become more extensive and more stringent.[7] The total debt and debt ratios should be expected to improve over time if the aid, as the original theory suggested, enhanced growth and enabled the debt to be retired.

AID AND ECONOMIC GROWTH: METHOD AND DATA

We have used two simple approaches to test the association of aid and output.[8] Our interest is in the impact of aid, as an aggregate variable, on economic growth. This is because policy leverage is conditional on the total sum of loan and grant aid. None the less, we also explored the separate impact of grants (with and without technical assistance) on economic growth.

Granger Causality Test for Aid–Output Association

Output could be positively influenced by aid by relaxing the saving and import constraint. On the other hand, higher output could be interpreted to be the outcome of the 'right' economic policies and rewarded by more aid.[9] Thus, success may breed more aid as donors tire of putting money in what are perceived as bottomless pits, and opt to back the winners.[10]

We use the Granger causality test to explore the direction of association between aid and output.[11] The logic of the Granger causality test is straight forward and based on the notion that the future cannot cause the past or the present. We apply this logic to the association of output (Y) and aid (A) in the two equations below.

$$Y_t = \alpha + \mathrm{B}A_t + \sum_{i=1}^{k} \delta_i A_{t-i} + \lambda Y_{t-i} + \varepsilon \qquad (1)$$

Thus in equation (1), we allow for aid to boost output contemporaneously and with lags. The lagged output terms allow for the possibility of a 'output momentum' effect which could be severed by exogenous shocks such as civil war or crop failure due to pests or floods. Equation (2) below is parallel to equation (1).

$$A_t = \alpha' + \mathrm{B}' Y_t + \sum_{j=1}^{n} \delta_i' Y_{t-j} + \lambda' A_{t-j} + \varepsilon' \qquad (2)$$

Thus, this time, we test for the association of contemporaneous and lagged output with aid and also for a possible 'aid momentum' effect captured by the lagged aid terms. In the above equations, on the one hand, if aid precedes an increase in output, i.e., the coefficient of A (instantaneous causality) or some lagged version of this variable is significant, then we do not know that aid 'causes' an increase in output but that this is possible. On the other hand, we can rule out causality if neither the current nor lagged version of A is significant.[12] This restricted notion of causality is referred to as Granger causality.

Test for Aid–Growth Association[13]

We start with a general production function explaining Y or GDP – defined over two inputs, capital (K) and labour (L) – for the economy as a whole and include in it a vector of other variables, C_i (which include aid), which can theoretically enhance economic growth.

$$Y = F(K, L, \sum_i C_i) \tag{3}$$

Differentiating equation (3) with respect to time, dividing through by Y and multiplying and dividing each term by itself (except K) we get the following equation to estimate:[14]

$$\mathrm{GY} = \mathrm{a} + \mu \frac{I}{Y} + \tau\,\mathrm{GL} + \theta\,\mathrm{GA} + \sum_i \phi_i \mathrm{GC}_i + \varepsilon \tag{4}$$

The manipulations above transform all variables, except the investment–GDP ratio, I/Y, into growth terms. GY and GL represent the growth rates of GDP and labour force respectively, and μ and τ represent the elasticity of output with respect to labour and the marginal productivity of capital respectively. The growth in aid, GA, has been taken out of the summation as the variable of particular interest. Its coefficient, θ, as well as the coefficients of other theoretically relevant variables in the summation, ϕ_i, represent output elasticities. These variables include export–GDP ratio, industry–GDP ratio, inflation, foreign direct investment and the terms of trade.[15]

This framework allows for a sensitivity analysis for testing the robustness of the aid coefficient as recommended by Levine and Renelt (1992). They examine the behaviour of the estimated coefficient of a variable of interest (aid in our case) as combinations of other potentially important explanatory variables are included on the right-hand side of the growth equation. The upper and lower extreme bounds of the coefficient of the variable of interest are chosen from these regressions as the maximum and the minimum values of the estimate plus or minus two standard deviations. An estimated coefficient is judged as fragile if the coefficient of interest is insignificant in any of the estimated equations and if either one of the extreme values has a different sign from the coefficient obtained in the base regression.

In our case, there are seven theoretically relevant additional variables apart from investment, growth of labour force, aid and the variable capturing supply-side shocks. Using combinations of two additional variables in an augmented growth model means estimating a total of 21 equations or aid coefficients as reported in Table 1.4. Thus, this is a rigorous test for determining coefficient robustness.

Data

The data on total debt outstanding, net transfers, and terms of debt were drawn from the World Bank database titled *World Debt Tables 1995*. Data on GDP, investment and other variables that are hypothesized as affecting growth are drawn from the World Bank database titled *World Tables 1995*. The labour force data are drawn from the World Bank database titled *Social Indicators of Development 1995*. Finally, aid disbursed in real terms is from the *Economic Survey 1994–95* (1995).[16]

FINDINGS

Aid–GDP Granger Causality Nexus

Apart from the variables described in equations (1) and (2), we have included a variable to capture supply shocks. Since Pakistan is predominantly a cotton based economy, most negative shocks (due to floods, droughts or agricultural viruses) or positive shocks (bumper crops) get transmitted to the economy via cotton production. We regressed cotton production on time and saved the residuals (RCOT) to use as a supply-side shock variable. We posit a positive relationship of RCOT and GDP since a positive residual could result from a positive shock and vice versa. One could expect a negative association of RCOT and aid, if the latter compensates for weather-related and other natural disasters. Neither expectation was borne out in either the Granger causality or the sensitivity analysis since RCOT is insignificant in both cases. Table 1.3 reports the results based on the Granger causality test for various lags (equations (1) and (2)).

Table 1.3 Granger causality test results

Direction of causality		F-value	P of F value	Decision
GDP← Aid	Aid lags			
	1	9.17	0.003	Do not reject
	2	6.25	0.000	Do not reject
	3	4.24	0.029	Do not reject
Aid← GDP	GDP lags			
	1	1.21	0.33	Reject
	2	1.30	0.31	Reject
	3	0.57	0.61	Reject

Notes: The regression results the above table is based on are reported as Appendix Table 1.5, at the end of this chapter

The results in Table 1.3 indicate that higher GDP does not Granger cause higher aid but that aid negatively Granger causes GDP. As the table indicates, this finding is not sensitive to the lag length. Appendix Table 1.5 indicates that in the set of GDP← Aid equations, the sign of the aid coefficient (lagged one period), its magnitude and its significance is not sensitive to the lag length. Thus we have confidence in this finding which suggests that, based on past experience, a 10 per cent increase in aid is associated with a 0.4 per cent decline in GDP.

Growth–Aid Association

The results from using this method reinforce the findings from the last subsection. We find that aid has a negative and significant association with economic growth when we estimated equation (4). We added subsets of the conditioning variables (two variables at a time) to the base regression equation with capital, labour and aid and estimated 21 augmented growth equations. These conditioning variables include size of exports as a percentage of GDP (SOE) as a proxy for openness, foreign direct investment (FDI), inflation (INF), size of industry (SOI), terms of trade (TOT), age dependency ratio (DR) and total debt stock as a percentage of GDP (DSR). As indicated by Table 1.4, the negative impact of aid on economic growth is robust.

The first 21 rows all show aid to have a negative and highly significant coefficient irrespective of the conditioning variable combination used.[17] As in Appendix Table 1.5, the base aid–output elasticity coefficient is 0.04. This elasticity varies from a high of 0.06 to a low of 0.03. Finally, the sensitivity test reported in the last three rows shows that there is no sign

Table 1.4 Sensitivity analysis to assess the negative growth–aid association. Equation estimated: $GY = \alpha + \mu\ (I/Y) + \tau GL + \theta GA + \Sigma_i \phi_i GC_i + \varepsilon$

	θ	Standard error	R bar sq.	Conditioning variables
	−0.0540*	0.0086	0.68	DFI, DR
	−0.0320**	0.0137	0.21	DFI, SOI
	−0.0489*	0.0106	0.46	DFI, SOE
	−0.0355**	0.0128	0.26	DFI, TOT
	−0.0338**	0.0132	0.22	DFI, DSR
	−0.0358**	0.0130	0.25	DFI, INF
	−0.0621*	0.0081	0.72	DR, SOI
	−0.0569*	0.0074	0.73	DR, SOE
	−0.0559*	0.0086	0.65	DR, TOT
	−0.0561*	0.0086	0.66	DR, DSR
	−0.0593*	0.0077	0.75	DR, INF
	−0.0599*	0.0095	0.61	SOI, SOE
	−0.0385*	0.0139	0.25	SOI, TOT
	−0.0593*	0.0119	0.46	SOI, DSR
	−0.0365**	0.0128	0.28	SOI, INF
	−0.0479*	0.0104	0.47	SOE, TOT
	−0.0489*	0.0098	0.52	SOE, DSR
	−0.0409*	0.0119	0.37	SOE, INF
	−0.0388*	0.0126	0.27	TOT, DSR
	−0.0378*	0.0123	0.29	TOT, INF
	−0.0380*	0.0125	0.26	DSR, INF
Sensitivity test: base and extreme values				
High	−0.0621*	0.0081	0.72	DR, SOI
Base	−0.0434*	0.0115	0.37	
Low	−0.0320**	0.0137	0.21	DFI, SOE

Notes: Table based on regressions available on request from the authors. The Cochrane–Orcutt method was used in cases of serial correlation. All the variables were I(0) except for GDP, LF, IR, DR and DSR. Using the Durbin Watson, Augmented Eagle–Granger and Johansen methods, we established all regressions to be cointegrating. Conditioning variables: SOE the share of exports in GDP, SOI the share of industry in GDP, INF the inflation rate, FDI the foreign direct investment, DR the age dependency ratio, TOT the terms of trade, DSR the debt stock ratio. The correlation coefficient of aid lagged one period and IR is −0.16. This was of concern since aid could be a major determinant of IR.

* = Significant at least at the one percent level.

** = Significant at least at the five percent level.

change when two standard errors are added or subtracted to the minimum and maximum coefficient of aid. We therefore conclude that our finding of a negative and significant association of aid with growth is robust.[18]

The debt/GDP ratio was not a robust variable. Fry (1992) showed that the debt/GDP ratio in excess of 50 per cent has a negative impact on economic growth due to capital flight and a decline in the quantity and efficiency of investment.[19] Also, foreign direct investment and export growth were not robust variables.

While we did not have data to estimate sector production functions, we were able to correlate project aid to the agricultural and industrial sectors with output in these sectors for the period 1972–3 to 1987–8. These sectors combined accounted for about a third of total cumulative project aid over this period, with industry drawing about double the amount drawn by agriculture.[20] Both partial correlation coefficients were very low and insignificant when aid was used as a contemporaneous variable. Aid lagged one period had a positive correlation with the agricultural sector (0.48) which was significant at the 10 per cent level but with industry it was negative (−0.37) and insignificant.[21] While the agricultural coefficient is positive, as a partial correlation coefficient it is low and only weakly significant. Thus there is little support for aid effectiveness even with sectoral disaggregation.

DISCUSSION AND CONCLUSION

There is little about the aid/debt scenario for Pakistan that is positive. With the intensive period of structural adjustment in the late 1980s, the debt/GDP ratio and the debt service/export ratio rose compared to the mid-1970s to late 1980s period. Concessional aid as a percentage of the total has fallen, the average interest rate is higher, the maturity period is lower and the grant element is lower. Thus not only is Pakistan heavily in debt, but also the changing terms of the debt are going to make it much harder to get out of the debt trap.

The harsher terms on which Pakistan gets aid make the debt trap more formidable, as does the economics of the aid–growth nexus. At first, our findings about the negative and statistically robust negative impact of aid on economic growth may appear odd. In fact, one could argue that these results imply that Pakistan would be progressively better off the more of its resources it gifted to another country. But such an argument represents a fundamental misunderstanding about the nature of aid. Aid represents a package including policy parameters such as prescriptions about fiscal, trade and exchange-rate policy. Had these policies suited Pakistan's economic environment, aid would have positively impacted GDP growth. Another way of looking at this is to expect the debt/GDP ratio to fall if aid was really successful. Table 1.2 shows that while this ratio declined in the late 1970s to the late 1980s, it rose again from the late 1980s to the early 1990s, reflecting Pakistan's inability to retire its debt. Coincidentally, this is a period of intensive structural adjustment.

There are several factors that could neutralize the effectiveness of aid. Aid goes to the public sector; and blockages, inefficiency, misuse and leakage are likely to reduce effectiveness in the use of these resources as is the case with other public sector expenditures. Additional reasons identified in the literature include project selections biased towards prestigious but economically unsound large projects, foreign exchange intensive projects, and infrastructure rather than productive projects.[22] The lack of government–donor and intra-donor coordination could similarly reduce the effectiveness of aid.[23] As is well known, much aid returns to the country of origin in the form of expensive consulting contracts.[24] Similarly, the effectiveness of aid can be reduced by 'tying' agreements whereby the purchase of equipment and materials from donors costs much more than cheaper alternatives of similar quality.[25]

The above factors explain why aid may not be as effective as it might otherwise be. For the negative association, one can turn to the earlier literature on the negative aid–saving association. This literature has been reviewed in detail in the surveys by Ridell (1987) and White (1992) referred to earlier. Prominent advocates of this negative association include Griffen and Enos (1970) and Weisskopf (1972). Using a two-stage least-square model with growth estimated in the first stage and the fitted growth used in a saving function in the second stage, we also identified a negative association of official transfers and the saving rate between the 1971 and 1990 period. However, the magnitude of the effect was small (see Chapter 3, Table 3.1).

In general, the negative aid–saving association may be one of the channels explaining the negative aid–growth association. However, other factors have also been identified in the literature as possible explanations. That there is a short-run recessionary impact of adjustment policies is unlikely to be questioned by any economist. In addition, aid and debt leads to a destructive 'foreign exchange drag'. As noted by Cassen et al. (1990, p. 1.16), debt repayment is an outflow of free-standing foreign exchange, in contrast to the conditional and tied inflow of foreign exchange that aid represents. Further, foreign exchange, relatively easily available in the short run, can induce the 'dutch disease' syndrome (making exports non-competitive due to the artificial appreciation of the exchange rate). Finally, the negative impact of commodity aid on local production has been discussed in the literature.[26]

Surprisingly, the notion that aid to the public sector induces inefficiency by providing a soft budget constraint has not been discussed in the literature. This concept was originated by Kornoi (1986) and is widely viewed as an important explanatory factor in the failing of socialist economies. The extension of this concept to aid-recipient governments seems quite self-evident, and this may be the most important explanatory factor in explaining the negative growth–aid association.

The public choice literature which discusses inefficient rent-seeking and empire building also provides a rationale for this association in so far as aid enables inefficient administrative structures to survive. The realization for the need for accountable government has not yet translated into effective institutional reform.

The reasoning above and our findings show that it is possible to rule out the counterfactual that matters may have been even worse without aid. Given the negative and significant statistical association of growth and aid, one can only expect Pakistan to get more and more indebted. As mentioned earlier, our method explores an aggregate association. Our findings thus are not inconsistent with the existence of effective (where the benefits outweigh the costs) donor programmes and projects initiated by bilateral and multilateral aid agencies.[27] Also, it is possible that we have identified a negative association in the 'second phase' of aid receiving, whereas in the 'first phase' of aid receiving, on more generous terms, the infrastructure base of later growth may have been established.

If aid in the aggregate sense is 'bad', why does Pakistan continue to solicit it? While aid may have a negative impact on the economy, it could benefit at least some of those who decide whether or not to solicit it. Even if one can rule out overt vested interests, aid represents the path of least resistance. Policy-makers in Pakistan jump from managing one crisis to the next one, and grasp at whatever straws they can in the process, no matter how harmful they are in the long run. Furthermore, sensible long-run policies are not avoided because they inflict pain on the *poor*. Pakistan's policy-makers have shown themselves quite adept at testing these limits. Sensible long-run policies are avoided because they inflict pain on the *elites*.

The only alternative to aid is to raise revenues internally and to institute just economies in expenditures. But this would mean sensible long-run policies like tax reform, including closing exemptions and other tax loopholes, asking legislators to start taxing their agricultural incomes, and the cutting of luxurious expenditures by politicians and the civil and military bureaucracies. The issue of cutting the military budget has also been raised many times by others. This and other economies are now more necessary than ever because the evidence does not suggest that continuing to get indebted is sustainable policy.

NOTES

1. Thanks are due to Safiya Aftab, Tariq Banuri and Zia Mian for comments on an earlier draft. Paper submitted to *Oxford Development Studies*.
2. Our analysis deals with economic aid since no data on military aid were available.
3. Empirical research in Pakistan by Kemal (1992), Chishti and Khan (1992), Khan and Rahim (1992) and McGillivray, White and Ahmed (1994) are subject to the same critique.
4. This result is based on the fitted value and residual of a cross-country regression using a sample of 49 LDCs, with long-term debt as the dependent variable and population, population squared and GDP in purchasing power parity terms as predictor variables.
5. The period after the creation of Bangladesh.
6. By this we mean that Pakistan will continue to have to push export growth, which gives a particular slant to the economy, and turn over the foreign exchange earnings as debt repayment.
7. See chapter 5 of Banuri, Khan and Mahmood (1997) for an account of these conditionalities and their social and economic impact.
8. We are exploring if there is a robust association between aid and economic growth, and not the channels via which aid can affect growth. Mosley, Hudson and Horrell (1987) model the channels via which aid can influence growth.
9. This amounts to viewing aid as an endogenous variable.
10. Such thinking could account for the new aid policy of the US AID. An empirical underpinning for such aid reorientation is provided by the research interpretation and recommendations reported in Mosley, Hudson and Horrell (1987).
11. For a different version of such a test using Pakistani data see McGillivray, White and Ahmed (1994).
12. Both Granger (1969) and Sims (1972), in an equivalent causality test, introduce an arbitrary lag length.
13. For a review of applied growth models and some reservations on practice see Edwards (1993).
14. Derivation details are reported in Appendix 1.1.
15. Complete time series on education variables were not available.
16. All values have been converted to real million rupees.
17. The results of the base regression were much weaker when only grants (with or without technical assistance) was used instead of the aid variable.

Also, the results were much weaker when aid was included in the base regression contemporaneously.

18. An advantage of cointegration analysis is that it helps in avoiding spurious results.
19. See Table 1.1 for Pakistan's debt/GDP ratio.
20. Cassen et al. (1990), Annex, Tables and Bibliography, Table 10z.
21. The contemporaneous and one-period lagged aid correlation coefficient was 0.32 ($p=0.23$) and 0.48 ($p=0.07$) with agricultural output and -0.14 ($p=0.59$) and -0.36 ($p=0.18$) with industrial output.
22. Ridell (1987, p. 114).
23. Cassen et al. (1990).
24. Cassen et al. (1990, p. 2A.9) report that consulting draws away about 10 per cent of all aid in Pakistan.
25. Cassen et al. (1990, p. 1.50) speculate, based on the findings of an earlier study, that 'tying' increases the cost of procurement in Pakistan by about 30 per cent.
26. Commodity aid was about a quarter of total non-military aid in 1987–8, the latest year for which such disaggregated data are available. Cassen et al. (1990, Annex, Tables and Bibliography, Tables 2z and 6z).
27. For examples see Cassen et al. (1990, pp. 1.12–1.22).

REFERENCES

Banuri, T., S. R. Khan and M. Mahmood (eds), 1997, *Just Development: Beyond Adjustment with a Human Face* (Karachi: Oxford University Press).

Cassen, R. and associates, 1986, *Does Aid Work?* (New York: Oxford University Press).

Cassen, R., A. Duncun, S. Guisinger, E. Hooper and O. Noman, 1990, *The Effectiveness of Aid to Pakistan* (Islamabad: Economic Affairs Division, Pakistan and UNDP)

Chishti, S. and M. A. Khan, 1992, 'Foreign Aid, Defense Expenditure and Public Investment in Pakistan', Eighth Annual General Meeting of the Pakistan Society of Development Economists, Islamabad.

Edwards, S., 1993, 'Openness, Trade Liberalization and Growth in Developing Countries', *Journal of Economic Literature*, 31, no. 3 (Sept.), pp. 1358–93.

Fry, M. J., 1992, 'Some Stabilizing and Destabilizing Effects of Foreign Debt Accumulation in Developing Countries', *Economic Letters*, 39, pp. 315–21.

Granger, C. W. J., 1969, 'Investigating Causal Relations by Econometric Methods and Cross-Sectoral Methods', *Econometrica*, Vol. 37 (July), pp. 424–38.

Griffen, K. B. and J. L. Enos, 1970, 'Foreign Assistance, Objectives and Consequences', *Economic Development and Cultural Change*, 18, no. 3, pp. 313–27.

International Monetary Fund, 1994, *International Financial Statistics* (Washington, DC: IMF).

Kemal, A. R., 1992, 'Self-Reliance and Implications for Growth and Resource Mobilizations', Eighth Annual General Meeting of the Pakistan Society of Development Economists, Islamabad.

Khan, N. Z. and E. Rahim, 1993, 'Foreign Aid, Domestic Saving and Economic Growth 1960–1988', Ninth Annual General Meeting of the Pakistan Society of Development Economists, Islamabad.

Kornai, J., 1986, 'The Soft Budget Constraint', *Kyklos*, 39, pp. 3–30.

Levine, R. and D. Renelt, 1992, 'A Sensitivity Analysis of Cross-Country Growth Regressions', *American Economic Review*, 82, no. 4, (Sept.), pp. 942–63.

McGillivray, M., H. White and A. Ahmed, 1994, 'Evaluating the Effectiveness of Structural Adjustment Policies on Macroeconomic Performance: A Review of the Evidence with Special Reference to Pakistan', paper prepared for presentation at AERC/Goethe Conference on Political and Socioeconomic Consequences of Policy Based Lending, Karachi, Sept. 21–4.

Mosley, P., J. Hudson and S. Horrell, 1987, 'Aid, the Public Sector and the Market in Less Developed Countries', *Economic Journal*, 97 (Sept.), pp. 616–41.

Ridell, R. C., 1987, *Foreign Aid Reconsidered* (London: Johns Hopkins University Press).

Sims, C. A., 1972, 'Money, Income, and Causality', *American Economic Review*, 62, no. 4 (Sept.), pp. 540–52.

Weisskopf, T. E., 1972, 'The Impact of Foreign Capital Inflows on Domestic Saving in Underdeveloped Countries', *Journal of International Economics*, 2, pp. 25–38.

White, H., 1992, 'The Macroeconomic Impact of Development Aid: A Critical Survey', *Journal of Development Studies*, 28, no. 2 (Jan.), pp. 163–240.

Appendix 1.1

Derivation of Equation 4:

$Y = F(K, L, \Sigma_i C_i)$

$\mathrm{d}Y/\mathrm{d}t = (f_k \,\mathrm{d}K/\mathrm{d}t + f_l \mathrm{d}L/\mathrm{d}t + \Sigma_{i.} f_c \mathrm{d}C_i/\mathrm{d}t)$

Divide both sides by Y

$(\mathrm{d}Y/\mathrm{d}t)/Y = (f_k \,\mathrm{d}K/\mathrm{d}t + \mathrm{f}_l \,\mathrm{d}L/\mathrm{d}t + \Sigma_{i.} f_c \mathrm{d}C_i/\mathrm{d}t)/Y$

Multiply and divide each term in the right hand parenthesis except K by itself.

$$(\mathrm{d}Y/\mathrm{d}t)/Y = 1/Y(\mathrm{d}Y/\mathrm{d}L^*\mathrm{d}L/\mathrm{d}t^*L/L) + 1/Y(\mathrm{d}Y/\mathrm{d}K^*\mathrm{d}K/\mathrm{d}t) + 1/Y(\Sigma_i \mathrm{d}Y/\mathrm{d}C^*\mathrm{d}C_i/\mathrm{d}t \, ^*C_i/C_i)$$

$$(\mathrm{d}Y/\mathrm{d}t)/Y = [(\mathrm{d}Y/\mathrm{d}L^*L/Y)((\mathrm{d}L/\mathrm{d}t)/L)] + (\mathrm{d}Y/\mathrm{d}K^*I/Y) + [(\Sigma_i \mathrm{d}Y/\mathrm{d}C_i{}^*C_i/Y)((\mathrm{d}C_i/\mathrm{d}t)/C_i)]$$

Since

$(\mathrm{d}Y/\mathrm{d}t)/Y = \mathrm{GY}$
$(\mathrm{d}L/\mathrm{d}t)/L = \mathrm{GL}$
$(\mathrm{d}K/\mathrm{d}t)/Y = I/Y$
$(\mathrm{d}C_i/\mathrm{d}t)/C_i) = \mathrm{GC_i}$

$$\mathrm{GY} = \alpha + \mu I/Y + \tau \mathrm{GL} + \theta \mathrm{GA} + \Sigma_i \phi_i \mathrm{GC}_i + \varepsilon$$

where

α = constant term
$\mu = \mathrm{d}Y/\mathrm{d}K$ = marginal productivity of capital
$\iota = \mathrm{d}Y/\mathrm{d}L^*L/Y$ = labour output elasticity
$\theta = \mathrm{d}Y/\mathrm{d}A^*A/Y$ = aid output elasticity
$\phi = \mathrm{d}Y/\mathrm{d}C_i{}^*C_i/Y$ = conditioning variable output elasticity
ε = error term

Appendix 1.2

Table 1.5 Granger causality between aid and growth

	LGDP AID LAGS			LAID GDP LAGS		
	1@	2@	3@	1	2	3
Constant	5.383*	3.947***	4.543	−50.101	−76.629	−8.81
	(3.54)	(2.22)	(1.16)	(0.91)	(1.24)	(0.21)
T	0.027*	0.190***	0.023	−0.240	−0.372	−0.019
	(3.57)	(1.79)	(1.19)	(0.96)	(1.21)	(0.14)
LAID	0.001	−0.007	−0.012			
	(0.12)	(0.55)	(0.60)			
LGDP				−0.243	−0.163	2.712
				(0.97)	(0.02)	(0.47)
LAID (−1)	−0.040*	−0.042*	−0.041*	0.043	−0.262	0.041
	(3.97)	(3.39)	(2.44)	(1.25)	(0.60)	(0.92)
LAID (−2)		0.012	0.013			
		(0.90)	(0.05)			
LAID (−3)			0.004			
			(0.02)			
LGDP (−1)	0.592*	0.708*	0.662**	4.780	1.565	−2.890
	(4.68)	(3.99)	(2.12)	(0.34)	(0.28)	(0.47)
LGDP (−2)					5.404	7.630
					(1.06)	(1.25)
LGDP (−3)						0.816
						(0.14)
R bar Sq.	0.99	0.99	0.99	0.67	0.63	0.80
F-Stat	6294*	3702*	2374*	9.97*	6.09*	8.23*
D. W.	2.18	2.16	2.09	2.20	1.95	1.97
n	19	18	17	19	18	17

Notes: Parentheses contain t-statistics.
@ = adjusted for autocorrelation using the Cochrane–Orcutt method
(−1) = one period lag etc.
* = significant at the 1% level.
** = significant at the 5% level.
*** = significant at the 10% level.
LAID = Log of aid etc.

All variables are I(1) or non-stationary. However, using the Durbin–Watson and Johansen methods, we established the GDP ← Aid equations were cointegrating. None of the Aid ← GDP regressions were cointegrating. Higher order lagged dependent variables were not significant in the first set of equations with LGDP as the dependent variable. The third order lagged dependent variable [LAID(−3)] was significant in the second set of equations with LAID as the dependent variable, but the equations were not cointegrating. We also estimated equation 1 and 2 using growth of GDP rather than GDP. The results were substantively the same. However, the R bar squared for the GDP ← Aid equations were essentially zero in both the logged and non-logged versions. Finally, we found the Granger causality relation in Table 1.3 holds only for the aggregate aid variable but not for grants, with or without technical assistance.

2 Devaluation and the Balance of Trade[1]

INTRODUCTION

Exchange-rate flexibility is generally recommended as part of structural adjustment packages to offset balance of trade deficits.[2] However, according to Burton and Gilman (1991, p. 19), the IMF is eclectic. For example, if countries confront a chronic current account deficit and inflation is not a serious problem, a market-determined exchange rate may be endorsed. Alternatively, if coping with inflation is the priority, a pegged exchange rate could be recommended as a nominal anchor. Problems in the real world rarely come singly. Pakistan has struggled with both price stabilization and current account deficits. It adopted a managed float in 1982 and, as part of its structural adjustment reforms, has occasionally made discretionary changes in the exchange rate when confronted with low foreign exchange reserves, or when the value of the dollar has appreciated substantially in relation to other currencies. The obvious question is whether the evidence supports such policy action. The answer is that the evidence is decidedly mixed.

Goldstein and Khan (1978) suggested that both export demand and supply as well as import demand are considerably responsive to the exchange rate. Their conclusions were based on a study of eight industrialized countries for the 1955–70 period. Hence they claimed that the Marshall–Lerner conditions would easily be satisfied. This result was challenged by Miles (1979), who tested the effects of devaluation on both the trade balance and the balance of payments for a mix of fourteen industrialized and less developed countries in the 1960s.[3] He found that devaluation is primarily a monetary phenomenon that does not affect the trade balance, but does reduce the balance of payments deficit. Balassa et al. (1989) found results similar to Goldstein and Khan for Korea (1965–79) and Greece (1960–78). Rose (1991) rejected the existence of a relationship between the balance of trade and the exchange rate for five major OECD countries using quarterly data for the 1974–86 period. Hughes and Singh (1991) also provide evidence questioning such an association for both industrialized countries for the 1956–76 period and for selected less developed countries.[4] Using a cointegration approach, Bahmani-Oskooee (1991) identified a long-run equilibrium relation between the trade balance and the real effective exchange rate for five out of the eight countries studied for the 1973–88 period.

For Pakistan, Khan and Hasan (1994) used annual data from 1972 to 1991 and estimated import and export demand functions, an export supply function and a price equation using 3SLS. Elasticities were then used to test the Marshall–Lerner condition. As the sum of the export and import demand elasticities exceeded 1, they concluded that the Marshall–Lerner condition was satisfied and that devaluation in Pakistan can improve the trade balance for Pakistan.

Athukorala and Riedel (1991; also Riedel and Athukorala, 1995) have convincingly raised serious methodological doubts about the empirical validity of conventional export demand functions and have suggested an alternative formulation. This represents the point of entry for our conceptual discussion. Our focus is on identifying the implications of their findings for exchange-rate policy and testing the resulting hypothesis. We argue that using the real effective exchange rates (EER) in disaggregate export demand functions is preferable for several reasons. First, EER represents the actual control variable used by policy-makers to influence relative prices. Second, using EER avoids a major specification flaw that results from the use of relative prices as indicated by Athukorala and Riedel. We also avoid the aggregation problem by estimating separate export demand functions for Pakistan's major exports.

The use of the Marshall–Lerner condition implies treating the trade balance as a partial equilibrium phenomenon. There is a debate on the broader macroeconomic effect of devaluations which is reviewed in Lizondo and Montiel (1989) and Nunnencamp and Schweickert (1990). These macroeconomic effects can have second-order effects on the trade balance via various channels, but the effects can be conflicting and, *a priori*, the final outcome is ambiguous.

Below we explain Pakistan's exchange-rate regime. Then we present a conceptual discussion and our estimation model. Our results are then presented, followed by a summary and concluding observations.

PAKISTAN'S EXCHANGE RATE REGIME[5]

Immediately after Independence, Pakistan's currency was linked to the pound sterling. The Pakistani rupee was devalued for the first time in 1955 during the post-Korean War recession. The second major change in the exchange rate was the devaluation of May 1972, which was precipitated by the oil crisis. The rupee was devalued from Rs 4.92 to Rs 11.00 to the US dollar. Subsequently, the rate was fixed at Rs 9.90 to the US dollar, an exchange rate which prevailed for ten years. In January 1982, the appreciation of the US dollar in international markets led the government to adopt a managed float based on a trade-weighted basket of currencies.[6]

As the term 'managed float' implies, the State Bank is free to adjust the value of the currency to contend with external imbalance. In particular, the State Bank has occasionally intervened to adjust the value of the rupee whenever the value of the US dollar has appreciated in international markets. However, these have been mild adjustments. In July 1993, however, the rupee was devalued by 3 per cent, to Rs 28.17 to the US dollar, followed by a further devaluation of 6 per cent one week later. This last devaluation was carried out as part of the structural adjustment reforms recommended by the IMF for promoting export growth and reducing the trade deficit.[7] A similar devaluation of 8.7 per cent occurred in October 1997.

CONCEPTUAL DISCUSSION AND ESTIMATION MODEL

The conventional export demand as specified by Reidel and Athukorala (1995) is

$$X_d = \varepsilon(P_x - P_w) + \eta Y_w, \qquad (1)$$

where X_d is export demand, ε is price elasticity, P_x is domestic export price, P_w is export price of competing nations, η is income elasticity and Y_W is the GDP of trading partners. Athukorala and Riedel (AR) convincingly argue that conventional estimates of price and income elasticity defy common sense. First, the low consensus price elasticities from equation (1) (0.5 to 1) suggest an optimal tax, even for small countries, which no one has seriously recommended. Second, for the terms of trade not to turn against an exporting nation, equation (1) implies that the growth in exports should not exceed the growth in world income.[8] AR show that for Hong Kong and Korea (machine and transport equipment) this was not the case, and yet exports did not have an adverse impact on the terms of trade. This was true because in both cases these countries were shown to be price takers. Third, if countries are price takers, equation (1) can be estimated only if there are measurement errors since $P_x/P_w = 1$. This error typically results in an overstatement of η.[9] Finally, if a country is a price taker, there is no demand constraint, so exports should be modelled on the supply side. Their simple solution is estimating an inverse demand function as follows:

$$P_x = P_w + (1/\varepsilon)X_d + (n/\varepsilon)Y_w \tag{2}$$

If the coefficient of P_w is not significantly different from 1, and if the other two coefficients are not significantly different from zero (suggesting ε to be infinitely elastic), the small country case is confirmed.

The policy implications are far reaching. A price taker confronts only a supply constraint and can promote exports of existing quantities without adversely affecting its terms of trade. The implications for applied research for trade policy are also far reaching. Researchers should begin by testing the small-country assumption, preferably by major export commodities.

Applied research seeks to inform policy, and it is best to inform policy-makers in terms of the control variables they manipulate. For trade policy, the real effective exchange rate (EER), or the ratio of traded to non-traded goods (P_T/P_{NT}), is the control or policy variable, and so our concern is with the implications of the above findings for the manipulation of the EER. This is of major policy significance since many countries on a fixed or some kind of floating exchange-rate regime, are often advised to devalue their currency to attain external balance in the context of structural adjustment programmes.

The AR results suggest that small countries confront an infinitely elastic demand curve. If the country is a price taker for all goods, the AR results, stretched to the extreme, suggest several possibilities.[10] First, if the EER is above parity, we should observe zero exports for the country. Second, devaluations to the parity levels should show big discontinuous jumps in exports, with the size of the jump dependent on the supply constraint. Third, if the country is at parity, a devaluation would simply result in a loss of export revenue. None of these scenarios is realistic, and they seem to make a mockery of the standard structural adjustment prescription of using devaluation to attain external balance.

In practice, even small countries are likely to confront very high rather than infinite elasticity. Second, there is an aggregation problem since all goods of different price responsiveness are lumped together. Thus it makes sense to estimate disaggregate export demand functions using EER as the price proxy. Policy-makers need to know the responsiveness of their major exports to changes in EER. As earlier argued, by using EER, which is not expected to be one, we avoid the specification problem resulting from the use of relative prices in conventional export demand functions. We use quarterly data to estimate aggregate and disaggregate export demand functions specified as follows:

$$\log X_d = a_0 + a_1 \log(EER) + a_2 \log GDPG6, \tag{3}$$

where the coefficients a_1 and a_2 are the 'price' and income elasticities of demand and *GDPG6* is an index of the GDP of six industrialized countries which are also among the country's major trading partners.[11]

To estimate equation (2), we start by determining whether EER is exogenous. If exogeneity is ruled out, we estimate export demand and supply within a system of simultaneous equations, using a method first adopted by Goldstein and Khan (1978). Export supply is specified as:

$$\log X_s = b_0 + b_1 \log(EER) + b_2 \log Y + b_3 W \tag{4}$$

where X_S is export supply and Y is a capacity variable, which in this case is the trend GDP. W represents a weather dummy since weather affects the production of Pakistan's major primary exports and related manufactured goods. We also specify an equilibrium condition

$$X_d = X_s \tag{5}$$

Equations (3) and (4) are then solved simultaneously using the instrumental variable approach. We also estimated an aggregate import demand function to identify the likely first-round effect of devaluation on the trade balance.

$$\log M_d = e_0 + e_1 \log(EER) + e_2 \log GDPP \tag{6}$$

where M_d is import demand and *GDPP* is Pakistan's GDP.[12]

RESULTS

Estimates of the aggregate export and import demand functions for Pakistan are reported below in Table 2.1. We had 42 quarterly observations spanning 1983Q1 to 1993Q3. For the export demand function, we used the Wu–Hausman test to determine if EER was exogenous, rejected the null of no simultaneity, and hence estimated the export demand equation using the instrumental variable method.[13] Also, we used Johansen's estimation to confirm the existence of a cointegrating vector in both cases, which suggest that the equations reported below represent a long-run association between the variables.[14]

Table 2.1 Aggregate export and import demand functions

Depen. var.	Regressors and test statistics						
	INPT	LGDPG6	LGDPP	LFEER	R-BAR-sq	F-Stat	DW
LX	−7.91*	1.63*		−0.32***	0.84	31.10*	1.53
	(2.25)	(6.79)		(1.68)			
LIM	−0.08*		2.13*	0.78*	0.85	37.28*	1.60
	(3.39)		(8.95)	(4.07)			

Notes: Estimates based on the Cochrane–Orcutt iterative method.
Parentheses contain t-statistics.
* Significant at the 1 per cent level of significance
*** Significant at the 10 per cent level of significance
LGDPG6 Log of GDP of industrialized countries
LGDPP Log of Pakistani GDP
LFEER Log of fitted effective exchange rate
LIM Log of total imports

The fit of the equations in Table 2.1 is reasonable, and all the signs are as expected. The coefficient of EER is significant only at the 10 per cent level, but barring that qualification, the sum of the two coefficients of EER comes to slightly more than one (1.1). This suggests that on an aggregate level, Pakistan could expect no change or a minor improvement in its trade balance following a currency devaluation. Since the Marshall–Lerner condition is derived assuming an initial trade balance, we re-derived this condition by relaxing this assumption and found it to be as follows:[15]

$$\varepsilon_x X/pM + \varepsilon_m > \qquad (7)$$

where ε_x and ε_m are the export and import demand elasticities, X and M are average exports and imports and p is the conversion factor. Our estimate shows that the modified Marshall–Lerner condition above sums to slightly less than one.[16]

To avoid the aggregation problem and to indicate to policy-makers the likely impact of devaluation on Pakistan's major exports, we estimated disaggregate export demand functions, which are reported in Table 2.2.[17]

There are several points to note in Table 2.2. Except for raw cotton, for which we also have a poor fit, the income elasticity, when significant, varies between 1.8 and 6.7. One needs to interpret these numbers carefully. An income elasticity of 7 for carpet exports means that a 1 per cent increase in the GDP of the G6 countries is associated with a 7 per cent increase in imports of carpets from Pakistan. Since average real quarterly

Table 2.2 Export demand functions using the IV method (dependent variable: LX)

Depen. var.	Regressors and test statistics						
	INPUT	T	LGDPG6	LFEER	R-BAR-sq	F-stat	DW
LXRC@	−446.94*	−0.49*	39.38*	2.83	0.32	3.33*	2.10
	(−2.68)	(2.87)	(2.75)	(1.28)			
LXF@	−24.33		2.70	−0.29	0.47	5.92*	1.37
	(0.35)		(0.59)	(0.49)			
LXCY	−6.53		1.80*	−1.60*	0.90	174.90*	1.9
	(0.53)		(2.60)	(2.79)			
LXTL	50.12*		−2.73*	−2.88*	0.75	56.48*	2.24
	(7.83)		(6.76)	(8.51)			
LXMOL	−5.07		1.07	−0.64	0.25	7.27*	2.09
	(0.21)		(0.64)	(0.50)			
LXCC	−25.40*		2.74*	0.27	0.89	147.77*	2.09
	(3.67)		(5.77)	(0.75)			
LXOC#	−5.44		1.87*	−2.33			
	(0.19)		(2.98)	(1.43)			
LXC@	−56.66	0.13*	6.70**	−2.61*	0.71	12.80*	2.04
	(1.45)	(−3.05)	(1.98)	(6.53)			
LXML	−29.50*		3.41*	−0.86**	0.96	492.98*	2.06
	(4.05)		(7.05)	(2.08)			
LXSG@	−14.06		2.13**	−0.97	0.73	16.41*	2.07
	(1.06)		(2.22)	(1.14)			
LXMED#	−3.28*		2.33*	0.37***			
	(4.03)		(5.96)	(1.19)			

Notes: @ Estimates based on the Cochrane–Orcutt iterative method.
Newey–White (Parzan weights) heteroscedasticity and autocorrelation consistent estimators.

*	Significant at 1 per cent level of significance
**	Significant at 5 per cent level of significance
***	Significant at 10 per cent level of significance
LXRC	Log of exports of raw cotton
LXF	Log of exports of fish
LXCY	Log of exports of cotton yarn
LXTL	Log of exports of tanned leather
LXMOL	Log of exports of molasses
LXCC	Log of exports of cotton textiles
LXOC	Log of exports of other textiles
LXC	Log of exports of carpets
LXML	Log of exports of manufactured leather
LXSG	Log of exports of sports goods
LXMED	Log of exports of medical equipment
LX	Log of exports

GDP of the G6 countries was about 7.5 trillion dollars, a one per cent increase in GDPG6 represents about 75 billion dollars. Average quarterly carpet exports from Pakistan amount to about 30 million dollars. Thus a 7 per cent increase in the exports of carpets from Pakistan represents only about 0.0003 per cent of the increase in GDPG6, which is minuscule. Thus while an income elasticity coefficient of 7 appears very large, viewed in the proper perspective, it can be quite modest. This explanation is necessary in view of the attention high income elasticity coefficients have been given in the literature.

Our real concern is with the responsiveness of Pakistan's major exports to a change in the exchange rate. An increase in the EER index represents an appreciation of the currency. For five out of the twelve major exports considered, we have a significant negative association of an exchange-rate appreciation with the corresponding exports. The coefficient is close to one (not significantly so) in one case (0.86) and considerably greater in the other three (1.60, 2.61 and 2.88). This indicates a considerable response in exports is likely in three out of the twelve cases. However, on average, these exports represent about one-third of the export value for twelve major exports we selected, and about a fifth of total export value. In view of these findings and the aggregate results reported in Table 2.1, one can assert that, as expected from the AR findings, there is little empirical support for Pakistan's attempt to increase exports by devaluing its currency.[18] The insignificant coefficients for textiles should not be surprising since textile exports are constrained by quotas in industrialized countries.

SUMMARY AND CONCLUSION

Most structural adjustment programmes require flexibility in the exchange rate. Typically, the reason for urging this flexibility is to redress balance of trade deficits. One method used in the literature to assess this recommendation is to test the Marshall–Lerner condition. This entails estimating export and import demand functions and checking to see if the sum of the price elasticity of exports and imports is greater than one. If the condition is satisfied, the inference is that the balance of trade is likely to respond positively to a devaluation or depreciation of the currency. Recently, conventional export demand functions have been criticized in the literature for ignoring the likelihood of countries being small with regards to their exports. Small countries face an infinite demand elasticity, and conventional estimates suffer from specification bias since the relative price ratio should be one. We argue that it is still possible to use conventional export demand functions by using the real effective exchange rate as a proxy for relative prices. This may also be preferable since the real effective exchange rate represents the actual control variable policy-makers use in trying to influence the external balance. We also demonstrate why high income elasticities need not be of great concern.

We jointly estimated an export demand function with an export supply function using an instrumental variable approach and also an import demand function. We found that the Marshall–Lerner condition is barely satisfied for Pakistan since the sum of import and export demand elasticities are only slightly greater than one. Also, the Marhsall–Lerner condition assumes an initial trade balance, and we re-derived the Marshall–Lerner condition by relaxing this assumption. We find that the modified Marshall–Lerner condition is not satisfied by a very small margin. Thus, past experience suggests that Pakistan can expect little or no change in its trade balance by devaluing its currency.

We believe that our findings are consistent with Athukorala and Riedel's (AR) findings. Evidence suggests that Pakistan's currency has been close to parity since there has been little difference between the official and free-market exchange rate. Under such circumstances, the AR findings suggest that there is little reason to expect a major change in the trade balance following a devaluation.

To address the aggregation problem and to ascertain the likely effect of a devaluation on Pakistan's major exports, we estimated disaggregate export demand functions. We found that only one–third of Pakistan's major exports are likely to respond positively to a devaluation. These findings reinforce the results from the aggregate export demand function.

Given the scant evidence that devaluation improves the trade balance, there is reason for caution. Devaluation could result in inflation since imports are more expensive in local currency. Also, for devaluation to work, the government must repress wages, or the competitive advantage devaluation gives to exports will be eroded. Society must judge if this distribution of income (away from low-income workers to export industrialists and agriculturalists) is fair. Scholars have argued that devaluation retards growth due to higher costs of production. Finally, in rupee terms, the debt burden immediately increases due to the devaluation (see Appendix 2.2). These are complicated issues we have not explored but note as related research issues.

The caution of Pakistani economic managers has often served the country well. Our findings here suggest that, based on past experience, they should not expect a major improvement of the trade balance with large currency devaluations such as the one adopted in the Summer of 1993 or

Fall of 1997. Capital market and other compulsions may still require maintaining a market-determined exchange rate. However, devaluation must be recognized as a sign of failure since it springs from the inability to contain fiscal deficits and inflation. In this regard, devaluation is clearly a soft option.

NOTES

1. This chapter was first prepared as a paper by Shahrukh R. Khan and Safiya Aftab for the international conference on 'Economic Liberalization in South Asia', 30 Nov.–2 Dec. 1994, organized by the Australian South Asia Research Centre. It has been published in *Economia Internationale*, XLIX, no. 2, 1996. Many thanks are due to Premchandra Athukorala, Warwick McKibben, Saqib Jafarey and Tariq Banuri for comments on earlier drafts.
2. Quick et al. (1987) pointed out that out of a total of 106 exchange-rate regimes approved by the Fund's executive board between 1983 and 1986, about two-thirds contained elements of exchange-rate flexibility.
3. Both Goldstein and Khan (1978) and Miles (1979) reviewed the earlier literature. Miles also pointed out that there are several approaches to explaining the association of the balance of trade with the real exchange rate. Apart from the elasticities approach embedded in the Marshall–Lerner conditions, there is an absorption and monetarist approach. Although the transmission mechanisms suggested by these approaches differ, they are observationally equivalent in terms of the reduced form equations estimated.
4. This study presented evidence in tabular form, whereas all the other studies cited used the regression method.
5. This section relies on data from the *Economic Surveys*.
6. The basket includes the currencies of Pakistan's trading partners.
7. Dorash (1988) presents a detailed account of the movements of Pakistan's nominal and real effective exchange rates.
8. The condition for stable terms of trade ($P_{\mathrm{x}} - P_w = 0$) is $0 = X_d/\mathrm{Y}_{\mathrm{W}}$.
9. AR also point out that η can be overstated if product diversification in aggregate functions and quality improvements are not accounted for.
10. Bear in mind that policy-makers manipulate EERs in an attempt to change export prices relative to non-traded goods and in the process the foreign currency price of domestic exports relative to those of competing nations.
11. For details on the description of our variables, please refer to the data appendix below.
12. A variable to capture the foreign exchange constraint is often used in the import demand function following the structuralist literature. For Pakistan, this ought to be constructed as the sum of remittances, export revenue, and net loan and grant inflows. Quarterly data were not available for these variables. Foreign exchange reserves are often used as a proxy variable. However, these reserves do not actually finance the imports but represent

the balance after imports have been financed. We none the less used it as a proxy variable but did not find it to be significant. Using annual Pakistani data, aggregate import demand functions have been estimated by Shabbir and Mahmood (1991) to test for structural stability, and disaggregate functions by Sarmad and Mahmood (1987).

13. For details of the Wu–Hausman test see Hausman (1978). This test consisted of solving equation (4) for EER. In the second stage, equation (3) is estimated with and without the residuals of the first stage regression. The F-statistic between these two estimations of equation (3) is Wu's T_2 statistic. The null-hypothesis of no simultaneity is rejected if the F-statistic is significantly different from zero. This procedure was also adopted for the disaggregate export demand functions reported in Table 2.2, and in all cases the null of no simultaneity was rejected.
14. We also found this to hold for the equations in Table 2.2.
15. For details of this derivation see Appendix 2.1.
16. In rupees, average exports and imports are 12.72 billion and 14.43 billion respectively.
17. The major exports represent about two-thirds of total exports in both the beginning and end quarters of our data. We selected the commodities by using Rs 100 million as the cut-off value for third quarter of 1993. Results for rice are not reported since the equation had no explanatory power as indicated by the F-test.
18. It appears that there was little reason for the big devaluation in 1993 or 1997, since the gap between the official and free-market exchange rate was small prior to the devaluation and not affected by the devaluation.

REFERENCES

Athukorala, P. and J. Riedel, 1991, 'The Small Country Assumption: A Reassessment with Evidence from Korea', *Weltwirtschaftliches Archiv*, Band 127, Heft 1, pp. 138–51.

Bahmani–Oskooee, M., 1991, 'Is There a Long-Run Relation Between the Trade Balance and the Real Effective Exchange Rate of LDCs?' *Economic Letters*, 36, pp. 403–7.

Balassa, B., E. Voloudakis, P. Fylaktos and S. T. Suh., 1989, 'The Determinants of Export Supply and Export Demand in Two Developing Countries: Greece and Korea', *International Economic Journal*, 3, no. 1, pp. 1–16.

Burton, D., and M. G. Gilman, 1991, 'Exchange Rate Policy and the IMF', *Finance and Development*, 28, no. 3, pp. 18–21.

Dorash, P., 1988, 'Exchange Rates and Trade Effects on Relative Prices in Pakistan', draft working paper, International Food Policy Research Institute.

Dornbusch, R., 1980, *Open Economy Macroeconomics* (New York: Basic Books).

Goldstein, M. and M. S. Khan, 1978, 'The Supply and Demand for Exports: A Simultaneous Approach', *The Review of Economics and Statistics*, May, pp. 275–86.

Government of Pakistan, Economic Affairs Division. *Pakistan Economic Survey*, various issues.

Government of Pakistan, Federal Bureau of Statistics, *Monthly Statistical Bulletin*, various issues, Islamabad.

Hausman, J. A., 1978, 'Specification Tests in Econometrics', *Econometrica*, 46, no. 6 (Nov.), pp. 1251–71.

Hughes, A., and A. Singh, 1991, 'Consequences of the World Economic Slowdown and the Asian and Latin American Economies: A Comparative Analysis of Economic Structure, Policy and Performance', in ed. T. Banuri, *Economic Liberalization: No Panacea* (Oxford: Oxford University Press).

Khan, A. H., and A. Hasan, 1994, 'Impact of Devaluation on Pakistan's External Trade: An Econometric Approach', Pakistan Society of Development Economists, Tenth Annual General Meeting, Pakistan Institute of Development Economics, Islamabad.

Khan, A. H. and B. Reza, 1989, 'The Demand for Money in Pakistan: Quarterly Results 1972–1987', *Pakistan Economic and Social Review*, 27, no. 1.

Lizondo, J. S. and P. J. Montiel, 1989, 'Contractory Devaluation in Developing Countries: An Analytical Overview', IMF Staff Papers, 36, no. 1, pp. 182–227.

Miles, M., 1979, 'The Effects of Devaluation on the Trade Balance and the Balance of Payments: Some New Results', *Journal of Political Economy*, 87, no. 3, pp. 600–20.

Nabi, I., forthcoming, 'The Competitiveness of Pakistani Exports', in ed. S. R. Khan, *Fifty Years of Pakistan's Economy* (Karachi: Oxford University Press).

Nunnencamp, P., and R. Schweickert, 1990, 'Adjustment Policies and Economic Growth in Developing Countries: Is Devaluation Contractionary?' *Weltwirtschaftliches Archiv*, 126, Heft 3.

Quick, P. J., B. V. Christensen, K. Huh and T. Sasaki, 1987, 'Floating Exchange Rates in Developing Countries: Experience with Auction and Interbank Markets', IMF Occasional Papers, no. 53, Washington, DC.

Riedel, J. and P. Athukorala, 1995, 'Export Growth and the Terms of Trade: The Case of Curious Elasticities', in eds D. Vines and D. Currie, *North South Linkages and International Macroeconomic Policy* (Cambridge: Cambridge University Press).

Rose, A, K., 1991, 'The Role of Exchange Rates in a Popular Model of International Trade: Does the Marshall–Lerner Condition Hold?' *Journal of International Economics*, 30, pp. 301–16.

Sarmad, K. and R. Mahmood, 1987, 'Disaggregated Import Demand Functions for Pakistan', *Pakistan Development Review*, 26, no. 1, pp. 71–80.

Saul, L. J. and P. J. Montiel, 1989, 'Contractionary Devaluation in Developing Countries: An Analytical Overview', *IMF Staff Papers*, 36, no. 1, pp. 182–287.

Shabbir, T. and R. Mahmood, 1991, 'Structural Change in the Import Demand Function for Pakistan', *Pakistan Development Review*, 30, no. 4, p. 1168.

Appendix 2.1: Derivation of a Modified Marshall–Lerner Condition

The trade balance is defined as the excess of exports over imports as follows:

$$T = X(p) - \flat M(\flat, Y)$$

where X is defined as the value of exports and $\flat M$ is the value of imports in domestic currency. Exports and imports are functions of a relative price variable p and $\flat$, for which the real effective exchange rates for export and import can be used as proxy variables, and imports are further dependent upon the domestic GDP, i.e Y.

$$\mathrm{d}T = \delta X/\delta p\,\mathrm{d}p - [\flat\,\delta M/\delta\flat + M]\,\mathrm{d}\flat$$

Multiply and divide by p and X.

$$\mathrm{d}T = \delta X/\delta p \cdot p/X \cdot X/p\,\mathrm{d}p - [\flat\,\delta M/\delta\flat + M]\,\mathrm{d}\flat$$
$$\mathrm{d}T = \varepsilon_x \cdot X/p\,\mathrm{d}p - [\flat\,\delta M/\delta\flat + M]\mathrm{d}\flat$$

Multiply and divide by M.

$$\mathrm{d}T = \varepsilon_x \cdot X/p\,\mathrm{d}p - [\flat/M\,\delta M/\delta\flat \cdot M + M]\mathrm{d}\flat$$
$$\mathrm{d}T = \varepsilon_x \cdot X/p\,\mathrm{d}p - [\varepsilon_m \cdot M + M]\,\mathrm{d}\flat$$

where

$$\varepsilon_x = \delta X/\delta p \cdot p/X > 0;$$
$$\varepsilon_m = -(\delta M/\delta\flat \cdot \flat/M) > 0.$$

$$\mathrm{d}T = \varepsilon_x \cdot X/p\,\mathrm{d}p - M[\varepsilon_m + 1]\,\mathrm{d}\flat$$
$$\mathrm{d}T/\mathrm{d}p = \varepsilon_x \cdot X/p$$
$$\mathrm{d}T/\mathrm{d}\flat = -M\,[\varepsilon_m + 1]$$
$$\mathrm{d}T/\mathrm{d}p + \mathrm{d}T/\mathrm{d}\flat = \varepsilon_x \cdot X/p - M[\varepsilon_m + 1]$$

$$\mathrm{d}T/\mathrm{d}p + \mathrm{d}T/\mathrm{d}\flat > 0 \text{ if } \varepsilon_x \cdot X/p - M[\varepsilon_m + 1] > 0$$

or $\varepsilon_x \cdot X/p - M\varepsilon_m > M$

divide through by M and

$\varepsilon_x \cdot X/p - \varepsilon_m > 1$ is the modified Marshall–Lerner condition. Note that ε_m is negative, so the condition

$|\varepsilon_x \cdot X/pM + \varepsilon_m| > 1.$

Appendix 2.2: Depreciation as a Currency Tax

INTRODUCTION

Poor countries generally continue to face currency depreciation relative to hard currencies. Why is a continued depreciation inevitable? Simply because in most cases the rich get richer. More resources means better social and physical infrastructure, more investment in R&D, and consequently stronger economies. Many products of such economies are usually indispensable for poor economies and hence they have an inelastic demand for rich-country products. This in turn leads to balance of trade deficits which is once source of pressure for currency depreciation. (As earlier suggested, poor macro management, resulting in higher inflation in poor countries relative to rich ones, is another source of pressure for currency depreciation.)

We coin the term 'currency tax' to designate that which is implicitly paid by poor countries every time they depreciate their currency. This tax occurs because the dollar denominated debt rises in local currency terms immediately and proportionately to the depreciation in the currency.

In the rest of this appendix we explain the simple method for quantifying the additional debt burden resulting from a currency depreciation; and then use Pakistani data, as an example, to show the loss over various time periods including the structural adjustment period.

METHOD

As mentioned above, each time an LCD depreciates, in local currency terms they have a higher foreign currency denominated debt. This represents a real resource transfer since governments could use these monies for development needs.

Consider the following:

$$LCD = DD^{*}R \tag{8}$$

where

DD = Nominal dollar (or foreign currency) denominated debt.
LCD = Nominal debt in local currency terms.
R = The nominal dollar exchange rate defined as local currency over dollars.

If the currency depreciates (R rises), LCD must rise given DD is unchanged. Thus the change in LCD that results from currency depreciation is

$$dLCD = DDdR + RdDD \tag{9}$$

To get an upper bound approximation of the impact of currency depreciation, for a period in question, on foreign debt liability in local currency, we take the average DD and multiply it by the currency depreciation (dR) over that period, and add to that the average exchange rate over the period (R) multiplied by the change in nominal dollar denominated debt (dDD) over the period.

RESULTS

Table 2.3 calculates the additional debt liability in nominal rupee terms for Pakistan due to the currency depreciation over the various periods in question.

The calculations in column 2 represent the difference in what the end-period debt stock actually is and what it would have been had the currency not depreciated over the period in question. Column 3 then shows what this additional burden is as a percentage of end-period GDP.

Note that these are upper bound estimates because we assume that there is a full real depreciation resulting from the nominal depreciation (i.e. no price adjustment). If prices adjusted instantaneously, the real debt burden would not change, which represents the other extreme. However, Nabi has demonstrated that the depreciation in the nominal exchange rate has more than compensated for the higher price level in Pakistan relative to its major trading partners. The impact of depreciation on the debt burden in rupee terms has thus been quite substantial in all periods.

Table 2.3 Estimates of the currency tax

Periods	Period Depreciation (Rs)	dLCD (nominal billion Rs)	Column 2 as a percentage of nominal end-period GDP
1970–7	5 (5)	63.0	60.8
1977–87	7 (10)	196.5	48.5
1988–95	15 (18)	645.9	47.7

Source: World Bank *World Tables, Economic Survey 1995–96.*
Note: Parentheses contain nominal rupee to dollar exchange rate at the start of the respective periods.

Appendix 2.3: Data

Data on value added of exports, imports and the unit value of exports were obtained from Pakistan's *Monthly Statistical Bulletins* and converted into quarterly form.

Since quarterly data on GDP are not available for Pakistan, annual data from the *Economic Survey* was converted into quarterly data according to the technique described in Khan and Reza (1989).

The data on GDP of the six industrialized countries were obtained from the monthly issues of the IMF's *International Financial Statistics* and were converted into US dollars with data on exchange rates from the same source. The six countries included in the index are Canada, France, Germany, Italy, the United States and Japan. These countries account for 37.2 per cent of total exports from Pakistan. For other major importers from Pakistan, quarterly data were not available. However, in the annual data, the correlation of exports to the G6 countries and total Pakistani exports was 0.99.

The data series for the real effective exchange rate was obtained from *International Financial Statistics* and the IMF Information Notice System. The exchange rate is calculated against a basket of currencies which includes the currencies of trading partners for both exports and imports, excluding oil trade partners.

3 Financial Sector Reform[1]

INTRODUCTION

Among the series of reforms accepted by policy-makers in Pakistan are financial sector reforms such as interest rate liberalization and the deregulation and privatization of banks.[2] We demonstrate in this chapter that there is very weak support at best for the neo-liberal hypotheses concerning interest rate liberalization and that such liberalization is regressive. There is, however, preliminary support concerning the efficiency of private sector banks.

McKinnon (1973) and Shaw (1973) were the major advocates of financial reform.[3] They argued that financial repression in the form of controlled, and hence often negative, real interest rates reduced incentives for saving and hindered financial intermediation. Liberalizing and allowing positive, market-driven interest rates would channel funds from consumption, cash holdings, less productive self-investment, and overly capital intensive investments to more productive investments.

Disputing this contention, neo-structuralists have argued that following financial liberalization the funds would be drawn from the informal credit markets (curb markets), which are actually more efficient at intermediating funds because there are fewer leakages and no reserve requirements.[4] Given the lack of data on intermediation in the informal sector and responses following bouts of liberalization, the debate is potentially difficult to resolve. However, Cho (1990) has disputed the validity of the neo-structuralist arguments on a conceptual level. The McKinnon–Shaw hypotheses have spawned a theoretical and empirical literature and currently represent the mainstream conventional wisdom.[5]

Pakistan has adopted several of the neo-liberal prescriptions for financial reform.[6] Included among these is making the real interest rate positive, hence reducing financial repression and privatizing the banking system. In the second section we state and test various neo-liberal hypotheses advocating interest rate liberalization. In the third section, we analyse the political economy of interest rate liberalization. In the fourth section we review bank privatization. We end with a summary and concluding remarks.

TESTING INTEREST RATE LIBERALIZATION HYPOTHESES

Since most of the fundamental financial reforms have occurred recently, one could argue that it is not as yet possible to determine their quantitative impact on the economy. Even so, some neo-liberal hypotheses have been tested in Pakistan by using historical data.[7] Inferring support from a pre-reform environment for the reform certainly appears to be a flawed method. None the less, we employed this method not to endorse it but to contrast our results with studies which have used this method to endorse neo-liberal reforms in Pakistan. In all these exercises, we took account of the non-stationarity of most of the variables we used.

Saving and Real Interest Rates

Cross-country evidence about a positive association of saving and interest rates is mixed.[8] None the less, to see if this holds for Pakistan, we used time series data from 1970–90.[9] Since growth is hypothesized to increase saving and is in turn affected by investment, we estimated the saving function, as is conventional, using the two-stage estimation procedure.[10] To compute the expected real interest rate, we estimated expected inflation as a polynomial distributed lag of current and past inflation rates. Similarly, we computed permanent or expected per capita GNP.[11] However, we found much stronger results from simply using the log of per capita GNP and the real interest rate. The results are reported in Table 3.1.[12]

We identified a statistically significant positive association of interest rate and saving, although the magnitude is virtually negligible. A 10 per cent

Table 3.1 Association of the saving rate with real interest rate (dependent variable is saving)

Regressor	Coefficient	T-Ratio
INPT	−1.3983	−2.21**
OTR	−0.6799E−5	−2.12**
R	0.0026	4.97*
LPCGNP	0.1842	2.36**
S(−1)	0.0389	0.19
FGR	0.0034	1.62

R-Bar-Squared = 0.85 F-Statistic = F(4,15) = 30.88
RSS = 0.0021 D-W Statistic = 2.12
*Significant at 1 per cent level of significance
**Significant at 5 per cent level of significance
OTR = Official Transfers
R = Real interest rate
LPCGNP = Log per capita GNP
FGR = Fitted Growth Rate
S(−1) = Saving rate lagged one period

increase in the real interest rate could be expected to be associated with a 0.03 per cent rise in saving.[13] A positive association of real saving with per capita GNP and a negative one with official transfers are as expected.

One could argue that the truly endogenous component of saving is household saving. Unfortunately, we did not have the complete data series, but we did find that between 1980 and 1981, and 1989 and 1990, household saving constituted at least three-fourths of total saving.[14] Private saving is defined as corporate plus household saving. Using private saving as a percentage of GNP as our dependent variable, we obtained results virtually identical to those reported in Table 3.1.

Interest Rates and Financial Deepening

The theory is that a positive real interest rate should deepen the market by encouraging more saving in the form of various financial assets. Thus even if a higher real interest rate does not lead to higher real saving, given the right incentives, households are expected to change the form in which they hold their saving, i.e. from real to financial assets. We tested the association of interest rates and financial saving by regressing the ratio of M_3/GDP as a measure of financial deepening (FD) on the real interest rate. The results are reported in Table 3.2.

While the interest rate coefficient is positive and highly significant, our results show that a 10 per cent rise in interest rate would lead to only about a 0.1 per cent rise in financial deepening.[15]

Table 3.2 Association of financial deepening with real interest rates (dependent variable is financial deepening)

Regressor	Coefficient	T-Ratio
INPT	−0.6077	−14.17*
T	−0.0102	−3.46*
R(−1)	0.0127	5.99*

R-Bar-Squared = 0.65
F-Statistic = F(2,16) = 17.98
RSS = 0.056 D-W Statistic = 0.77
*Significant at 1 per cent level of significance
R(−1) = Real interest rate lagged one period
T = Time trend

Financial Deepening and Investment Productivity

Higher financial saving or financial deepening is not viewed as an end in and of itself. The hypothesis is that financial saving is intermediated towards real investment with beneficial effects for the economy. Financial deepening is also viewed as a worthy goal because it is expected to lead to a more efficient allocation of financial resources towards real investment.[16] The inverse of ICOR or incremental capital output ratio is used as a proxy for investment productivity, and since real interest rate is positively associated with financial deepening, the hypothesis is that investment productivity should also be positively associated with the real interest rate. This hypothesis was tested and the results are reported in Table 3.3.

Given that the model estimated is log linear, a 10 per cent increase in the real interest rate is associated with about a 5 per cent decline in investment efficiency as measured by the inverse of ICOR.

Interest Rate Liberalization and Growth

A greater availability of credit via financial liberalization is also asserted by proponents of interest rate liberalization to have a positive impact on growth. Alternatively, the higher cost of capital could have a negative impact on growth. We tested this hypothesis by including the real interest rate in a standard neo-classical growth equation, and the results are reported in Table 3.4.[17]

The dependency ratio and log of the terms of trade index are significant and have the expected signs. The interest rate, however, has a small but significant negative association with the growth rate which could be resulting

Table 3.3 Association of inverse ICOR with the real interest rate (dependent variable is inverse ICOR)

Regressor	Coefficient	T-Ratio
INPT	−2.8937	−6.76*
T	0.0996	3.31*
R	−0.0492	−2.13**

R-Bar-Squared = 0.39 F-Statistic = F(2,17) = 5.53
RSS = 7.08 D-W Statistic = 1.06
*Significant at 1 per cent level of significance
**Significant at 5 per cent level of significance
R = Real interest rate

Table 3.4 Association of the growth rate with the real interest rate (dependent variable is the growth rate)

Regressor	Coefficient	T-Ratio
INPT	97.1808	2.14**
T	−0.2295	1.15
GLF	0.3973	−0.26
R	−0.1312	−2.64**
LTT	10.8817	2.90**
DR	−152.6843	−3.77*

R-Bar-Squared = 0.63   F-Statistic = F(5,14) 7.40
RSS = 23.8518   D-W Statistic = 2.57
*Significant at 1 per cent level of significance
**Significant at 5 per cent level of significance
GLF = Growth in Labour Force
LTT = Log of Terms of Trade Index
DR = Dependency Ratio

from the higher cost of capital.[18] This negative association could also be explained by the crowding out of the more efficient private sector investment, as the state issued various high-yielding financial assets to cover its own expenditures. Data on bank advances to the public and private sector are reported in Table 3.5.

Table 3.5 shows how starting from the early 1980s, the government has steadily decreased its dependence on bank borrowing (column 1). It has managed to do this by borrowing directly from the capital market. Column 2 shows the steady decline in the loans to public sector enterprises from 17 per cent in 1982 to about 6 per cent of total loans to domestic constituents in 1995. Conversely, column 3 shows the steady rise in loans to the private sector from about half in 1982 to about three-fourths of total domestic loans granted in 1995. Loans to the private sector jumped in the mid-1980s and peaked at four-fifths of total loans granted in 1992 after which point they declined somewhat. Even so, it is not possible to make the conventional argument concerning the crowding out of the private sector to explain the negative association of the interest rate and investment efficiency and economic growth.

Neo-liberal economists would be justified in countering that banks were not privatized until the early 1990s and so that political patronage and influence rather than profit could well have been the criteria for giving loans. There is evidence that this did indeed happen in Pakistan. Lists of defaulters from among the business, political and military elites, who

Table 3.5 Percentage distribution of bank advances

Year	Government*	Public enterprises	Private sector†
1982	22.0	17.0	51.1
1983	20.1	19.1	50.7
1984	14.0	16.6	58.6
1985	12.6	16.2	62.4
1986	5.0	16.6	69.7
1987	4.3	12.3	74.1
1988	7.0	11.2	72.5
1989	7.1	8.6	74.9
1990	11.1	7.4	71.8
1991	7.9	7.0	76.1
1992	8.9	7.3	79.5
1993	9.4	5.6	75.4
1994	8.2	5.6	75.9
1995	8.7	5.7	73.6

Sources: State Bank of Pakistan, *Annual Report*, various issues.

Notes: Rows do not add to a hundred because of various other minor categories of loans.

* Loans to government include loans for commodity operations and local bodies.

† These are business loans.

together owed the banking system about a fourth of the total loans it made since its inception, have been made public several times starting in 1993. Less than 5 per cent of their outstanding debt has been collected by the three state banks (see next section). Interestingly, the two privatized commercial banks fared much better. We will return to the issue of bank privatization, but first we explore the political economy of interest rate liberalization.

POLITICAL ECONOMY OF INTEREST RATE LIBERALIZATION

Since no economic reason appears to have been established, at least to date, to liberalize the interest rate in Pakistan, it is all the more important to discuss the political economy of this reform. In other words, who gains and who loses from interest rate liberalization.

In a newspaper interview, the Governor of the State Bank asserted that financial repression hurts the small saver.[19] It is not clear what size of deposit represents that of the small saver. If we view the top 15 per cent of depositors as large savers and the rest as small savers, even then the small savers account for only a third of total deposits.[20] Thus a disproportionate percentage of the benefit from higher deposit rates probably accrues to upper income groups, who therefore stand to lose most from financial repression.

Given the high prevalence of tax evasion, one could consider financial repression as an implicit tax on the rich. This is clearly not a first best solution, but years of attempts at reforming the tax administration have not made much headway.[21] Giovannini and De Melo (1993) have made a case for viewing financial repression as a tax and demonstrated that it can yield substantial revenue, equivalent in some cases to that derived from seigniorage. They estimated that the revenue from financial repression for Pakistan for 1993 was 20.5 per cent of total tax revenue.

On the one hand, the evidence suggests that containing the interest rate is likely to have limited negative repercussions on real and financial saving. On the other hand, high interest rates are likely to result in a ballooning of the fiscal deficit if selected government projects on average have a social rate of return less than private sector and government projects that are consequently denied funds.[22] We explored the association of the real interest rate on government bonds with the deficit and the results are reported in Table 3.6.

Our results show that a one per cent rise in the interest rate on government bonds increases the deficit by about 3 billion rupees. There are several options for containing the deficit. One option is to keep term deposit rates low until fiscal balance is attained. If term deposit rates rise, the deficit has to be curtailed by sharper cuts in expenditure and/or higher tax rates. If the government can raise revenues via progressive taxation, which is unlikely, that is the first best option from a progressive viewpoint. If it

Table 3.6 Association of the budget deficit with the yield on government securities (dependent variable is the budget deficit)

Regressor	Coefficient	T-Ratio
INPT	−7673.9	−1.01
T	−3419.1	−13.57*
RPAK	2885.4	3.15*

R-Bar-Squared = 0.92 F-Statistic = F(2,15) 92.79
RSS = 4.15E+08 D-W Statistic = 1.19
*Significant at 1 per cent level of significance
RPAK = Yield on government securities

opts for expenditure cuts, the poor are likely to be hurt the most. 'Progressive expenditures', such as targeted food subsidies and social sector spending, are viewed as the most vulnerable budget items, and so the poor bear a disproportionate burden of the deficit cuts. If neither of these deficit reduction options is pursued, an inflation tax resulting from deficit financing is almost inevitable, and researchers have shown that the poor once again bear the greater burden.[23] It therefore appears that in the short run, repressing the interest rate is a progressive option for containing the deficit while fiscal balance is being restored.[24]

PRIVATIZATION AND EFFICIENT BANKING

The hypothesis that denationalization will lead to more efficient banking cannot be tested yet in a satisfactory manner because there are too few years of experience to draw on since the two commercial banks were denationalized. None the less, what we find might be indicative of future trends. We compare the before and after record of these two banks in terms of the profit/assets ratio, deposit growth, loan recoveries and the ratio of non-performing loans. We also compare the recent record of the denationalized banks with commercial banks still in the public sector using these performance criteria. Finally we cite evidence on the performance of nationalized commercial banks relative to foreign commercial banks. The relevant tables are reported in the Appendix as Tables 3.7–3.10.

In April 1991, the Muslim Commercial Bank became the first public sector bank to be privatized. Fifty per cent of the bank's shares were acquired by the National Group, a consortium of industrialists. This was followed by the privatization of the Allied Bank in September 1991. The bank was restructured as an institution jointly owned by its employees through the Employees' Stock Ownership Plan (ESOP), formulated by the Allied Management Group.

The profit/asset ratio of the MCB, reported in Appendix Table 3.7, actually fell after the bank was privatized but picked up in a couple of years and jumped from 0.46 in 1993 to 0.72 in 1994. The value of net assets of the bank rose by 38 per cent, as it invested heavily in Federal Investment Bonds and in Treasury Bills following the implementation of Prudential Regulations. The profit/asset ratio of the Allied Bank immediately showed a considerable improvement, rising to almost one in 1993. The rate of growth of pre-tax profits was particularly impressive, averaging just over 250 per cent.

The growth rate of deposits after denationalization, reported in Appendix Table 3.9, was impressive in both the newly privatized banks.

The average growth rate of deposits for both privatized banks dropped prior to privatization but then picked up and increased from 26.5 and 36.1 per cent in 1988–90 to 132.5 and 65.5 per cent respectively for the MCB and ABL for 1991–4. In contrast to the substantial gains made by these banks, primarily as a result of extensive deposit mobilization campaigns, the performance of the nationalized banks remained fairly constant.[25] Whether the growth of bank deposits will continue remains to be seen. Even so, the newly privatized commercial banks immediately captured the lion's share of the increased liquidity in the market. This seems to be due to a more efficient approach towards deposit mobilization.

The privatized banks have also been more successful in loan recovery. The total value of outstanding loans from all commercial banks and development finance institutions was Rs 80.35 billion on June 30 1993; of which Rs 51 billion were owed to the three nationalized commercial banks. This state of affairs may have arisen because loan disbursement in the nationalized commercial banks became increasingly politicized, with commercial banks being pressurized to extend loans to influential applicants without adequately enforcing collateral requirements. As can be seen from Appendix Table 3.9, their loan recovery drive has not been very successful. The three Nationalized Commercial Banks (NCBs) have collectively recovered only about 3.8 per cent of their outstanding debt.

The two newly privatized commercial banks fared better. Both the Muslim Commercial Bank and the Allied Bank launched campaigns to recover their outstanding debt immediately after their respective denationalizations. The MCB formed a Special Assets Management Group for the recovery of outstanding debt, while the Allied Bank designated 1992 as the year of 'recoveries', and award schemes were introduced to encourage staff to formulate programmes for the recovery of 'problem loans'. This initiative was taken at a time when loan recovery had not yet become an issue on the national scene.

Appendix Table 3.10 reports non-performing loans as a proportion of total loans disbursed by the five major commercial banks. Once again, the NCBs are in an unfavourable position relative to the newly privatized commercial banks, as 'bad' loans constitute 25 to 30 per cent of their total credit advancements.

Lari (1993) used various performance indicators including profitability, efficiency, leverage and capital adequacy ratios to develop rankings of NCBs relative to foreign banks. Out of 25 banks ranked for 1990, the five major NCBs secured the twentieth to the twenty-fourth positions. The next chapter is entirely devoted to privatization, and we review the experience of recently privatized firms in the industrial sector compared to similar units still in the public sector.

CONCLUSION

Our primary objective in this chapter was to test a series of neo-liberal hypotheses about the likely benefits of financial liberalization and to investigate if privatization enhanced banking efficiency. Financial deepening and investment efficiency are the channels via which a higher interest rate is expected to benefit the economy. In addition, a direct positive impact on growth is anticipated as credit becomes more readily available.

Judging from Pakistan's experience, the association of real interest rates and real saving, while positive, was negligible. We found the expected positive association of real interest rates and financial saving but one of modest magnitude. Neo-liberal theory posits that financial deepening can contribute to efficiency of investment, and we tested this hypothesis by regressing the inverse of incremental capital output ratio, as a proxy for the efficiency of investment, on real interest rates. We found a significant but negative association between the two variables. We also found a negative and significant association of growth rates and interest rates contrary to the neo-liberal hypothesis of a positive association via more credit becoming available. Among other reasons, it is possible that the adverse impact of a higher cost of capital and the quality of the investment could explain this negative association. Evidence suggests that one can rule out the crowding out of private sector investment as a causal factor.

Perhaps one reason to refrain from liberalizing interest rates in Pakistan is the enormous size of the budget deficit and the large contribution of interest payments to this deficit. If real and financial saving rate is only modestly responsive to interest rates, as the evidence in this paper suggests, the government could view an interest ceiling as an implicit tax on the upper and upper-middle classes without impeding real or financial saving. Our reasoning indicates this to be the most progressive way of dealing with the deficit.

The one unambiguously positive reform appears to be the denationalization of two state-owned banks. In terms of the growth of assets their performance improved dramatically compared to their past performance and also relative to the nationalized banks. They also outperformed the nationalized banks in recovering loans and in terms of their ratio of bad loans. If better management is more likely to be associated with privatization, the evidence to date suggests there is a strong case for denationalization. However, the same cannot be said for interest rate liberalization.

NOTES

1. This chapter was first written by Shahrukh R. Khan and Safiya Aftab as a paper for a Conference on Economic Reforms and the Role of Government organized by the Applied Economic Research Institute, Karachi, Nov. 18–20, 1993. The paper was subsequently published in volume 10, nos. 1 & 2 of the *Journal of Applied Economics*. Thanks are due to Hafiz A. Pasha for comments on an earlier draft.
2. We view financial reform as the broader term which includes liberalization of interest rates and credit, but also includes denationalization, privatization, public sector debt management and prudential regulations. Our focus is on the impact of interest rate liberalization and privatization, and we do not deal here with related issues of capital flows, exchange-rate or foreign investment liberalization.
3. See Fry (1995) for an extensive discussion.
4. Wijnbergen (1983) and Taylor (1983). Also see Bencivenga and Smith (1992) on the optimal degree of financial repression.
5. McKinnon revised his initial position and based on a synthesis of the experience of East Asian and Southern Cone countries advocated a sequencing of interest rate liberalization such that it should follow macro stabilization (1988). Villaneuva and Mirakhor (1990) develop this argument, suggesting that liberalization should take macro stabilization and prudential regulation into account.
6. Ul Haque and Kardar (1993) present a detailed interpretive account of financial sector reforms in Pakistan which began in 1990.
7. Fry (1984), Khan (1982, 1988). To justify their analyses, they could conceivably have argued that term deposit rates, the variable of interest, has varied a great deal from more to less negative and even positive for several years.
8. Lee (1991), pp. 6–7.
9. When revising this chapter, additional data were available until 1993. Since banking sector reform began in 1990, we decided to let the focus remain only on the pre-reform period. There were not enough observations to test for post-reform structural changes.
10. Apart from investment ratio and labour force growth, the exogenous variables included in the estimation of the first-stage growth function were the long-run terms of trade, dependency ratio, growth in exports, export ratio, official transfers, real interest rate and log of per capita GNP. The fitted growth rate from the first stage was used in the second-stage saving function. The exogenous variables represent the variables conventionally used as saving rate predictors. Saving was defined as gross national saving divided by gross national product. Following the explanation in Appendix 3 of Asian Development Bank (1985), p. 51, we selected gross national saving over alternative measures to define the saving ratio. Given our sample size, we used variable deletion tests to identify the robust and significant predictors of the saving rate. Data on the dependency ratio and labour force were extracted from the data diskette of the World Bank *Social Indicators of Development*. The nominal interest rate series was constructed as a

weighted average of rates of return on scheduled banks deposits. The figures were taken from various issues of the State Bank of Pakistan *Annual Reports*.

11. The inflation and income adjustment coefficients were 0.92 and 0.94 respectively.
12. All variables except the fitted growth rate and the interest rate were non-stationary, as evident from Augmented Dicky Fuller tests for unit roots. Using the Johansen Maximum Likelihood Procedure, we identified the existence of a cointegrating vector for the saving function which captures a stable long-run association between the series.
13. This coefficient is smaller than that identified by Fry (1984), p. 49. We essentially used the same method so the results are comparable, although Fry used annual data from 1960–81. For a more recent review of evidence on this issue see Fry (1995), p. 188. Fry interprets the cross-country evidence as suggesting that there is virtually no direct effect of real interest rates on the level of saving.
14. State Bank *Annual Reports*, various years.
15. From a money demand equation (not reported) we found the short-run impact of real interest on financial saving to be identical. We used the significant coefficient of lagged money to estimate the long-run equilibrium effect. A 10 per cent increase in the interest rate can be expected to be associated with a 0.2 per cent rise in financial saving, still a modest effect.
16. A statement of this and the previous hypothesis on financial deepening and investment productivity is contained in World Bank (1987), p. 32.
17. We substituted the real interest rate for the ratio of investment to GDP normally included in the growth equation to capture the positive impact of interest rate on investment as more funds become available. Except for growth and interest rate, all other variables are non-stationary. However, we identified a cointegrating vector, which suggests a stable long-run association between the series. Lagged interest rate was not significant.
18. Fry (1995), pp. 178–89, reports cross-country evidence of positive association of real interest rates and growth.
19. 'Dr. Yaqub Says Banking System Exploitative, Inefficient and Corrupt', *Dawn, Economic and Business Review*, 18 Nov. 1993.
20. Data are drawn for 1990 from the State Bank *Annual Report 1991–92*, Statistical Appendix, p. 63. Since individuals do not report income and assets when opening bank accounts, conjecture is the best one can do. Not even the Governor of the State Bank is privy to the information about the distribution of depositors by income group. Such information can be ascertained from a survey of deposit holders, although misreporting of income and assets is likely.
21. This is conceded even in government sources, *Economic Survey 1992–93*, p. 55.
22. Interest payments amounted to one-fifth of total federal government expenditure in 1991–2 or about four-fifths of the overall deficit of Rs 78.7 billion ($1 = Rs 31.5) in 1991–2. This represents about 6.5 per cent of GDP at market prices. *Economic Survey 1992–93*, Statistical Appendix, p. 116 and p. 118.
23. Afridi, Qadir and Zaki (1984).

24. The case for caution in liberalizing interest would be further reinforced if it results in a significant curtailment of either informal private (curb market) or public investment finance. Unfortunately, data are not readily available to investigate this issue more thoroughly. The data reported in Table 3.6 shows that, over the 1980s, bank financing was increasingly directed to the formal private sector and away from the public sector.
25. The growth of deposits of the two newly privatized commercial banks should be interpreted with caution. The substantial increases in the value of bank deposits is at least partially attributable to the collapse of the cooperatives in the Punjab province (accounting for roughly 65 per cent of Pakistan's population) and the resulting slump in property prices, which rendered investment in real estate largely unprofitable. Another reason for these high deposit growth rates could be stock-market volatility and bearish trends resulting from political instability.

REFERENCES

Afridi, U., A. Qadir and J. Zaki, 1984, 'Effects of Dual Sector Inflation Across Income Levels in Pakistan', *Pakistan Development Review*, 23, nos 2 & 3, pp. 381–90.

Asian Development Bank, 1985, *Improving Domestic Resource Mobilization Through Financial Development* (Manila: Asian Development Bank).

Bencivenga, V. R. and B. D. Smith, 1992, 'Deficits, Inflation and the Banking System in Developing Countries: The Optimal Degree of Financial Repression', *Oxford Economic Papers*, 44, pp. 767–90.

Cho, Yoon Je, 1990, 'McKinnon–Shaw vs the Neo-Structuralists on Financial Liberalization: A Conceptual Note', *World Development*, 18, no. 3, pp. 477–80.

Fry, M. J., 1984, 'Econometric Analysis of National Saving Rate' and 'Financial Saving, Financial Intermediation and Economic Growth', in *Improving Domestic Resource Mobilization through Financial Development*, Appendixes II and III, Asian Development Bank, Economics Office, Manila.

Fry, M. J., 1995, 2nd edn, *Money, Interest and Banking in Economic Development* (Baltimore: Johns Hopkins University Press).

Giovannini, A. and M. de Melo, 1993, 'Government Revenue from Financial Repression', *American Economic Review*, 83, no. 4, pp. 953–63.

Government of Pakistan, *Economic Survey*, Economic Advisors Wing, Ministry of Finance, various issues.

International Monetary Fund, 1992, *International Financial Statistics Yearbook*, vol. XLV (Washington, DC: International Monetary Fund).

Khan, A. H., 1982, 'Permanent Income, Inflation Expectations and the Money Demand Function in Developing Countries', *Pakistan Development Review*, 21, no. 4, pp. 259–73.

Khan, A. H., 1988, 'Financial Repression, Financial Development and Structure of Savings in Pakistan', *Pakistan Development Review*, 27, no.4, pp. 701–13.

Lari, Raeena, 1993, 'Commercial Banks in Pakistan: A Performance Evaluation', National Development Finance Corporation Research Report Financial Liberalization Series, vol. III, Karachi.

Lee, J., 1991, 'Financial Sector and Economic Development, A Survey', Asian Development Bank, EDRC Report Series no. 55.

McKinnon, R. I., 1973, *Money and Capital in Economic Development* (Washington, DC: Brookings Institution).

McKinnon, R. I., 1988, 'Financial Liberalization in Retrospect: Interest Rate Policies in Retrospect', in eds Gustav Ranis and T. Paul Schultz, *The State of Development Economics: Progress and Perspectives* (Oxford: Blackwell), pp. 386–410.

Shaw, E., 1973, *Financial Deepening in Economic Development* (New York: Oxford University Press).

State Bank of Pakistan, *Annual Report*, various issues.

Taylor, L., 1983, *Structuralist Macroeconomics: Applicable Models for the Third World* (New York: Basic Books).

Ul Haque, N. and S. Kardar, 1993, 'The Development of Financial Markets in Pakistan', Sustainable Development Policy Institute Working Paper no. 15, Islamabad.

Villanueva, D. and A. Mirakhor, 1990, 'Strategies for Financial Reforms: Interest Rate Policies, Stabilization and Bank Supervision in Developing Countries', *International Monetary Fund Staff Papers*, 37, no. 3, pp. 509–36.

Wijnbergen, S. Van, 1983, 'Interest Rate Management in LDCs', *Journal of Monetary Economics*, 12, no. 3, pp. 433–52.

World Bank, 1989, *World Development Report* (New York: Oxford University Press).

Appendix 3.1: Comparative Privatized and Nationalized Bank Performance

Table 3.7 Profit–asset ratios of commercial banks

Banks	1988	1989	1990	1991	1992	1993	1994
MCB	0.80	0.77	0.44	0.47	0.42	0.46	0.72
ABL	0.31	0.28	0.26	0.35	0.93	0.99	0.73
HBL	0.53	0.52	0.32	0.26	0.27	0.26	0.22
UBL	0.29	0.27	0.25	0.19	0.19	0.17	0.03

Sources:
Habib Bank Ltd. (HBL) *Annual Report* 1994
Muslim Commercial Bank (MCB) *Annual Report* 1994
Allied Bank Ltd. (ABL) *Annual Report* 1994
United Bank Ltd. (UBL) *Annual Report* 1994

Table 3.8 Commercial banks' deposit growth rates

Banks	1988–90	1991–4
Muslim Commercial Bank (MCB)	26.5	132.5
Allied Bank Ltd. (ABL)	36.1	65.5
Habib Bank Ltd. (HBL)	30.1	34.6
United Bank Ltd. (UBL)	23.4	36.9

Sources:
Habib Bank Ltd. (HBL) *Annual Report* 1994
Muslim Commercial Bank (MCB) *Annual Report* 1994
Allied Bank Ltd. (ABL) *Annual Report* 1994
United Bank Ltd. (UBL) *Annual Report* 1994

Table 3.9 Loan recovery in major commercial banks

Banks	Total Outstanding Debt (Rs)	Amount Recovered till 21 Sept. 1993 (Rs)	Amount Recovered till 29 Sept. 1993 (Rs)	Proportion of Total Debt Recovered
National Bank of Pakistan	13.72 billion	14.3 million	15.9 million	1.16%
Habib Bank Ltd.	24.69 billion	108.1 million	134.6 million	5.45%
United Bank Ltd.	12.48 billion	32.3 million	58.9 million	4.72%
Muslim Commercial Bank	4.67 billion	33.7 million	34.9 million	7.47%
Allied Bank Ltd.	1.96 billion	n.a	26.4 million	13.5%

Source: *Dawn*, 21 and 29 Sept. 1993.

Table 3.10 Non-performing loans as a proportion of total loans disbursed

Banks	Proportion of Bad Loans (%)
National Bank of Pakistan	31.3
Habib Bank Ltd.	30.0
United Bank Ltd.	25.1
Muslim Commercial Bank	17.2
Allied Bank	11.7

Source: *Dawn*, 29 Sept. 1993.

4 Comparative Privatization Experience: Employee and Private Ownership[1]

INTRODUCTION

Does privatization lead to greater economic efficiency? Is privatization inevitably regressive? Do employee-owned firms represent a way of ameliorating the regressive social impact of privatization without compromising economic efficiency? These issues are empirically investigated in this chapter by comparing the performance of employee-owned privatized units with those conventionally transferred to an individual or a corporate group by comparing the before and after privatization performance of both kinds of units.

Privatization is understood as a process whereby the public sector divests itself of its holdings in a firm, bank or any other enterprise and relinquishes ownership and control to the private sector. The 'private sector', in most cases, is a corporate group which arranges financing for the venture, and, once the deal is done, begins the process of hiring labour and management, or in some cases, makes decisions on whether or not to retain existing labour and management. In an employee takeover, the corporate group who bids for the enterprise is not an extraneous party, but is composed of employees of the firm, who jointly formulate a stock ownership or 'takeover' plan, arrange financing for the venture, and compete in the open market to become the majority shareholders of the firm.

Cooperatives in one form or another have existed in Pakistan practically since the inception of the country, but mainly in the agricultural sector. The incidence of employee takeover in manufacturing industry through a well-formulated plan of stock ownership is a new occurrence. The study of such enterprises is of interest for a variety of reasons. First, this form of ownership of private capital may be the least likely to disturb the existing pattern and level of employment in the firm. This is an important consideration when unemployment rates are high and rising. Second, this form of divestment could be an important additional option when financial markets are neither well regulated nor broad and deep.[2] Third, this form of industrial organization, if successfully managed, can minimize labour unrest and lead to productivity gains.[3]

The testable hypotheses for us were that higher worker productivity may result from participation in management and from profit-sharing, that there may be fewer retrenchments under the employee-owned option, and that profits may be higher under conventional privatization. While we did not have the data to do rigorous hypothesis testing, we believe that the case material and evidence we present about the process of alternative forms of privatization make a contribution.[4]

Below we describe the stimulus for alternative forms of privatization. Then we describe the sample selection, our method and the data; report and discuss the findings; and end with a summary and concluding remarks.

STIMULUS FOR ALTERNATIVE FORMS OF PRIVATIZATION IN PAKISTAN

The process of deregulation began in Pakistan in 1977 soon after the military takeover. Although the government expressed a commitment to privatize state-owned enterprises and initiate a process of divestment, the pace of this operation remained sluggish throughout the 1980s. It was not until Pakistan became a recipient of loans from the IMF under the structural adjustment facility (SAF) in 1988, that the government came under pressure to begin divesting holdings in manufacturing enterprises. According to the terms of the agreement reached between the IMF and the government of Pakistan in 1988, privatization and deregulation were to be the cornerstone of the reform process. The government was to begin the process of auctioning government-owned industrial and financial concerns as soon as possible.

The process of divestment began in earnest in 1991. The Privatization Commission, set up in January 1991, identified over a hundred industrial units which could be transferred to private control. According to the terms of reference given to the Privatization Commission, the process of transfer of firms to private ownership could take a variety of forms. Industrial units could be auctioned off to the highest bidder by calling for either open or sealed bids. Alternatively, privatization could be accomplished by divesting shares of the public sector industries on the stock exchange at an agreed share price.

Industrial relations in the private sector in the pre-nationalization days were always a cause for concern for industrialists, workers and the government.[5] As the process of privatization began, labour–management relations once again became an issue, and workers of state-owned enterprises expressed serious reservations about privatization. Not surprisingly, labour's overriding concern was job security. Many public sector industrial units are acknowledged to be overstaffed, and workers of such units anticipated a wave of layoffs and staff reductions soon after privatization. The government had agreed to guarantee job security of all workers in privatized units for a period of one year, but at the same time, many employees were also expected to opt for the lucrative golden handshake schemes offered by the new management of the privatized enterprises.

As a means of addressing labour concerns, the government adopted a policy of encouraging workers of state-owned enterprises to take over the firm upon privatization.[6] Employee groups were given the first option to match the highest bid in case of sealed bidding. The possibility of entering into a lease management contract with employees for a specified period was also open. In spite of these efforts, only eight privatized units have been transferred to the control of employees.[7] The primary reason for this appears to be financial constraints confronted by workers as explained later.

SAMPLE SELECTION, METHOD AND DATA

A total of eight firms were initially selected for analysis. All eight were originally state-owned firms which were recently privatized. These firms were selected as follows: First, those industry groups were identified in which at least one firm had been taken over by an employees' group. There were four such industries, i.e., chemicals, tractor, cement and ghee manufacturing. In three of these industries, there was only one firm that had been transferred to employee ownership, and these firms were automatically selected for analysis.[8] These firms were Sind Alkalis, Millat Tractors and Dandot Cement. A total of three ghee mills were transferred to employees, of which Sh. Fazal-ur-Rehman and Sons was chosen for analysis.[9]

The next stage entailed the selection of privatized firms from these industries which had been transferred to private ownership. To select such firms, two factors had to be taken into consideration. First, only those firms could be selected for analysis whose product was comparable to the product of the employee-owned firm. Second, the value of fixed assets of the two firms had to be comparable. Sind Alkalis effectively has no local competition in the public or the private sectors. The only other producer of soda ash and soda bicarbonate in the country (Sind Alkalis's two major products) is ICI, a multinational company, with a wide range of products in addition to the two mentioned above. In case of the tractor industry, only one firm was comparable with Millat Tractors and that was Al-Ghazi Tractors.[10]

Kohat Cement was chosen as suitable for comparison with Dandot Cement on the basis of the value of fixed assets of both firms. Kakakhel Industries was considered as suitable for comparison with Rose Ghee Mills because of similarities in capacity and size of the firm and the time of privatization.

During the course of the study, we discovered that Dandot Cement was no longer under employee control: they had sold their shares to a private company, as they had been unable to run the firm. The present owners of the company were not keen to be part of our study. The cement industry was thus excluded from the analysis. We take up the case of each remaining three industries separately and investigate the pre- and post-privatization performance of the selected firms.

The performance evaluation consists of a comparative analysis of profitability, labour productivity, capacity utilization and employment changes, and also an analysis of differences in management styles.[11] We use the rate of return on total assets as the profit rate to work with.[12] The relevant opportunity cost of this capital investment is 15 per cent, approximately the maximum rate of interest that could be earned on government bonds. The faith one can place on profit and value added data, especially when comparing across public and private domains, has to be tempered given the differing compulsions governing accounting. Thus we have also provided data on sales revenue as a percentage of total assets and sales revenue per employee.

FINDINGS

We start with presenting a brief case history of each company. Following this, comparative performance statistics of employee-owned and conventionally privatized firms are presented and discussed. Finally, we review post-privatization management, with a focus on the nature and extent of employee participation in the case of employee-owned firms, and on labour retrenchment and welfare in the case of conventionally privatized firms.

THE CHEMICAL INDUSTRY

1. Firm Case History

Sind Alkalis Ltd

Sind Alkalis started operating in Karachi in 1967 under the name of Indus Chemicals and Alkalis Ltd. It was, and still is, the country's only indigenous producer of soda ash and soda bicarbonate. The company was nationalized in 1972, and was taken over by the Federal Chemical and Ceramics Corporation (Pvt.) Limited, a public sector conglomerate of fourteen firms. The company was offered for sale to the private sector in 1992 through sealed bidding. Ninety-eight per cent of the employees of the company had become members of the Sind Alkalis Employees Management Group (SAEMG) and had expressed an interest in making a bid to buy out the company.[13]

SAEMG set to work about a year before the auction of the company and arranged for financing for an employee buy-out. Originally it gave in a bid of Rs 60 per share. The highest bid received for the firm was Rs 102 per share. In accordance with the privatization law, SAEMG was given the option of matching this bid, which produced an increased bid of Rs 103 per share.[14] The bid was financed partly through personal contributions from employees and partly by the use of provident and gratuity funds. A cash payment worth 40 per cent of the total was made at the time of transfer of the company in October 1992, and the remaining 60 per cent was to be paid over a period of three years.

The primary motivating factor behind this employee buy-out was job security. Workers were distrustful of assurances by the government that job security would be maintained. Sind Alkalis was one of the companies that had been plagued by confrontational labour–management relations in the pre-nationalization era, and workers were wary of working under private management again.

2. Performance

The Table 4.1 gives the data for Sind Alkalis from 1988 onwards. The company was privatized in 1992, so we have data for just two years after privatization. The return on total assets declined the year prior to privatization, rose the year after privatization, and then declined sharply. Post-privatization profits could have been affected by, among other things, the imposition of an export tax in 1993 and the erratic supply of gas. The political situation in Karachi, the city where the plant is located, has also been extremely unstable and this is also likely to have affected the company's performance. In any case, except for 1990–1, prior to privatization the return on total assets was only marginally higher than our reference point of 15 per cent as the opportunity cost of capital. More observations in a stable environment are needed to draw a reasonable conclusion about the impact of privatization on our measure of the profit rate.

The capacity utilization of the company was exceptionally high and rising post-privatization.[15] Again, the two years following privatization reveal

Table 4.1 Performance of Sind Alkalis before and after privatization

Firms	Before privatization			After privatization		
	1988–9	1989–90	1990–1	1991–2	1992–3	1993–4
Return on total assets	15.2	15.9	16.9	15.4	15.7	13.4
Capacity utilization (per cent)*	93.1	96.5	93.7	97.4	94.1	92.7
Labour productivity (1988–89 = 100)	100	110.5	129.1	155.4	170.0	181.6
Net sales revenue per employee (Rs. million)	0.32	0.36	0.40	0.47	0.52	0.60
Sales revenue/total assets (per cent)	112	121	113	122	135	141
Employees	744	748	744	737	706	698

Source: *Annual Report*, Ministry of Production, Experts Advisory Cell, various issues. Sind Alkalis *Annual Reports*.
Notes: * = capacity utilization for soda ash, the company's prime product.

falling capacity utilization. The index of labour productivity has shown a notable rising trend which was not deterred by the privatization. However, the productivity increase in the last two years should be viewed in the context of a 6.7 per cent decline in the labour force compared to the pre-privatization high. Labour productivity may also have been affected by the changes in management structure. Another crude measure of labour productivity is the net sales revenue per employee. Like value added per worker, this increased appreciably over the period under study, from less than a quarter of a million rupees in 1988–9 to over half a million in 1993–4. Sales revenue as a proportion of total assets also increased steadily in the post-privatization phase.

3. Management

After privatization, the Sind Alkalis Employees Management Group held 37.1 per cent of the shares, while financial institutions and companies held 37.9 per cent and the remaining shares were held by the general public. Of the shares held directly by employees, 60 per cent were held by workers and 40 per cent by management. Shares were issued to all employees in their names, and all employees signed a pledge giving SAEMG the first right to buy shares if the employee decided to sell or to leave the company.

There is a distinction between the employees' status as shareholders and as paid employees. Wage increments, for example, are fixed independently through bi-yearly negotiations with the collective bargaining authority.[16]

Post-privatization, two of the nine directors were elected from among the workers by the general body and two directors were elected from among the management by the general body. There were some important changes in the post-privatization structure of the company. All major financial and managerial decisions were referred to a body known as the Internal Management Board (IMB – which like the board met quarterly) before they go to the board for the final approval. The IMB consisted of twenty employees, ten of whom were from the management cadre of the company while ten were workers. The members from the management were nominated by the managerial staff, while the representatives of the workers were nominated by the union. The IMB also conducted the performance evaluation of the company.

In addition to the IMB, the firm also increased the number of committees dealing with various administrative issues at the shop-floor level as well as at the managerial level. Thirteen shop-floor committees were formed consisting of representatives of workers, one junior executive and a senior manager. The shop-floor committee met every three to four months and its function was to apprise the workers of the affairs of the company. The shop-floor committees were particularly important as they gave a sense of ownership to the shop-floor workers who invested in the employee buy-out. These, and the formation of the IMB represent significant modifications in the management structure of the company after it was taken over by employees. These modifications may well partly account for the continued post-privatization increase in labour productivity.

Post-privatization, the company embarked upon an extensive expansion programme. However, it faced some difficulty in securing financial backing for the undertaking, since banks are hesitant to finance employee-owned firms as opposed to large private conglomerates.[17]

THE TRACTOR INDUSTRY

1. Firm Case Histories

a. *Millat Tractors*

The company was formed as Rana Tractors and Equipment Ltd. in 1964. It was nationalized in 1972, taken over by Pakistan Automobile Corporation Ltd. and renamed Millat Tractors. Millat has by all accounts been a success story in the automobile industry. Initially, the company assembled tractors from imported SKD (Semi-Knocked Down) kits. Since 1982, however, the company has gradually moved towards assembling tractors from CKD (Completely Knocked Down) kits, and even to manufacturing components. In May 1991, the management of the company, upon being notified of plans to privatize the company, immediately set about formulating an Employees' Stock Ownership Plan. The chief executive circulated a letter to all employees setting out the salient features of the buy-out. Employees opted to give cash contributions based on their willingness to acquire share holdings. Unlike Sind Alkalis, where the government corporation controlled only 33 per cent of the share holdings, 51 per cent of the shares of Millat Tractors Ltd. were divested. Sealed bids were invited, and Millat Tractors won the bidding at the price of Rs 107.8 per share.[18]

b. Al-Ghazi Tractors

Al-Ghazi Tractors has a chequered history of ownership. The company was formed in 1983 as a joint venture. Pakistan Automobile Corporation (PACO) held 46 per cent of the shares, Fiat (a British subsidiary) held 5 per cent and the Habib Group of Industries held 24 per cent. The remaining shares were held partially by investment companies and partially by the public. Although PACO was the majority shareholder of the company, management was entirely in the hands of the Habib Group, with input from Fiat. This was a new experiment in the public sector, wherein private companies were responsible for the management of a public enterprise. This experiment continued for a period of seven years. In 1990, the agreement with the Habib Group expired, and the government took over the management. The Habib Group sold off their share holdings, and withdrew from the company.

PACO held the management of the company for almost two years. The company's performance at this time was unsatisfactory, and it became one of the first companies to be privatized. PACO's share holdings in the company were divested by the government and were bought by the Al-Futtaim group of the United Arab Emirates. By the time the company came up for privatization, it had suffered such heavy losses that its equity had been eroded from over Rs 80 million in 1990–1 to Rs 4 million in 1991–2. It was perhaps for this reason that only one bid was received for the company.

2. Performance

For Millat tractors, the return on total assets shows a declining trend for the three years prior to privatization; this continued for the first year after

Table 4.2 Comparative performance indicators for the tractor industry

Firms		Before privatization			After privatization		
		1988–9	1989–90	1990–1	1991–2	1992–3	1993–4
Millat Tractors	Return on total assets	20.8	13.9	12.0	9.4	16.1	15.2
	Capacity utilization (per cent)*	140.6	114.7	73.4	63.0	66.8	58.4
	Index of Labour Productivity (1988–9 = 100)	100	96.9	96.2	n.a	228.8	223.9
	Net sales revenue per employee (Rs million)	2.6	2.4	1.8	2.6	4.2	4.5
	Sales revenue /total assets (per cent)	294	205	143	120	203	241
	Employees	840	852	830	568	555	553
Al-Ghazi Tractor	Return on Total assets	7.9	11.2	7.9	−0.4	22.0	30.5
	Capacity utilization (per cent)*	n.a.	44.0	37.8	22.2	41.2	37.0
	Index of Labour Productivity (1989–90 = 100)	n.a.	100	95.8	45.0	234.4	298.7
	Net sales revenue per employee (Rs million)	2.01	1.98	2.29	1.45	2.83	2.91
	Sales revenue/total assets (per cent)	152	201	207	135	219	243
	Employees	706	691	600	600	600	600

Source: *Annual Reports*, Ministry of Production, Experts Advisory Cell. *Annual Reports*, Millat Tractors.

privatization. For the second and third years after privatization there is a recovery, although the profit rate is only slightly higher than the 15 per cent return on government bonds. As mentioned earlier, Al-Ghazi Tractors has gone through numerous management changes since its inception. Above, we report data for the last three years under PACO management when the profit rate was well under 15 per cent. The company suffered a record loss in 1991–2, when almost all of its equity was eroded and it registered a negative profit in the first year after privatization. The data reveal a subsequent dramatic textbook turn around with recorded profits at 22 and 30 per cent which are well above the return on government bonds.[19]

Capacity utilization in Millat Tractors was low and has declined continuously since 1988–9. Capacity utilization at Al-Ghazi tractors was even lower, but the declining trend was reversed after privatization.[20] The index of labour productivity rose dramatically for Millat Tractors, but even more so for Al-Ghazi Tractors. Once again, this may have been the result of the downscaling of the work force that has taken place since privatization. The variable on sales revenue per employee corroborates the labour productivity index as this shows an increase of almost a hundred per cent for Millat Tractors in the post-privatization phase. Sales revenue per employee increased sharply for Al-Ghazi after 1992, but the magnitude is still much lower than Millat. Sales revenue as a proportion of total assets does not differ significantly for the two companies in the last two years of our analysis. The decline in the labour force relative to the highest pre-privatization employment was 35 per cent for Millat Tractors and about half of that (18 per cent) for Al-Ghazi Tractors.

3. Management Structure

a. Millat Tractors

Post-privatization, investment firms (both local and foreign), and insurance companies and financial institutions held approximately 40.5 per cent of the shares, while 8.1 per cent were invested in provident and gratuity funds and the balance were held by individuals. This last category includes the shares held by the Millat Tractors Employees Group. Seventy per cent of total employee contribution came from management, while workers contributed 30 per cent. The shares were not issued to workers at the time of the survey as they were pledged to banks as collateral. It was expected that the company's outstanding loan would be paid off and shares would be issued in the employees' names by 1996.

The composition of the board of directors of Millat Tractors had not altered to labour's advantage. There were a total of ten board members, of whom one was the managing director of the company and one was co-opted from the Muslim Commercial Bank, the official bank of the company. Of the remaining eight members, one was nominated by the government to represent the workers, while two were representatives of investment companies. The remaining five directors represented government departments such as PACO and the Ministry of Production. After privatization, there was no change in three of the positions, i.e., the investment companies and MCB still nominate their directors on the board. The management now nominated six directors, while the workers nominated one. Thus workers' representation on the board remained unchanged.[21]

Millat Tractors did not introduce any formal institutional changes in its decision-making structure after privatization either. One significant move was the constitution of a shareholders' trust which acted as an advisory body to the board of directors. However, the trust's recommendations were not binding on the board of directors. The trust consisted of two representatives of workers and five of management. The trust had a subcommittee consisting of seven workers and seven managers who were supposed to initiate the formation of shop-floor committees to ensure a smooth flow of information to the workers at the shop-floor level and to apprise the management of the views of the workers. However, the meetings of the trust were infrequent and the role of the trust had not been clearly delineated. Not surprisingly, there was dissatisfaction on the part of the workers regarding the lack of any significant change in management.

As mentioned before, the management in Millat Tractors, who form about 30 per cent of the total work force, contributed over 70 per cent of the employee funds needed to undertake the buy-out. As the risk was unevenly distributed, the management felt that it was not appropriate to initiate any drastic changes in the management structure. The management also felt that it was impossible to get financing from commercial banks unless a small group of about five to six people hold controlling shares within the employees' group.

b. Al-Ghazi Tractors

There was a drastic restructuring of the organization immediately after privatization whereby the chief executive and all general managers and department heads were replaced. In addition to this, 15 managers were relieved of their duties. Workers were offered a golden handshake scheme, and 39 left the company. The management changed the cost and price structure of the firm. Costs were downscaled significantly, and prices were rationalized gradually, until they stabilized in October 1992. Since then, there has been no further price increment, except for one adjustment for an increase in sales tax.

There were two unions in the company. As required by corporate law, elections were held once a year for representation in the collective bargaining authority. However, there did not seem to be a serious problem in labour–management relations. Privatization was actually welcomed by the unions, possibly because of the dismal period under PACO management. Also, the unions in the company had initially been used to working under private management when the Habib Group was in charge. The fact that the company was taken over by an Arab conglomerate also created a favourable impression, particularly amongst the workers in Dera Ghazi Khan, an impoverished district of Southern Punjab.

Since privatization, the management contributed towards improving living conditions for workers in the factory area in D. G. Khan by the provision of recreational and educational facilities and medical benefits. The management also claimed that salaries had doubled at all levels since 1992. This may have contributed to the dramatic productivity increases. However, decision-making was entirely viewed as the prerogative of management, as is the norm in other privately owned companies.

THE GHEE INDUSTRY[22]

1. Firm Case Histories

a. Rose Ghee Mills (Sh. Fazal-ur-Rehman and Sons)

Rose Ghee Mills is one of the oldest industrial units in the country. It was set up in 1959 and operated under private management until it was converted into a public limited company in June 1970. Thereafter it was nationalized along with other ghee manufacturing units in September 1973. It operated under the auspices of the Ghee Corporation of Pakistan until it was privatized in April 1992, when the government divested 51 per cent of its share holdings.

The privatization of Rose Ghee Mills has not been smooth. The company's performance had been dismal in the recent past, and although five private corporations had expressed interest in the company, including the ex-owners, only one bid was forthcoming, and that was from the employees' management group. The bid price offered was Rs 101 per share, and the Privatization Commission decided to transfer ownership to the group.

The employee takeover in this case proved to be totally unsuccessful. The rising prices of raw material and the imposition of sales tax combined to cause a sharp rise in running costs and hence huge losses. The employees' group could not salvage the situation, and in October 1994, the employees' group decided to transfer management to a private entrepreneur, with the intention of transferring all shares pledged in the name of their group to the new management as soon as the bank guarantee was paid off. An agreement to this effect was signed with the industrialist concerned. However, a dispute arose and the management was not transferred. In fact, the employees' group continued to run the company's affairs and were looking for a new investor to buy out the company when this research was being conducted. The company could therefore be considered temporarily employee-owned. The old managing director of the company subsequently left, and the company's affairs were being managed by the labour union leaders.

In addition to managerial inefficiency and changes in the cost structure, the employees also felt that one reason for the failure of the company was the discriminatory treatment of the government. They claimed that while other employee-owned groups were given some form of rebate by the Privatization Commission, such concessions had not been extended to them. Also, they claimed that unlike other employee-owned firms, they did not reschedule payment, and they believed that this partly explained why they ran into financial difficulties so soon after the takeover.[23]

b. Kakakhel Industries Ltd.

Kakakhel Industries began operations in March 1968. Fifty-one per cent of the company's shares were offered for divestment. There have been two changes in ownership of the firm since privatization. The unit was initially bought by Mr Inayatullah Chaudhry and his nominees. One of the first things that the new management did upon taking control, was to negotiate with the workers and the representatives of the Privatization Commission to implement a golden handshake scheme.[24] The management paid a sum of over Rs 11 million to workers under the scheme, while the Privatization Commission also gave a matching grant of over Rs 14 million for the purpose. The management relieved the entire body of workers of their services and an entirely new labour force was recruited.

The company, however, could not sustain the financial costs of the above transaction, and that, combined with a host of other financial and managerial constraints, forced the management to put up its shareholdings for sale. During this time, the company remained closed for a period of two and a half months and no production was possible. A new management took control in October 1992. These disturbances undoubtedly affected the company's immediate post-privatization performance.

2. Performance

The profit rate in Rose Ghee Mills dived after privatization into large negative numbers. Performance in 1993–4 was particularly poor, possibly because of the problems regarding the transfer of management. The representatives of the employees' management group cited a number of reasons for their failure to run the unit successfully. They claimed that the prices of raw materials rose because of the imposition of import duty on vegetable oil.[25] Sales dropped in the last year of our study because of marketing problems and cuts in the budget for advertisements. The employees also felt that there had been administrative difficulties since the employee takeover as there were clashes between the managing director and the president of the labour union, which affected the process of decision-making as well as managerial performance.

The profit rate of Kakakhel Industries also dropped into negative numbers (−62.8) immediately after privatization. Like Rose Ghee Mills, one of the factors contributing to the reduced profitability for Kakakhel Industries was the rationalization of the price of imported crude oil. This, combined with the cost of the golden handshake scheme, reduced the profit rate immediately following privatization. However, like Al-Ghazi tractors, their classic textbook strategy of cutting losses following privatization appear to have paid off and, in 1993–4, their reported profit of 30 per cent was twice the return on government bonds.

Capacity utilization in Rose Ghee Mills reveals a sharply declining trend starting two years prior to privatization. The fall in profits and the consequent shortage of operating finance are likely reasons for this. The same is true for Kakakhel Industries, although the declining trend is less sharp. Neither of the two units could operate at full capacity until the companies were reorganized to adjust to the new input price structure in the market. Labour productivity in Rose Ghee Mills also fell sharply, particularly in the last year of our analysis, despite an employment decline of 36 per cent. Sales revenue per employee declined by about 16 per cent for Rose Ghee Mills for the last year of our analysis, although it was significantly higher than average in 1991–2 and 1992–3. Thus increase was due to the reduction in the number of employees. We could not calculate sales per employee for Kakakhel Industries because of the absence of data on the number of employees. Sales revenue as a proportion of total assets is unusually high in Rose Ghee Mills, as the value of total assets has dwindled.

Table 4.3 Comparative performance indicators for the ghee industry

Firms		Before privatization			After privatization		
		1988–9	1989–90	1990–1	1991–2	1992–3	1993–4
Rose Ghee Mills	Rates of return on total assets	22.2	28.9	23.2	−21.9	−12.5	−92.3
	Capacity utilization (per cent)*	81.4	92.9	98.1	94.3	71.6	46.8
	Index of Labour Productivity (1988–9 = 100)	100	129.3	128.8	43.3	64.2	6.8
	Net sales revenue per employee (Rs million)	1.14	1.35	1.51	1.90	1.99	1.67
	Sales revenue/total assets (per cent)	860	879	905	1,198	1,388	2,815
	Employees	340	338	336	258	223	219
Kakakhel Ghee Ind.	Rate of return of total assets	22.5	15.9	18.8	−62.8	−4.9	29.9
	Capacity utilization (per cent)*	95.0	110.2	102.5	87.2	60.0	51.4
	Sales revenue/total assets (per cent)	448	466	478	743	305	460

Source: *Annual Reports*, Rose Ghee Mills and Kakakhel Industries Ltd.
Notes: Data on labour productivity and number of employees were not available for Kakakhel Industries.

3. Management Structure

a. Rose Ghee Mills

The pattern of shareholdings since privatization was as follows: The Employees Provident Fund Trust held 37.8 per cent of the shares and 6.9 per cent were held by the Gratuity Fund Trust. Of the remaining shares, the largest share, 21.4 per cent, was held by financial institutions while individuals held 13.3 per cent. The remaining shares were held by investment and insurance companies and joint stock companies.

The total value of the shares divested by the government was Rs 25.7 million. The employees' group had problems in securing bank guarantees for the payment of the amount, and also could not make the downpayment of 40 per cent required by the Privatization Commission. Finally, the Muslim Commercial Bank (MCB) emerged as a bank guarantor, and also loaned an amount of Rs 5 million towards the first payment. One million rupees were provided by the managing director of the company, while the rest of the money for the downpayment came from the provident and gratuity funds. No individual contribution was taken from the employees. Shares have not been transferred to the employees as they are still being held in trust with the bank.

The composition of the board of directors changed twice after privatization. When the employees' group took over the company, they changed four of the members of the board (of the three members who did not change, one was the managing director and the other two were representatives of financial institutions). Of the four members added by the employees' management group, two were workers while two were from management. But the distinction between workers and management was not clear in the company. There were only seven people in the firm who could be considered managers *per se*, and most of them had worked as shop-floor workers at some time. After the transfer of management, an agreement was signed with the prospective new owners in October 1994, and the composition of the board of directors changed yet again. However, as has been pointed out, this arrangement did not last for long and the old system was reverted to. The board did not meet regularly.

The company had not made any alterations at all in its management structure since privatization. The salaries and benefits schemes of the employees were also exactly the same. The company's affairs after privatization were so unsettled that the employees' group has not had the chance to bring about any substantive changes. In any case, since it was felt that the company will have to be sold out to a private investor again, the employees were not interested in carrying out any transformations.

b. Kakakhel Industries Ltd.

As mentioned earlier, the entire work force of the unit was replaced after privatization, and the owners went through a long period of negotiation with the labour union to finalize the modalities of the golden handshake scheme. Since the employment of a new work force, labour–management relations were smooth.

SUMMARY AND CONCLUSIONS

Although our sample is small of necessity, some generalizations are possible. The primary motivation for encouraging employee takeovers in the privatization process was to preserve the work force, but the number of employees decreased for employee-owned firms as well in the post-privatization phase. Both the conventionally privatized firms in the sample implemented golden handshake schemes after privatization, and in at least one case, relieved their entire work force of their services. This gives credence to employees' concerns about job loss resulting from privatization.

In two of the four cases that we investigated, employee ownership could be considered a successful mode of privatization. Sind Alkalis is successfully operating and, inspired by the Mondragon model, has instituted interesting changes in the management structure to make it more democratic and participatory. These changes may well partly account for the rise in labour productivity following privatization. Productivity also rose in Millat Tractors, but this is probably due to sharp labour retrenchment, since they did not institute any managerial innovation. Profit rates for Sind Alkalis fell post-privatization to 13.5 per cent and, while profit rates in Millat Tractors increased post privatization, at 15.2 per cent, they just barely matched the return of 15 per cent on government bonds.

Privatization experience in the tractor and ghee industries shows that classic textbook firm restructuring following privatization can bring about quick reversals in profitability. Such restructuring in Al-Ghazi Tractors and Kakakhel Ghee Industries resulted in profits shooting up from negative numbers to 30 per cent in the third year following privatization. This represents evidence in support of the hypothesis that traditional privatization can generate a sharp turn-around in profitability.

We do not believe that our findings rule out the employee takeover option. The performance of such firms may be constrained in several ways. First, both workers and management are severely hampered by the lack of education amongst workers at the shop-floor level. Second, in conversation we gleaned a lack of clarity on the part of management on the dual nature of workers in employee-owned firms, i.e., that of owners and employees. As shareholders, workers have a right to demand transparency and a free flow of information. However, their role as employees is no different from employees in any public or private firm, and their demand for retaining unions to represent their interests is legitimate. Finally, all employee-owned firms, even market leaders like Millat Tractors, complained of the difficulties they faced in getting access to credit. While credit is accessible to both public sector firms as well as to large private conglomerates, most employee-owned firms faced severe problems in securing financing. Government support in the form of training and equal access to credit needs to accompany the employee ownership option.

The comparison in this study is based on changes that have taken place over a short period, since privatization data were available for only two or three years. It would be worth repeating the exercise after some time (perhaps another five years), when the situation has had time to stabilize under the new management.

NOTES

1. This chapter is based on a paper written by Safiya Aftab and Shahrukh Rafi Khan at the urging of Karamat Ali (chief executive, Pakistan Institute of Labour Education Research). Many thanks are due to him for suggesting this study and for financial support for our data collection. The paper has been published in the *Canadian Journal of Development Studies*, 17, no. 3 (1996).
2. Naqvi and Kemal (1991, p. 106) pointed out that the government failed to divest itself completely or even partially of public industrial enterprises largely for this reason. Although the Karachi Stock Exchange experienced a tremendous increase in market capitalization due to the entry of foreign investors in early 1994, the momentum could not be maintained for a variety of both domestic and international reasons.
3. The Mondragon cooperative model is the inspiration for the employee-owned privatization option in Pakistan. The Pakistan Institute of Labour Education and Research (PILER) has been actively involved in creating linkages between the Mondragon cooperatives and Pakistani employee-owned firms. See Henk and Logan (1982) and Whyte and Whyte (1988) for studies of the Mondragon Cooperative Complex.
4. For reviews of the relevant literature see Bonin, Jones and Putterman (1993).
5. See Amjad and Ahmed (1984), p. 228 for statistics on number of strikes and workers involved in strikes.

6. An attempt was also made to safeguard workers' interests in case of a corporate takeover. It was decided in consultation with the All Pakistan State Enterprises Workers' Action Committee (APSEWAC) that 10 per cent of shares of all units, offered for privatization, would be offered to the employees of the particular unit, in case the unit were taken over by a private investor. This compensation for workers may partially have reduced the incentive for an employee takeover.
7. To date, approximately 70 manufacturing units out of a total of 108 offered for sale have been transferred to the private sector.
8. National Cement was the second cement manufacturing unit to be transferred to the employees' group, but the unit was still in the process of transfer at the time research for this paper was being conducted.
9. The other two mills, Bengal Vegetable Oil Industries, Karachi, and Hydari Ghee Industries, Hyderabad, were not in operation due to disputes over ownership and various other financial matters.
10. This was the only other tractor manufacturing firm which had previously been in the public sector.
11. Pre-tax profits = Net profit + prior periods adjustment
    Total assets = Total fixed assets (tangible) + intangibles + long-term investments + long-term deposits + long-term loans or advances + current assets
    Labour productivity = Value added/No. of employees
    Value added = Pre-tax profits + salaries and wages + depreciation + financial expenses.
12. A systematic reevaluation of assets prior to privatization would affect the pre- and post-privatization comparisons. Discussion with staff members of the Privatization Commission indicate that they maintain a roster of chartered accountants from whom one is selected to evaluate the firms assets prior to privatization. Since these are the most prominent firms, and generally the same firms used by public and private sector corporations, it is very unusual (except in the case of overt wrongdoing) for the evaluation to result in significant differences in the valuation of assets from that conducted by the firms' accountants. This is also evident from the data on total assets, since there is no systematic change in the value of total assets post-privatization.
13. Eighteen employees did not join the SAEMG, but continued to be employed in the company and were expected to be issued shares.
14. This was over ten times the par value of the share.
15. In particular, the company formulated an expansion plan for the soda ash manufacturing facilities. It was expected that the new facilities would be in place in another two to three years, and the capacity of the company for the production of soda ash would increase from 51,000 metric tons to 75,000 metric tons.
16. Sind Alkalis has two labour unions, and elections are held every two years for one union to be the collective bargaining authority for the next two years.
17. In conversation, the general manager revealed that the management is thinking of getting together with other employee-owned firms to form a bank.
18. There was a difference of opinion amongst some employees and the management of the firm on the modalities of the bidding. A group of employees

claimed that they had not been consulted on the details of the takeover in accordance with the rules of the Privatization Commission. After the decision of the Commission was announced, a legal battle ensued as the decision was challenged in the superior courts by this group of former employees. The management of the company was finally transferred to the employees' group who had quoted the highest bid in January 1992. At this point, some of the workers availed themselves of the golden handshake scheme supported by the company, and 230 employees thus left Millat Tractors to start their own transport company. However, some employees who were initially members of the group opposing the takeover by Millat Tractors Employees Group, stayed on in the company and were issued shares.

19. Al-Ghazi's value of total fixed assets is less than half that of Millat Tractors. However, even in the mark-up on sales, which is a rough measure of profitability but is not affected by scale, Al-Ghazi's return in 1993–4 at 12.6 per cent is about double that of Millat Tractors (6.3 per cent). The tractor industry faced some serious problems in the early 1990s. The Agricultural Development Bank of Pakistan (ADBP), which extends loans to farmers to buy tractors, was forced to cut back on its credit schemes. Also, the Awami (People's) Tractor Scheme initiated by the PPP government probably adversely affected performance of local firms, since the market was flooded with cheaper products from Eastern Europe.
20. The post-privatization decline for the last year in both cases reflects the slump in the tractor industry (see n. 19).
21. The Board of Directors in any company is not involved in day-to-day management decisions. The role of the Board is normally to oversee company policy and performance in a broader perspective. The constitution of the Board of Directors is therefore more symbolic than indicative of changes in day-to-day management.
22. *Ghee* is hydrogenated fat.
23. From the information available to us, we cannot confirm that Millat Tractors and Sind Alkalis received concessions from the Privatization Commission or rescheduled payments.
24. According to the accord signed by the Privatization Commission and the All Pakistan State Enterprises Workers Action Committee (APSEWAC), no labour lay-offs could take place within a year of privatization. However, management had the option to offer a golden handshake plan to employees, in which workers were given the option of getting a lump-sum payment and leaving the company within a year of privatization.
25. The average price of imported crude oil rose from Rs 9.59 per kg in 1991–2 to Rs 12.34 per kg in 1992–3.

REFERENCES

Al-Ghazi Tractors Ltd, *Annual Reports*, various issues.

Amjad, Rashid and Viqar Ahmed, 1984, *The Management of Pakistan's Economy* (Karachi, Oxford University Press).

Bonin, John P., Derek C. Jones and Louis Putterman, 1993, 'Theoretical and Empirical Studies of Worker Cooperatives: Will the Twain Ever Meet?', *Journal of Economic Literature*, 31, pp. 1290–1320.
Government of Pakistan, Ministry of Production, Experts Advisory Cell, *Annual Reports*, various issues, Islamabad.
Henk, Thomas and Chris Logan, 1982, *Mondragon: An Economic Analysis*, (Institute of Social Studies, The Hague, George Allen and Unwin).
Kakakhel Industries Ltd., *Annual Reports*, various issues.
Millat Tractors Ltd., *Annual Reports*, various issues.
Naqvi, S. N. H. and A. R. Kemal, 1991, 'The Privatization of the Public Industrial Enterprises in Pakistan', *Pakistan Development Review*, 30, pp. 105–44.
Rose Ghee Mills, *Annual Reports*, various issues.
Sind Alkalis Ltd., *Annual Reports*, various issues.
Whyte, William Foote and Kathleen King Whyte, 1998, *Making Mondragon: The Growth and Dynamics of a Worker Cooperative Complex*, Cornell International Industrial and Labor Relations Report no. 14.

5 Structural Adjustment, Industrialization and Export Promotion[1]

INTRODUCTION

One of the nationalistic fears of structural-adjustment induced trade liberalization is that it may lead to de-industrialization, and one of the expected gains of such structural adjustment is export promotion.[2] The objective of this paper is to test if de-industrialization has occurred in Pakistan, and whether Pakistan has been able to successfully promote exports since the onset of structural adjustment. Neither industrialization nor export promotion should be viewed as ends in and of themselves. Thus the links of industrialization and export promotion to economic growth are also empirically investigated.

A nationalistic perspective is that structural-adjustment induced tariff cutting would result in a flood of cheap and high quality imports which are the products of advanced technology and which would result in de-industrialization. Also, structural reforms induce a sudden and sharp increase in the costs of production, because of higher utility and borrowing costs, and could have at least a short-term adverse impact on industrial growth. The original concern with de-industrialization occurred in the context of the 'Dutch Disease', whereby prosperity strengthened the currency, made imports cheaper and resulted in a decline in local industrialization. To an extent, structural adjustment can have a similar effect since it can stabilize the currency and make imports more attractive. Remittances could have a similar effect by strengthening the currency.

The theory of infant industry protection suggests that developing countries need time to build themselves up to face competition. However, the fear is now expressed that conditionality-driven trade reforms will make them indefinitely dependent on primary products with declining terms of trade.[3] An alternative empirically based perspective is that developing countries have spoiled industrialists, who have refused to become competitive and are hence a drain on the rest of the economy. Thus no further protection is warranted and it is high time that this sheltered industrial sector confront competition via trade liberalization. Competitiveness would also be induced by expecting this sector to break into export markets and economic benefit would result from the higher profitability and from the earning of much-needed foreign exchange. Proponents of this view fail to distinguish between a protected manufacturing sector that faces internal competition and one which is both externally protected and internally shielded from competition via numerous special privileges.

In this chapter we briefly present evidence on whether trade liberalization has occurred in Pakistan. We present the case for industrialization and export orientation in more detail. Next, we empirically estimate the contribution of domestic demand, import substitution and export promotion to industrial growth. Then we review the change in industrialization and export orientation over time, and also review Pakistan's industrialization and export orientation relative to cross-country experience. Finally, we investigate the association of industrialization and export orientation with economic growth. We end with a summary of findings.

TRADE LIBERALIZATION

We draw on two sources to indicate that trade liberalization has indeed taken place. A study conducted by Aftab (1994) computed scarcity premia based on a survey of importers for 85 commodities. The theory is that high scarcity premia result from trade restrictions such as quotas and licences and when these are removed, the premia vanish. Aftab found that over half the commodities had a scarcity premium of less than 10 per cent, whereas an earlier study by Kemal et al. (1981), based on a similar sample, showed these premia to cluster between 20 to 40 per cent for almost three-quarters of the products. This result is even more clearly demonstrated with weighted averages which show that the premia fell considerably between 1979 and 1994 as indicated in Table 5.1.

Table 5.1 Weighted average mark-ups on imported goods, by commodity group

Commodity group	1979	1994
Consumer goods	37.5	2.9
Intermediate goods	25.6	15.4
Capital goods	33.4	6.3

Sources: Kemal et al. (1981, p. 5) and Aftab (1994).
Note: Aftab pointed out that titanium dioxide and sulphur had a disproportionate effect in the relatively high premia for intermediate goods in 1994.

Scarcity premia are an input into computing effective protection rates (EPRs). EPRs in turn are the usual tool to investigate trade liberalization, since they measure what the protection to value added is after netting out the effect of tariffs on inputs. Kemal (1997, table 7) has shown industrial EPRs to have declined from 125 in 1968–9 to 77 in 1990–1, once again suggesting that considerable liberalization has occurred.[4]

The Finance Supplementary Amendment Bill, 1997, has furthered the process of trade liberalization considerably. The maximum slab of duty of 65 per cent was reduced to 45 per cent (except for automobiles). The minimum across-the-board tariff was set at 10 per cent (essentials exempted). Most SRO (special revenue orders) exemptions were withdrawn. The import regulatory duty of 10 per cent and additional regulatory duties (5 per cent to 20 per cent) were abolished.

THE CASE FOR INDUSTRIALIZATION AND EXPORT ORIENTATION

The literature establishing the case for industrialization goes far back. The first generation of development economists believed that industrialization was central to or the lead sector in development because of its dynamic potential for generating externalities, high growth and even labour absorption. Hirschman (1958) expected linkages to be overwhelmingly of greater importance in industry than in other sectors. Lewis (1954) was careful to point out the importance of agricultural growth, but this was so that wage good prices would not rise and constrain capital accumulation in the more dynamic industrial sector. Broadly speaking, these writers originated the structuralist case for encouraging industrialization. Industrialization was believed to generate both technical and pecuniary externalities and hence contribute to economic growth beyond its share in GNP. Scitovsky (1958) distinguished between the two. Technical externalities occur when the production function of a firm includes the production decisions of other firms. Pecuniary externalities are mediated through the market and occur when the profit function of a firm includes production decisions of other firms. Thus pecuniary externalities are broader and defined particularly in the context of industrialization in LDCs. Scitovsky pointed out that examples of technical externalities are limited, while those of pecuniary externalities are wide ranging.[5]

We view externalities to include both pecuniary and technical externalities, as encapsulated in what are referred to in Weiss (1988) as linkages and dynamic increasing returns. These externalities are viewed as resulting from interactions within and across industries. One mechanism for such externalities is the mobility of unskilled, skilled and managerial labour, which leads to attitudinal changes, skill formation and knowledge diffusion. The capital goods sector has been noted to be another potential mechanism for the generation of and transmission of technological innovations and upgradations. In addition, these externalities include increased complementarities, specializations and spin-offs with the ensuing expansion of markets allowing for economies of scale.

Externalities could be categorized into 'own-effect' and 'cross-effect'. In other words, industrialization could generate externalities that are internalized within the industrial sector, but there can also be a transmission of externalities from the industrial sector to the non-industrial sector. Many, but not all, of the externalities cited above are likely to be realized within the industrial sector. However, attitudinal changes, enhanced knowledge, technological innovations, larger markets, lower input prices and incentives to save and accumulate may benefit the non-industrial sectors as well. Weiss (1988, pp. 98–116) has reviewed the empirical literature on industry externalities.

The seminal contribution was by Kaldor (1967), who posited and tested for a positive association between output growth and productivity growth within manufacturing. The output growth generates the externalities mentioned above and hence is hypothesized to lead to productivity growth within that sector. An alternative approach is to estimate static intersectoral linkages across sectors using an input–output model.

Khan and Bilginsoy (1994) test for the existence of cross-sector industry externalities on a macroeconomic level that incorporate linkages using cross-country data and a two-sector framework. They found empirically robust support for the structuralist belief in the likelihood that manufacturing and industry generate dynamic externalities that are transmitted to other sectors in the economy. Moreover, their coefficients suggested that these externalities are quantitatively significant, with the manufacturing externalities contributing almost up to a third of total non-manufacturing growth. This figure for industry externalities was almost one-fourth. Indeed, it was striking that when industrialization or manufacturing were included in the growth equation, export share or the growth in exports as right-hand side variables were insignificant.

In another cross-country study, Khan, Bilginsoy and Alam (1997) use an aggregate production function framework to capture the overall growth impact resulting from the growth of the manufacturing and industrial sector. They postulate the existence of both kinds of externalities (own- and cross-effects) if the coefficient of the growth in manufacturing exceeds its share in GDP. Using four different cross-country data sets spanning 1965 to 1990, growth in industry was found to be a robust predictor of overall growth, and its coefficient was found to be significantly larger than its share in GDP. Again, trade policy variables such as export share in GDP or export growth did not prove to be robust growth predictors. Thus, there is evidence of the positive impact of industrialization on an economy. It is no surprise then that the acronym Newly Industrialized Countries (NIC) is honorific rather than pejorative.

In comparison to the earlier writings, the method of industrialization has fallen into disrepute in the more recent development literature. Neo-liberal economists switched the focus by marshalling evidence to show that industrialization was induced by trade and domestic distortions, and nurtured by a misallocation of resources and hence not cost effective. The most significant contribution to such a view was that of Little, Scitovsky and Scott (1970). Among other ills, distorted industrialization was viewed as responsible for increased inequality via the extraction of surplus from agriculture, unemployment, and balance of payment problems. While Little, Scitovsky and Scott conceded that the contribution of industry may have been understated due to their inability to measure externalities, the overall impact of their work, and that of many other prominent neo-liberal economists writing in a similar vein, created a new orthodoxy that is still dominant.

Neo-liberal economists view trade liberalization as beneficial for several reasons. Export-oriented development is viewed as preferable because it induces productivity growth via competitive pressures, access to technology, enhanced capacity utilization and economies of scale and access to imported inputs of superior quality. There is a substantial empirical literature on this issue based mostly on cross-country evidence. Studies suggesting that exports are growth enhancing include Tyler (1981), Feder (1982), Kavoussi (1984), Balassa (1985), Chow (1987) and Dollar (1992). Scholars who have questioned these findings include Jung and Marshall (1985), Dodaro (1991), Sheehey (1992) and Khan and Bilginsoy (1994). In addition, in demonstrating a robustness test, Levine and Renelt (1992) incidently show that exports are not a robust growth predictor. (We replicated this finding for Pakistan in Chapter 1 above.)

For now, we view export growth as a contributor to industrial growth, and in the next section examine the various determinants of industrial growth, including export growth. Later we examine their separate contribution as a source of externality and in using resources more efficiently.

EXPORTS AND OTHER DETERMINANTS OF INDUSTRIALIZATION

The method utilized to decompose industrial growth is taken from Lewis (1969, pp. 17–22). This can be summarized in the following equation:

$$\Delta X = \mu_1 (\Delta D) + \mu_1 (\Delta E) + (\mu_2 - \mu_1) Z_2 \quad (1)$$

Where,

X = Domestic production
D = Domestic final demand
E = Exports
Z_2 = Total supply in terminal year
μ_1 = Domestic production to total supply in base year
μ_2 = Domestic production to total supply in the terminal year

Equation (1) represents the decomposition of total industrial production resulting from a change in domestic demand, exports and import substitution. The detailed derivation is presented in Appendix 5.1.[6] The results of this exercise are presented in Table 5.2 for the three periods generally used throughout the book. The last period, 1987–8/1990–1, represents the intensive bout of structural adjustment.[7] The sample of industrial goods we selected to compute Table 5.2 accounts for 85 per cent of the total value of industrial production.

Table 5.2 Sources of industrial growth (percentages)

Ind.	1970–1/1980–1			1980–1/1987–8			1987–8/1990–1		
	IS	X	DD	IS	X	DD	IS	X	DD
Con.	−0.14	0.10	1.04	−0.01	0.14	0.88	0.11	0.48	0.41
Int.	0.29	0.16	0.55	0.10	0.06	0.84	−0.49	−0.04	1.55
Cap.	0.22	0.00	0.78	0.18	0.00	0.82	0.20	0.00	0.80
Total	0.10	0.11	0.80	0.09	0.08	0.86	−0.12	0.15	0.97

Sources: Computations by authors based on *Census of Manufacturing Industries*, Federal Bureau of Statistics, Islamabad, various years.
Notes: IS = Import substitution.
X = Export promotion.
DD = Domestic demand.
Ind. = Industry type.
Con. = Consumer good industries.
Int. = Intermediate good industries.
Cap. = Capital good industries.

All numbers are weighted averages and the rows for all industry categories for all periods add to about 1. We were unable to exactly match the items in the electric machinery and equipment and non-electric machinery categories of the capital good industries for the 1987–8/1990–1 period to the earlier periods. Thus there is not complete comparability in the last and earlier two period estimates for capital goods.

The story that emerges from the numbers in Table 5.2 is plausible and consistent with policy changes that have historically been taking place. In the consumer goods industry, import substitution was already declining (negative) as a source of industrial growth in the base period (1970–81); i.e., imports increased their share of the domestic market. Exports accounted for 10 per cent of industrial growth in the base period and this increased to 14 per cent in the 1980–8 period. This trend continued in the structural adjustment period (1987–91) where export promotion was a very important part of industrial growth (48 per cent) and import displacement accounted for 11 per cent of industrial growth.[8] Thus Pakistan appears to have managed to deal with trade liberalization in the consumer goods industry rather well, over the time period under study, by displacing imports and promoting exports.

The intermediate goods industry is where the fears of de-industrialization at first appear more well founded. In the base 1970–81 period, import substitution accounted for 29 per cent of industrial growth. This declined to 10 per cent in the 1980–8 period and a negative 49 per cent in the structural adjustment period. Thus it appears that imports penetrated the domestic market following liberalization. On closer examination of the disaggregated findings, it is evident that much of the change has occurred due to the petroleum product group for which import substitution contributed 38 per cent as a source of industrial growth in 1970–81 but −17 per cent in 1987–91 (see Appendix 5.4, tables). This is not an industry for which Pakistan is resource rich. Market penetration is also evident for the pesticides, insecticides, fungicides and herbicide group and the compressed liquified and solidified gas group, although these product groups made no contribution to industrial growth in the base year. Thus while liberalization is associated with de-industrialization for the intermediate good category, the disaggregated data show the high negative number (−0.49) overstates the case.[9]

Export promotion in the intermediate goods sector consistently declined with exports accounting for 16 per cent of industrial growth in the first period, 6 per cent in the second period and −4 per cent in the third period (i.e. ΔX was negative). The negative exports could have resulted both from Pakistan's losing export markets to fierce international competition, after having got a leg up earlier, and also from domestic demand absorbing intermediate goods that might otherwise have been exported.

There has been little change in the capital goods sector. Import substitution accounted for roughly a fifth of industrial growth throughout the period, and exports, as one might expect, accounted for nothing, so domestic demand explained the rest of industrial growth. In aggregate terms, there has been negative import substitution or import penetration over the period because of the intermediate goods industry. Export promotion declined somewhat in the second period (due to intermediate goods) and then picked up in the third period (due to consumer goods). This mirrors findings we demonstrate in the next section.

INDUSTRIALIZATION AND EXPORT ORIENTATION IN PAKISTAN IN A CROSS-COUNTRY CONTEXT

This last section contained an analysis of change in the determinants of industrialization. However, so far, there has been no mention of the magnitude and change in industrialization itself, both in absolute terms and relative to cross-country experience. We now turn to these issues.

In Table 5.3 we present the broad changes that have taken place in Pakistan with respect to industrialization and export orientation. Both are

Table 5.3 Size and annual average growth rates of industry, manufacturing and export ratios

Period	SOI	SOM	SOE
1970–7	21.38	14.39	11.69
	(0.59)	(−0.41)	(−6.04)
1978–87	23.06	16.66	11.26
	(0.40)	(1.32)	(2.79)
1988–93	25.39	17.38	12.14
	(1.19)	(0.80)	(2.74)

Source: World Bank, *World Tables 1994*.
Notes: Parentheses contain annual average growth rates for the period.
SOI = Size of industrial sector defined as real value added in industry over real GDP.
SOM = Size of manufacturing sector defined as real value added in manufacturing over real GDP.
SOE = Size of exports defined as the real value of good and non-factor services over real GDP.

measured in terms of the ratio of the value added in industrial, manufacturing and exports sectors relative to GDP.

The evidence in Table 5.3 is again mixed. Overall, there has been a steady but small increase in the mean industry and manufacturing ratio across the three periods. However, the annual average growth rate of manufacturing and exports declined in the liberalization period compared to the earlier period.[10] Also, the performance across the board is feeble compared to the performance of the new NICs.[11]

The export ratio increased over the three periods by less than 1 per cent. However, there has been an improvement in growth rates from the negative 6 per cent in the base period to close to positive 3 per cent in the 1988–93 period.[12] The decline in export share in the second period and rise in the third structural adjustment period is broadly consistent with the finding in Table 5.2. The data reported in Table 5.4 sets Pakistan's performance in a cross-country perspective.

Table 5.4 shows that both in the base year, 1988, prior to structural adjustment, and in the terminal year, 1995, after several years of intensive structural adjustment, their is a substantial gap in Pakistan's industry ratio and those representing the mean for low income countries. The export ratio slipped from being slightly above the mean export for low income countries in 1988 to notably below it in 1995.

Another way of approaching this issue is to investigate how Pakistan is doing relative to its potential. One method of estimating potential is by using cross-country data and, based on that, inferring how Pakistan could be expected to perform based on its population and per capita GDP. We conducted empirical exercises to examine Pakistan's industrialization and export orientation in the context of cross-country experience, again using 1970–7, 1978–87 and 1988–93 as the three time periods.

Table 5.4 Pakistan's industry, manufacturing and export ratios compared to those of low income countries

Ratios	1988		1995	
	Pakistan	Low income countries	Pakistan	Low income countries
SOI	24	36	24	38
SOM	17	na	17	27
SOE	14	13	16	19

Source: *World Development Report 1997* (1997, pp. 236, 212) and *World Development Report 1990* (1990, pp. 182, 194).

The method used for these exercises is a straightforward one devised by Chenery and Sryquin (1975) to identify structural changes in economies. Among other variables, they estimated the size of the industrial sector as a function of per capita GNP and population and the squares of these variables. This was referred to as a 'structural equation', and per capita GNP and population are viewed as proxies for both resource endowments and the size of the market. The estimating equation is as follows:

$$\begin{aligned} \text{SOI} = \alpha + \beta_1 \text{POP} + \beta_2 \text{POP} + \beta_3 \text{POPSQ} + \beta_4 \text{PCGDP} \\ + \beta_5 \text{PCGDPSQ} + \beta_6 \text{DI} + \mu \end{aligned} \quad (2)$$

Where

SOI = Size of industry defined as industrial value added divided by GDP.
POP = Population.
POPSQ = Population squared.
PCGDP = Per capita GDP.
PCGDPSQ = Per capita GDP squared.

Once such an equation is estimated, it is possible to see how any country in the sample is performing relative to the cross-country experience by looking at the residual. For example, a positive residual for a country suggests its actual ratio (SOI or SOE) is a certain number of percentage points above its potential ratio as suggested by cross-country experience.

We used two data sets. The first was the data tape of the World Bank *World Tables 1994* from which we drew our left-hand side variables, SOI and SOE. While per capita GDP was also available in the World Bank *World Tables*, this was not in purchasing power parity terms. Thus we used the *Penn World Tables* (Mark 5.6a) compiled under the supervision of Summers and Heston (1991) to extract PCGDP adjusted for purchasing power parity.[13]

The sample we used has been reported as Appendix 5.2. We excluded countries which had a population of less than one million in the starting period, the ex-socialist bloc countries and countries that experienced a sustained high-intensity civil war in the relevant period. Countries for which there were some missing data also got excluded. This happened to include the high petroleum-exporting countries. Data for manufacturing were not available for several countries and so we have done this exercise only for industry and exports. The results from estimating equation (2) on this data set and sample are reported in Appendix 5.3, Table 5.6.[14]

Population is only a mildly significant positive predictor of the size of the industry in the 1988–93 period. In all periods, it has a negative and highly significant impact on the size of exports, suggesting that a larger population may result in more production for the non-traded sector and concomitant greater resource use in the non-traded sector. However, the magnitude of the impact is very small suggesting a 0.03 per cent decline in the export ratio for a ten million increase in the population.

PCGDP and the square of this variable has the expected positive/negative sign as predictors of industrialization in all periods. The Chenery and Sryquin stylized facts, verified here, suggest that industrialization is expected to be positively associated with the increase in per capita GDP but, beyond some threshold, as the service sector expands, its relative importance in terms of its share in GDP is expected to decline.[15]

The main purpose of conducting this exercise was to explore if Pakistan's industrialization and export orientation was above or below potential and if this changed over time. Based on the regressions reported in Appendix 5.3, Table 5.6, we computed the relevant residuals and the results are reported in Table 5.5.

Table 5.5 shows that the actual industry ratio is below its potential in the three periods. The export ratio has been notably below potential in the first two periods but fell from 15.3 per cent below potential in the first period (1970–7) to only 3.7 per cent below in the intensive structural adjustment phase. Once again, this is consistent with earlier findings of increased export promotion in the structural adjustment period. Also, Pakistan falling further below its industrial potential in the structural adjustment period is consistent with earlier findings. It is not encouraging that the provisional large-scale manufacturing growth estimate for 1996–7 was negative (–1.43) for the first time in Pakistan's economic history.[16]

Table 5.5 The extent to which the actual size of industry and export GDP ratios differ from potential based on cross-country experience (percentages)

Period	SOI	SOE
1970–7	–3.02	–15.34
1978–87	–0.21	–13.75
1988–93	–1.04	–3.66

Source: Based on cross-country regressions reported in Appendix 5.3, Table 5.6.
Notes: The percentages are calculated by dividing the residuals by the fitted values, where the fitted values are viewed as the potential.

TESTING THE ECONOMIC CASE FOR INDUSTRIALIZATION AND EXPORT PROMOTION IN PAKISTAN

Of course, industrialization and export orientation cannot be viewed as ends in and of themselves. In fact, both of them have been criticized in the progressive literature; industrialization for negative environmental consequences; export orientation for this, and for resulting in minority-enriching and labour-displacing enclave economies with few linkages with the domestic economy. Given these reservations, the endorsement of industrialization (with safeguards) and export orientation needs to based on demonstrating at least their positive contribution to GDP growth.

Following a method proposed by Khan and Bilginsoy (1994), we test if exports, industry or manufacturing have an externality impact on the rest of the economy and whether factors are used more productively in these sectors compared to the rest of the economy. These tests entail estimating the following equation, which represents a two-sector model whose derivation and other details are explained in the reference cited above.

$$\mathrm{GY} = \mathrm{a} + \mathrm{G_k}\frac{\mathrm{I}}{Y} + \lambda\mathrm{GL} + \theta\mathrm{GX} - \frac{1}{1-\delta}\,\mathrm{sGX} + \frac{\phi}{1+\delta}\,\mathrm{s} + \varepsilon \tag{3}$$

where GY is GDP growth net of the variable X whose externality and productivity we want to estimate, i.e. exports, industry and manufacturing. GL and I/Y are labour force growth and gross domestic investment over net GDP, and their coefficients G_k and λ are marginal productivities. GX represents the growth in either exports, industry or manufacturing, and their coefficient θ represents the externality elasticity. Finally s is X/Y in nominal terms and δ represents the productivity of the variable of interest relative to the rest of the economy. Thus $\delta > 0$ implies that exports, industry or manufacturing is more productive than the rest of the economy and welfare gains can be reaped by reallocating resources to these sectors from the rest of the economy. Unfortunately, since we only have data from 1970 to 1993, we cannot have a great deal of confidence in the results, and present them only as suggestive findings in Appendix 5.3, Table 5.7.

We have reported only the industry and manufacturing equations since the export equation was not cointegrated.[17] For neither industry nor manufacturing do the data suggest that externalities are transmitted to the rest of the economy. Also, there is no evidence so far that resources are used more efficiently in industry or manufacturing compared to the rest of the economy.[18]

SUMMARY

The major focus of this paper is on the impact of trade liberalization on industrialization and exports. Considerable trade liberalization took place over the period under study. This is evident from the much smaller premia on imported goods and from the sharp reduction in the effective rates of protection. While we have only been able to study part of the liberalization period, so far the evidence concerning de-industrialization and export promotion is mixed. We rely on several different kinds of evidence to reach this conclusion.

We found that export orientation has become an increasingly important source of industrial growth in the consumer goods industry (about half of total industrial growth), particularly in the structural adjustment period. Correspondingly, import substitution declined in importance and the trend suggests a displacement of imports. However, there is evidence of displacement of domestic production by imports in the intermediate goods sector.

The mean size of industry as a percentage of GDP at 25 per cent in the structural adjustment period (1988–93) has increased by 4 per cent compared to the base period (1970–7), while the size of the manufacturing sector increased by 3 per cent (from 14 to 17 per cent). Overall, mean exports as a percentage of GDP barely increased from 11.7 per cent in the base period to 12.1 per cent in the structural adjustment period. While the annual average growth rate of industry and manufacturing in the 1988–93 period was 0.6 per cent and 1.2 per cent above and below the base period (1970–7) respectively, that of exports was 8.8 per cent greater than the base period.

While industrial and export growth has occurred, the evidence suggests that in neither case is Pakistan realizing its potential or even matching the performance of low income countries. The growth of industry was 1.04 per cent below its potential in the structural adjustment period compared to 0.2 per cent below potential in the 1978–87 period. Also, compared to the category of low income countries in which Pakistan is included, Pakistan's industry and export ratios were substantially below the mean of low income countries in 1995. Finally, for the last year for which data were available (1996–7), large-scale manufacturing growth rates were negative for the first time in Pakistan's economic history.

There has been a steady improvement in export performance. Exports were 15.3 per cent below potential in the base period but only 3.7 per cent below potential in the structural adjustment period. The latter finding should not be cause for much celebration, since Pakistan's export ratio had also fallen behind the mean of low income countries in 1995 compared to being slightly ahead in 1988.

Of course, the real issue is how industry and exports contribute to growth. We tested to identify if the industrial and export sector contribute externalities to the rest of the economy and if resources are more productively used in these sectors compared to the rest of the economy. On both counts, we found no supporting evidence. However, we only had 23 years' data (1970–93), and conclusive results would require many more observations. Thus for now, one would have to rely on cross-country results to emphasize the importance of industrialization in Pakistan.

To conclude, the performance of the consumer goods sector in promoting exports and displacing imports has been robust. Other evidence also points to an improvement in export performance, although Pakistan is still not meeting its export potential or matching the mean performance of even low income countries. Also, our findings cannot reassure those in Pakistan who feared that structural adjustment would usher in de-industrialization. There is evidence of imports displacing domestic production in the intermediate goods sector, of average annual growth in industry declining, and of industry growth falling further behind potential in the period of economic liberalization compared to the earlier period. The negative (provisional estimate) growth rate of 1.43 per cent in 1996–7 will only add to such fears, and with some justification.

NOTES

1. This work was first presented by Shahrukh Rafi Khan and Shaheen Rafi Khan at the Twelfth Annual General Meeting of the Pakistan Society of Development Economists, 14–16 Dec. 1996. A summarized version of the paper appeared in the conference proceedings. Thanks are due to Javed Akbar Ansari, Tariq Banuri and Mohsin S. Khan for comments and also to Sajid Kazmi for extensive and able research assistance.
2. Industry comprises value added in mining, manufacturing, construction, electricity, water and gas. Since manufacturing constitutes the largest component of industry and is viewed as having special significance, it is also used as a separate category for the analysis.
3. For a brief review of the terms-of-trade controversy see Singer (1989).
4. Kemal (1997) estimated that EPRs declined to 66 in 1980–1. Thus, they appear to have actually increased over the 1980s, although they are considerably

lower in 1990–91 compared to 1968–69. Unfortunately, more point estimates are not available to compare EPRs in the mid to the late 1980s and early 1990s with the EPRs in the early 1980s.

5. For more recent discussions and examples of externalities see Weiss (1988, p. 116) and Stewart and Ghani (1991).
6. Thanks to Tariq Banuri for suggesting the derivation.
7. The structural adjustment period is still under way in 1997, although the new government of Nawaz Sharif has altered the macro focus from demand restraint to both demand restraint and supply incentives. The latest *Census of Manufacturing Industries* available is for 1990–1.
8. A positive number for import substitution could represent both more production due to protection, or import displacement via greater efficiency and competitiveness. By looking at long-term trends, it becomes possible to identify which force is operative.
9. Intermediate goods accounted for 42 per cent of the total 1990–1 value of production in our sample and the petroleum product group accounted for 23 per cent of this value of production. The pesticides, insecticides, fungicides and herbicide group and the compressed liquified and solidified gas group together accounted for less than 1 per cent of the value of production in the intermediate group category.
10. The negative growth in manufacturing and exports in the base period coincides with the nationalization of industry.
11. SOI and SOM for Malaysia, Thailand and Indonesia in 1994 were 43, 40 and 42 per cent and 32, 29 and 24 per cent respectively. *World Development Report 1997* (1997, pp. 236–7).
12. The export ratio reached a low of 9.0 per cent in 1977. Thus a positive growth rate of 2.79 per cent in the second period was only able to barely make the mean in the second period equivalent to the mean in the base period.
13. Data were only available until 1992 for the PPP per capita GDP.
14. The slight difference in the equations we estimated is the exclusion of the population square term for which we got a zero coefficient. The diagnostics of the straight OLS based on chi-squared tests suggested a specification error and the related non-normality in the error term. These problems were resolved by logging the dependent variable. We corrected for hetroscedasticity where it was present.
15. It is implicitly assumed in the Chenery–Sryquin method that all countries follow the same industrialization trajectory. We tested for this by using intercept and slope dummies for low and middle income countries and were able to reject separate trajectories.
16. *Economic Survey 1996–97*, Statistical Appendix (1997, p. 33).
17. The absolute value of the Eagle–Granger t-statistics at the 5 per cent level for the export, industry and manufacturing equations are 5.51, 5.94 and 5.51 and the estimated t-values are 4.52, 6.95 and 5.94 respectively. Thus industry and manufacturing equations are cointegrated, but this is not the case for the export equation.
18. We computed the parameter δ to equal to 3.84 in industry and -0.77 in manufacturing, but both coefficients were insignificant.

REFERENCES

Aftab, S., 1994, 'Scarcity Premia on Imports in Pakistan: An Update', Sustainable Development Policy Institute, Islamabad, mimeo.

Agarwala, R., 1983, 'Price Distortions and Growth in Developing Countries', World Bank Staff Working Papers no. 575 (Washington, DC: World Bank).

Balassa, B., 1985, 'Exports, Policy Choices, and Economic Growth in Developing Countries after the 1993 Oil Shock', *Journal of Development Economics*, 18, pp. 23–35.

Chenery, H. B. and M. Sryquin, 1975, *Patterns of Development* (London: Oxford University Press).

Chow, P. C. Y., 1987, 'Causality Between Export Growth and Industrial Development,' *Journal of Development Economics*, 26, pp. 55–63.

Dodaro, S., 1991, 'Comparative Advantage, Trade and Growth: Export-Led Growth Revisited', *World Development*, 19, pp. 1153–65.

Dollar, D., 1992, 'Outward-Oriented Developing Economies Really do Grow More Rapidly: Evidence from 95 LDCs, 1976–1985', *Economic Development and Cultural Change*, 40, pp. 523–44.

Feder, G., 1982, 'On Exports and Economic Growth', *Journal of Development Economics*, 12, pp. 59–73.

Greenway, D. and C. H. Nam, 1988, 'Industrialization and Macroeconomic Performance in Developing Countries Under Alternative Trade Strategies', *Kyklos*, 41, Fasc. 3, pp. 419–35.

Hamid, N., 1992, 'Industry and Trade', in eds W. E. James and S. Roy, *Foundations of Pakistan's Political Economy* (New Delhi: Sage).

Hirschman, A. O., 1958, *The Strategy of Economic Development* (New Haven: Yale University Press).

Jung, W. S. and P. S. Marshall, 1985, 'Exports, Growth and Causality in Developing Countries', *Journal of Developing Economics*, 18, pp. 1–12.

Kaldor, N., 1967, *Strategic Factors in Economic Development* (Ithaca: Cornell University Press).

Kavoussi, R. M., 1984, 'Export Expansion and Economic Growth: Further Empirical Evidence', *Journal of Development Economics*, 14, pp. 241–50.

Kemal, A. R., forthcoming, 'Patterns and Growth of Pakistan's Industrial Sector', in ed. S. R. Khan, *Fifty Years of Pakistan's Economy* (Karachi: Oxford University Press).

Kemal, A. R., N. Burney and S. Hameed, 1981, 'Quota Restrictions, Tariffs and the Scarcity Premia on Licences', Pakistan Institute of Development Economics, Statistical Paper Series, no. 2.

Khan, S. R. and C. Bilginsoy, 1994, 'Industry Externalities Revisited', *Kyklos*, 47, pp. 67–80.

Khan, S. R., C. Bilginsoy and M. S. Alam, 1997, 'Dynamic Efficiencies of Industrialization and Economic Growth: An Aggregative Analysis', *Economia Internationale*, 50, no. 1.

Levine, R. and D. Renelt, 1992, 'A Sensitivity Analysis of Cross-country Growth Regressions', *American Economic Review*, 82, pp. 942–63.

Lewis, S. R., 1969, '*Economic Policy and Industrial Growth in Pakistan* (London: George Allen and Unwin Ltd.).

Lewis, W. A., 1954, 'Economic Development with Unlimited Supplies of Labor', *The Manchester School*, 22, pp. 139–91.

Little, I., T. Scitovsky and M. Scott, 1970, *Industry and Trade in Developing Countries: A Comparative Study* (London: Oxford University Press).

Rosenstein-Rodan, P. N., 1943, 'Problems of Industrialization in Eastern and South Eastern Europe', *Economic Journal*, 53, pp. 202–211.

Sheehey, E., 1992, 'Exports and Growth: Additional Evidence', *Journal of Development Studies*', 28, pp. 730–4.

Singer, H. W., 1950, 'The Distribution of Gains between Investing and Borrowing Countries', *American Economic Review*, 40, pp. 473–85.

Singer, H. W., 1989, 'Terms of Trade and Economic Development', in *The New Palgrave: Economic Development* (New York: W. W. Norton).

Scitovsky, T., 1958, 'Two Concepts of External Economies', in eds A. N. Agarwala and S. P. Singh, *The Economics of Underdevelopment* (New York: Oxford University Press).

Stewart, F. and E. Ghani, 1991, 'How Significant are Externalities for Development', *World Development*, 19, pp. 569–94.

Summers, R. and A. Heston, 1991, 'The Penn World Table (Mark 5): An Expanded Set of International Comparisons, 1950–1988', *The Quarterly Journal of Economics*, 106, no. 2, pp. 327–68.

Tyler, W. G., 1981, 'Growth and Export Expansion in Developing Countries', *Journal of Development Economics*, 11, pp. 121–30.

Weiss, J., 1988, *Industry in Developing Countries: Theory, Policy and Evidence* (New York: Routledge).

World Bank, 1997, *World Development Report 1997* (New York: Oxford University Press).

Yotopoulos, P. A. and J. B. Nugent, 1976, *Economics of Development: Empirical Investigations* (New York: Harper and Row).

Appendix 5.1: Industrial Growth Accounting

$$\Delta Q = \Delta Z \quad \text{(i)}$$

Z = Total supply
Q = Total demand

$$\Delta Z = \Delta X + \Delta M \quad \text{(ii)}$$

X = Domestic production
M = Imports

$$\Delta Q = \Delta \text{DFD} + \Delta W + \Delta E \quad \text{(iii)}$$

DFD = Domestic final demand
W = Domestic intermediate demand
E = Exports

Due to a lack of data, the two categories of domestic demand are merged into D so that

$$\Delta Q = \Delta D + \Delta E \quad \text{(iv)}$$

Starting with equation (i), we can write

$$X_1/Z_1 * \Delta Q = X_1/Z_1 * \Delta Z$$
$$X_1/Z_1\,\Delta Q = X_1/Z_1 * Z_2 - X_1/Z_1 * Z_1$$
$$\mu_1\,\Delta Q = \mu_1\,Z_2 + (X_2 - X_1) - X_2$$
$$\mu_1\,\Delta Q = \mu_1\,Z_2 + \Delta X - X_2/Z_2 * Z_2$$
$$\mu_1\,\Delta Q = \mu_1\,Z_2 + \Delta X - \mu_2\,Z_2$$
$$\mu_1\,\Delta Q = (\mu_2 - \mu_1)\,Z_2 + \Delta X$$
$$\Delta X = \mu_1\,\Delta Q + (\mu_2 - \mu_1)\,Z_2$$

Substituting for ΔQ from equation (iv) we get

$$\Delta X = \mu_1 \Delta D + \mu_1 \Delta E + (\mu_2 - \mu_1)\,Z_2 \quad \text{(v)}$$

Equation (v) is what has been estimated. If import substitution is constant, the change in total production that would result from a change in domestic demand is $\mu_1(\Delta D + \Delta E)$. Where $\mu_1 = X_1/Z_1$ or domestic production to total supply in base year. Thus $\mu_1\,\Delta D$ explains the change in domestic production that results from a change in domestic demand and $\mu_1\,\Delta E$ explains the change in domestic production that results from a change in export demand. Finally, there is a change in domestic production that can be ascribed to a change in import substitution holding demand constant which is captured by $(\mu_2 - \mu_1)\,Z_2$. Here $\mu_2 = X_2/Z_2$, or domestic production to total supply in terminal year. If the ratio of domestic production to total supply increases in the terminal year compared to the base year, it can be attributed to domestic production displacing imports.

To repeat for emphasis, in equation (v), the first two terms represent the partial change in domestic production resulting from a change in domestic demand and the change in exports; and the third term represents the change in domestic production resulting from a change in import substitution.

Appendix 5.2: Country Sample

Algeria
Argentina
Australia
Austria
Bangladesh
Belgium
Benin
Bolivia
Brazil
Burkina Faso
Burundi
Cameroon
Canada
Central African Republic
Chad
Colombia
Congo
Costa Rica
Côte d'Ivoire
Denmark
Dominican Republic
Ecuador
Egypt
El Salvador
Finland
France
Germany
Ghana
Greece
Guatemala
Haiti
Honduras
India
Indonesia
Iran
Italy
Jamaica
Japan
Kenya
Korea
Republic
Lesotho
Liberia
Madagascar
Malawi
Malaysia
Mali
Mauritania
Mexico
Morocco
New Zealand
Niger
Nigeria
Norway
Pakistan
Panama
Papua New Guinea
Paraguay
Peru
Philippines
Rwanda
Senegal
Sierra Leone
Singapore
South Africa
Sri Lanka
Sudan
Sweden
Syria
Tanzania
Thailand
Togo
Trinidad and Tobago
Tunisia
Turkey
Uganda
United States
Uruguay
Venezuela
Zaire
Zambia
Zimbabwe

Appendix 5.3

Table 5.6 Cross-country regression to identify potential size of industry and exports

Time period	1970–7		1978–87		1988–93	
Dependent variable	LSOI	LSOE	LSOI	LSOE	LSOI	LSOE
Constant	2.76*	3.12*	2.82*	2.97*	−1.75*	2.85*
	(32.71)	(22.57)	(34.64)	(23.23)	(22.22)	(22.63)
Per Capita GDP	0.3E-3*	0.1E-4	0.2E-3*	0.8E-4	0.2E-3*	0.2E-3*
	(5.69)	(0.89)	(6.23)	(1.26)	(6.38)	(2.89)
Per Capita GDP	0.2E-7*	−0.2E-8	−0.1E-7*	−0.5E8	−0.1E-7*	−0.8E-8**
Squared	(4.46)	(0.79)	(5.40)	(1.02)	(5.60)	(2.39)
Population	0.6E-6	−0.3E-5*	0.5E-6*	−0.2E-5*	0.4E-6***	−0.2E-5*
	(1.37)	(3.69)	(1.64)	(3.45)	(1.66)	(2.89)
R-Bar-squared	0.37	0.13	0.37	0.13	0.38	0.19
N	78	80	81	81	79	80
F	12.32*	5.07*	16.98*	5.05*	16.64*	7.21*

Source: World Bank, *World Table 1994* for population, GDP value added in industry, Exports of goods and non-factor services. Penn World Tables (5.6a) were used for per capita GDP in purchasing power party (PPP) terms.

Notes: LSOI = Size of the industrial sector defined as value added in industry over GDP. The ratio was logged.
LSOE = Size of exports defined as the value of goods and non-factor services exported over GDP. The ratio was logged.
Parentheses contain t-ratios.
* = Significant at least at the 1% level
** = Significant at least at the 5% level
*** = Significant at least at the 10% level

Table 5.7 Growth equations: externality and productivity effect of the industry and manufacturing sectors

	Coefficient estimates	
Regressor	Industry	Manufacturing
T	0.206**	
	(2.32)	
CON	50.48**	39.51***
	(2.57)	(2.05)
IR	−78.42**	−52.77
	(2.19)	(1.64)
GLF	2.31***	0.78
	(1.78)	(0.62)
GX	−2.29	−2.92
	(1.26)	(1.39)
sGX	8.43	16.89
	(1.34)	(1.51)
s	−115.36**	−132.07
	(2.23)	(1.53)
R-bar-squared	0.29	0.29
DW-statistic	2.64	2.27
F-statistic (5, 17)	2.51***	2.82**

Notes: Time trend in the manufacturing equation was not significant.

X − Variable of interest (industry in column 2 and manufacturing in column 3)
Y = GDP
GY = GDP growth net of X
GL = Labour force growth
I/Y = Gross domestic investment over net GDP
GX = Represents the growth in either industry or manufacturing
S = X/Y
* = Significant at the 1 per cent level
** = Significant at the 5 per cent level
*** = Significant at the 10 per cent level

Appendix 5.4: Disaggregated Sources of Industrial Growth

Table 5.8 Exports

	1970/1–1980/1	1980/1–1987/8	1987/8–1990/1
Consumer Goods			
Grain Milling	−0.00	0.00	0.00
Sugar Refining	−0.00	0.00	0.00
Edible Oils	0.00	0.00	0.00
Tea Blending	0.00	0.00	0.00
Beverages	−0.00	0.00	0.00
Tobacco Mfg.	−0.00	0.01	0.07
Cotton Fabrics	0.06	0.09	0.13
Silk and Synth. Tex.	0.03	0.03	−0.04
Woollen Tex.	0.00	0.00	0.08
Woollen Rugs	0.00	−0.00	0.25
Footwear	0.00	0.01	0.00
Printing and Publ.	0.00	0.00	0.00
Drugs and Medicines	−0.00	0.00	0.00
Perfumes and Cosmetics	−0.00	0.00	0.00
Soaps and Detergents	0.00	−0.00	0.00
Intermediate Goods			
Cotton Ginning	0.09	0.08	−0.00
Cotton Yarn	0.04	0.07	−0.08
Jute Textiles	0.01	0.00	0.00
Leather and Leather Prod.	0.02	0.03	0.04
Paper and Paper Prod.	0.01	0.00	−0.00
Rubber Prod.	−0.00	0.00	−0.00
Fertilizers	0.00	0.00	0.00
Paints and Varnishes	0.00	0.00	0.00
Petroleum Prod.	0.00	−0.12	0.01
Glass and Glass Prod.	0.00	0.00	0.00
Acids, Alkalis and Salts	0.00	0.00	0.00
Dyes, Colours and Pigments	0.00	0.00	0.00
Comp., Lique., and Solidified Gases	0.00	0.00	0.00
Pest, Insect, Fung. and Herbicides	0.00	0.00	0.00
Synth. Resins, Plastic Materials and Man Made Fibres	0.00	0.00	0.00

Table 5.8 (*Continued*)

	1970/1–1980/1	1980/1–1987/8	1987/8–1990/1
Capital Goods			
Cement	−0.00	0.00	−0.00
Basic Metals	0.00	0.00	0.00
Metal Products	−0.00	0.00	0.00
Electrical Machinery and Equipment	0.00	−0.00	0.00
Non-Electrical Machinery	−0.00	0.00	−0.00
Transport Equipment	0.00	0.00	0.00

Table 5.9 Import substitution

	1970/1–1980/1	1980/1–1987/8	1987/8–1990/1
Consumer Goods			
Grain Milling	−0.01	0.00	0.01
Sugar Refining	−0.01	0.02	0.00
Edible Oils	−0.06	−0.04	0.08
Tea Blending	−0.05	0.00	−0.00
Beverages	0.00	−0.00	0.00
Tobacco Mfg.	0.00	−0.00	0.00
Cotton Fabrics	0.00	0.00	0.00
Silk and Synth. Tex.	−0.00	0.00	0.00
Woollen Tex	0.00	0.00	0.00
Woollen Rugs	0.00	0.00	0.00
Footwear	0.00	0.00	0.00
Printing and Publ.	0.00	0.00	0.00
Drugs and Medicines	−0.01	−0.00	0.02
Perfumes and Cosmetics	−0.00	0.00	0.00
Soaps and Detergents	0.00	0.00	0.00
Intermediate Goods			
Cotton Ginning	−0.00	−0.00	0.00
Cotton Yarn	0.00	0.00	0.00
Jute Textiles	−0.01	0.00	0.00
Leather and Leather Prod.	0.00	0.00	0.00
Paper and Paper Prod.	−0.01	−0.00	0.01
Rubber Prod.	−0.00	−0.00	0.00
Fertilizers	−0.07	0.07	−0.01
Paints and Varnishes	0.00	−0.00	−0.01
Petroleum Prod.	0.38	0.03	−0.17
Glass and Glass Prod.	0.00	0.00	0.00
Acids, Alkalis and Salts	−0.00	0.00	0.01
Dyes, Colours and Pigments	0.00	−0.00	0.05

Table 5.9 (*continued*)

	1970/1–1980/1	1980/1–1987/8	1987/8–1990/1
Comp., Lique., and Solidified Gases	−0.00	−0.00	−0.14
Pest, Insect, Fung. and Herbicides	−0.01	−0.01	−0.23
Synth. Resins, Plastic Materials and Man Made Fibres	−0.01	0.01	−0.00
Capital Goods			
Cement	0.00	−0.00	0.00
Basic Metals	0.04	0.11	0.11
Metal Products	0.02	−0.00	0.02
Electrical Machinery and Equipment	0.06	−0.01	−0.02
Non-Electrical Machinery	0.04	0.02	0.08
Transport Equipment	0.06	0.06	0.00

Table 5.10 Domestic demand

	1970/1–1980/1	1980/1–1987/8	1987/8–1990/1
Consumer Goods			
Grain Milling	0.08	0.09	0.02
Sugar Refining	0.17	0.13	0.15
Edible Oils	0.30	0.26	0.11
Tea Blending	0.13	0.05	0.07
Beverages	0.03	0.03	0.02
Tobacco Mfg.	0.13	0.09	0.00
Cotton Fabrics	0.03	0.01	0.00
Silk and Synth. Tex.	0.01	0.04	0.14
Woollen Tex.	0.02	0.01	−0.06
Woollen Rugs	0.00	0.01	−0.24
Footwear	0.02	0.02	0.02
Printing and Publ.	0.01	0.02	0.03
Drugs and Medicines	0.09	0.09	0.09
Perfumes and Cosmetics	0.01	0.01	0.02
Soaps and Detergents	0.02	0.02	0.02

Table 5.10 (continued)

	1970/1–1980/1	1980/1–1987/8	1987/8–1990/1
Intermediate Goods			
Cotton Ginning	0.03	0.06	0.12
Cotton Yarn	0.10	0.13	0.38
Jute Textiles	0.02	0.01	0.02
Leather and Leather Prod.	0.01	0.03	0.01
Paper and Paper Prod.	0.04	0.05	0.04
Rubber Prod.	0.02	0.02	0.02
Fertilizers	0.18	0.03	0.08
Paints and Varnishes	0.01	0.01	0.02
Petroleum Prod.	0.01	0.40	0.47
Glass and Glass Prod.	0.05	0.01	0.01
Acids, Alkalis and Salts	0.02	0.03	0.01
Dyes, Colours and Pigments	0.00	0.01	−0.04
Comp., Lique., and Solidified Gases	0.03	0.00	0.15
Pest, Insect, Fung. and Herbicides	0.01	0.03	0.24
Synth. Resins, Plastic Materials and Man Made Fibres	0.03	0.00	0.01
Capital Goods			
Cement	0.13	0.14	0.14
Basic Metals	0.24	0.19	0.15
Metal Products	0.04	0.04	0.02
Electrical Machinery and Equipment	0.11	0.17	0.19
Non-Electrical Machinery	0.12	0.13	0.08
Transport Equipment	0.15	0.15	0.22

Note: Sources of growth are reported across time for ease of comparison, so the rows do not add to 1.

Part II Assessing Impact

6 Structural Adjustment, Labour and the Poor[1]

INTRODUCTION

This chapter draws together some of the important evidence with regard to the impact of structural adjustment on labour and the poor, and identifies other areas where much research still needs to be done. Should the poor worry about structural adjustment? The answer is probably yes, although again this is an empirical issue. As mentioned above, one of the more stringent conditionalities of the SAF loans is that government should reduce the budget deficit through suitable demand management policies and by specific reforms aimed at cutting expenditures and increasing revenues. Curtailing expenditure invariably translates into cuts in subsidies and in expenditure on social sectors. Both these measures are easier to undertake than, say, a substantial reduction in military expenditure.

But these expenditure cuts are likely to adversely affect the poorer sections of society, as do wage restraints and increases in utility charges, which are also recommended by the Bank and the Fund. The imposition of a comprehensive General Sales Tax and the subsequent inflation may also hurt the poor more. Structural adjustment programmes also tend to be followed by widespread unemployment. In a country like Pakistan, where the government is the largest employer, a reduction in government expenditure immediately translates into a freeze on recruitment in government offices or into downsizing.[2] The imposition of greater taxes on the business community also tends to lead to large-scale laying off of industrial workers, as does privatization (see Chapter 4). Inflation, the withdrawal of subsidies and, consequently, higher food prices in urban areas and greater unemployment are all part and parcel of adjustment programmes. It is not surprising that social unrest, and in many cases rioting, tends to follow intensive versions of them.

Is the assumption about excessive and wasteful state expenditure warranted? Sometimes, but not always. Once again, this is an empirical issue. It could be that inadequate physical and social infrastructure results in a shortfall in production. In this case, the answer would be to focus primarily on boosting production rather than cutting expenditure.

We present evidence of the likely impact of structural adjustment on labour and the poor in the next section, and end with some concluding remarks.

EVIDENCE OF REGRESSIVE STRUCTURAL ADJUSTMENT IMPACTS

Since the onset of the medium-term structural adjustment programme in 1988, the socio-economic conditions of labour and the poor seem to have deteriorated. We start by reviewing the overall household economic progress by income group.

As shown in Table 6.1, real income in all income groups declined over the period under study. The magnitude of the decline is highest for the

Table 6.1 Changes in household monthly real income[3]

Income groups	Household monthly income in real terms	
	1987–8	1992–3
I	634.5	416.6
II	1084.2	966.5
III	1744.1	1583.2
IV	2742.2	2416.11
V	5250.6	5110.4

Source: Calculated from *Household Income and Expenditure Survey, 1987–88* (1990, p. 183), *Household Integrated Economic Survey 1992–93* (1996, p. 254).

Notes: The income groups across the two years respectively represent 8.9, 36.7, 20.5, 23.4, 10.5 per cent and 9.5, 31.9, 23.1, 22.1 and 13.4 per cent of the population. We assume an equal number of earners per *household*. Banuri et al.'s (1997, Table 4.8, p. 72) findings suggests that his assumption is only partially borne out since the mean earners for rich and poor households are 2.1 and 1.2 respectively. Thus there is some bias resulting from referring to a household as rich based on it having more earners. Per capita household classification, when possible, is preferable. Thanks to Haris Gazdar for pointing this out.

lowest income group (34 per cent) and lowest for the highest income group (3 per cent). The Federal Bureau of Statistics gives inflation-adjusted classifications of what income levels constitute low, middle and high income households in various years. The table above was calculated using the income categories defined in the *Household Integrated Expenditure Survey*. This ensured that the data would be comparable over the period under study.

The income distribution evident from household sample survey data is typically compressed. This is because the poorest in the lowest income group, that do not have fixed dwellings or reside in *kachi abadis* (shanty towns), get excluded. Such exclusion is also the case for the very rich, since a mean real monthly income of about Rs 5,000 for the upper income bracket for 1992–3 is unrealistically low. This also explains the apparent contradiction of a recorded increase in real per capita income during a period for which our results show mean household real income falling across the board for all income groups. It appears that all the recorded increase in per capita income for the country is accounted for by the increase in the income of the super rich.

Although structural adjustment may not be a cause of observed changes in standards of living, yet it is not possible to rule out an association. This is particularly the case with regard to employment and wages in the public sector. Responding to calls for fiscal discipline, the government pared down the work force and froze wages.

There is a steady decline in the public sector employment cost starting in 1988–9. This resulted from freezing nominal wages of government employees, bans on recruitment, and the encouragement of early retirements via golden handshakes.[4] While reducing the size of the public sector *per se* may not be injurious, expecting the labour market to somehow

Table 6.2 Share of public sector employment cost in public expenditure and GDP

Years	Share of public sector employment cost in:	
	Public expenditure	GDP
1988–9	35.3	7.9
1989–90	34.5	7.5
1990–1	32.3	7.0
1991–2	30.6	6.7
1992–3	28.7	5.9

Source: Adopted from Kemal (1994, p. 8).

Table 6.3 Unemployment rates by occupational categories

Occupational groups	1987–8	1990–1	1993–4
Professional and Technical	5.3	6.7	6.1
Administrative and Managerial	n.a.	15.9	9.8
Clerical and Related	3.2	15.1	13.5
Sales	3.2	2.6	3.7
Services	3.2	9.6	8.3
Agricultural	0.9	1.9	1.0
Production and Related Services	7.1	13.3	10.5

Source: Calculated from various *Labour Force Surveys*, 1987–8 (1989, p. 232), 1990–1 (1993, p. 335) and 1993–4 (1994, p. 421).

absorb larger numbers is unrealistic. This is evident even from the much doubted official unemployment statistics as reported in Table 6.3.[5]

One would expect a concentration of the poor in the clerical, sales, services, agricultural, and production and related services categories. In all of these, the unemployment rate has risen dramatically between 1987–8 and 1990–1.[6] However, in most cases, unemployment in 1993–4 was lower than in 1990–1, although still much higher than 1987–8. More spot observations over time are needed to see if this represents a continuing trend.

In addition to a decline in unemployment, real wages for skilled and unskilled labour over this period also declined dramatically, as reported in Table 6.4.

For unskilled workers, there is a convergence of wages in Peshawar, where they were the lowest, with those in Karachi, where they were the highest. This is to be expected, as migration south to Karachi could be expected to gradually cause the wages in the northern urban centres to rise. However, real wages for unskilled workers in Karachi declined by about 1 per cent in the 1980–1 to 1986–7 period and about 25 per cent in the 1987–8 to 1994–5 period.

The decline in real wages for skilled workers occurred in both cities and in both periods, although more in the later period. Between 1980–1 and 1986–7, real wages for masons declined by 16.5 per cent and 7.0 per cent, while during the 1987–8 to 1994–5 period, they declined by 18.0 and 19.2 per cent in Peshawar and Karachi respectively. One would also expect increasing unemployment and a decline in real wages to be accompanied by increasing inequality and poverty. This is indeed the case, as is evident from Table 6.5.

Table 6.4 Nominal daily wage of skilled and unskilled workers deflated by the food price index (1980–1 = 100)

Years	Unskilled workers (labourer)		Skilled workers (mason)	
	Peshawar (lowest)	Karachi (highest)	Peshawar (lowest)	Karachi (highest)
1980–1	18.0	27.5	60.0	65.0
1981–2	19.3	24.7	60.6	67.4
1982–3	18.7	25.4	62.6	67.0
1983–4	20.0	23.6	63.9	63.5
1984–5	18.4	22.6	53.9	58.5
1985–6	17.8	28.2	55.3	57.1
1986–7	20.4	27.3	51.1	61.4
Period change (%) (1980–1/1986–7)	(+13.3)	(−0.7)	(−16.5)	(−7.0)
1987–8	17.2	31.0	48.8	63.6
1988–9	18.5	30.6	44.8	67.0
1989–90	20.0	30.1	48.0	63.8
1990–1	18.3	27.9	48.9	59.6
1991–2	21.0	26.2	40.1	58.2
1992–3	20.0	26.1	40.4	60.2
1993–4	17.6	25.8	40.0	56.9
1994–5	17.8	23.3	40.0	51.4
Period change (%) (1987–8/1993–5)	(+0.8)	(−24.8)	(−18.0)	(−19.2)

Source: *Economic Survey 1995–96*, Statistical Appendix (1996), pp. 25–6 for nominal wages and p. 146 for the food price index.
Note: Peshawar and Karachi were selected as the two major cities with the lowest and highest daily wages in the base period.

Table 6.5 Inequality and absolute poverty

	Income share	Overall		Rural		Urban	
		Gini	Poverty	Gini	Poverty	Gini	Poverty
1984–5	6.2	0.43	18.3	0.35	21.1	0.38	11.1
1987–8	5.5	0.35	16.6	0.31	19.6	0.37	8.7
1990–1	6.1	0.41	17.2	0.41	20.6	0.39	9.8

Source: Adopted from Malik et al. (Tables II.1 and II.5). Recent estimates in Gazdar (1994) based on the 1991 Pakistan Integrated Household Survey (PIHS) are much higher.

Table 6.5 shows that inequality, as reflected by income share ratios and gini coefficients, has increased, as has absolute poverty. Income-share ratios represent the ratios of the income share of the richest 20 per cent of the households divided by the income share of the bottom 20 per cent. The numbers show an equalization trend in the mid to late 1980s that was reversed in the early 1990s. The same story is evident from the gini coefficients. The urban–rural disaggregation shows a sharp rise in inequality in the rural areas relative to the urban areas.

The poverty numbers are based on a head count of the percentage of the population below a calorie-based poverty line. Not surprisingly, the numbers reflect the pattern evident from measures of inequality. There is the same pattern of decline in absolute poverty from the mid to late 1980s and then a rise in the early 1990s. Second, poverty is strikingly more a rural than an urban phenomenon and has become more so over time.

A study by Malik on nutrition (1992), based on data from the *National Nutrition Survey 1985–87* and the *Demographic and Health Survey 1990–91*, shows that there has been an improvement in nutritional status over time for children below the age of two years. However, this trend has been reversed for the age group of four to five years. In any case, the prevalence of malnutrition among children in the country is extremely high.[7]

Unemployment could account for much of the increase in inequality and poverty, although this issue needs further exploration. Given the consumption pattern of the poor and the incidence of taxes and subsidies which prevailed prior to the recent structural adjustment measures, one could have anticipated the increase in poverty and can certainly explain it with hindsight. We first look at how spending on subsidies and social services have fared as a per cent of total expenditures. We have also included expenditures on defence and interest payments in Table 6.6.

It is of interest that defence expenditures have been contained and that interest payments continue to expand. Our focus here is on social services and subsidies. Expenditures on social services have steadily increased and it therefore seems that more than lip-service is being paid to the increase in focus on the social sectors. There is an implicit subsidy involved in social sector expenditures, since the government is not recovering all such expenditures in user charges. Education is an important component of social services, and given the major shift during the *Seventh Five Year Plan* away from expenditures on higher education and towards primary education, the rural poor are thus recipients of this subsidy due to expenditure reallocation.[8]

However, as shown in Table 7.6 of Chapter 7 (below), the combined expenditure on education and health as a percentage of GDP remained virtually unchanged between 1987–8 and 1995–6.

Table 6.6 Proportion of total government spending on subsidies, social sectors, interest payments and defence

Years	Current subsidies	Social services	Interest	Defence
1987–8	4.4	9.6	18.4	26.1
1988–9	6.6	9.6	18.9	25.4
1989–90	4.1	9.1	21.1	26.5
1990–1	4.1	10.8	19.2	24.8
1991–2	2.5	14.1	19.4	23.6
1992–3	2.1	15.7	22.6	25.0
1993–4	1.4	15.5	24.9	25.2
1994–5	1.5	16.5	23.8	23.4

Source: *Economic Survey 1996–97*, Statistical Appendix (1997, p. 127).

Table 6.7 Subsidies on wheat, sugar and edible oil as a percentage of current subsidies

Years	Subsidies on wheat and sugar	Subsidies on edible oil
1987–8	49.3	—
1988–9	54.9	21.4
1989–90	50.0	—
1990–1	43.3	21.1
1991 2	51.0	2.0
1992–3	52.7	—
1993–4	70.4	9.0
1994–5	44.9	5.4

Source: *Economic Survey 1996–97*, Statistical Appendix (1997, p. 127)

The picture with regard to the steady decrease in subsidies is not so sanguine. As Table 6.7 indicates, the bulk of the subsidies were on wheat, sugar and edible oil, which are important components of the total consumption basket of the poor.

Table 6.7 shows that not only have total subsidies declined but the share of wheat, sugar and edible oil in these subsidies has also declined sharply. This decline in subsidy accompanied an increase in the support price of wheat, which rose from Rs 64 per 40 kg in 1983–4 to Rs 173 per 40 kg in 1995–6, an increase of 170 per cent. Between 1984 and 1994, nominal wages for unskilled labour in Karachi increased 157 per cent.[9]

Table 6.8 Expenditure on wheat and fuel as a proportion of total household expenditure (percentages)

Income groups	Wheat		Fuel	
	1987–8	1992–3	1987–8	1992–3
I	12.07	24.71	7.76	17.65
II	10.82	13.34	7.06	10.16
III	9.21	10.19	6.19	7.67
IV	7.34	7.97	5.57	6.38
V	6.02	4.15	4.49	3.89

Source: Calculated from *Household Income and Expenditure Survey, 1987–88* (1989, pp. 183, 233, 263) and *Household Integrated Economic Survey 1992–93* (1996, pp. 254, 287, 322).
Note: As in Table 6.2.

The increase in wheat price is of concern since the lowest income group derive 70 per cent of their protein and 55 per cent of their calories from this source.[10] Also of concern is the changing share of wheat in the consumption basket of the lowest income group as reported in the Table 6.8.

In Table 6.8, observe that expenditure on wheat increased sharply for low and middle income households. This is contrary to past trends and expectations and could be accounted for by a substitution away from other foods. Ender, Wasay and Mahmood (1992, p. 1164) show a declining trend in the consumption of wheat in the past for the lowest income quartile and argue that this is expected with a rise in prosperity.

Looking at the consumption pattern of the poor shows that they have been hurt many times over. Not only have they borne a disproportionate burden of the cuts in employment, cuts in subsidies and the rise in prices, but they have also started bearing more of the tax burden. Using consumption patterns, Kemal and Mahmood (*Just Development*, ch. 4) showed that the burden of taxes on the poor increased by 10.3 per cent while that on the richest group declined by 4.3 per cent between 1987 and 1988. Taking only the poorest and richest income categories into account, the indirect tax structure remained mildly progressive with the poor paying 7.8 per cent of their income in taxes and the richest 11.0 per cent in 1990–1.

During this period, the share of indirect taxes in total taxes also declined from 87 to 84 per cent, and it has declined further to 61 per cent by 1995–6.[11] However, a simple decline in indirect taxes as a percentage of the total is not enough. The real issue is how sensitive the indirect tax structure (now referred to as the Generalized Sales Tax) is to the consumption pattern of the poor (via exemptions), and how this subsequently affects their tax burden.

CONCLUDING REMARKS

Our approach to structural adjustment is not ideological. We believe that some sensible policies may be recommended as part of the structural adjustment package, as we indicated in Part I of this book. We have also argued that the national interest needs to be kept in mind when assessing structural reform. However, in this chapter, which focuses primarily on the impact of the post 1987–8 bouts of structural adjustment policies on labour and the poor, we have demonstrated that it may not always be helpful to think on such a broad level. This is because the impact of structural adjustment is likely to differ a great deal by income group, and indeed by gender, as we indicate in the next chapter.

The evidence on the socio-economic condition of labour and the poor to date is not heartening. Due to privatization, golden handshakes, and an employment and wage freeze, the share of public sector employment cost in total public sector employment decreased from 35.3 to 28.7 per cent. In the presence of excessive underemployment and public sector inefficiency, this could be considered a positive outcome. However, one would hope that the private sector is then picking up the slack. Even taking into account the recognition by the Federal Bureau of Statistics that they were understating unemployment rates prior to 1990–1, the increase in unemployment rates by occupational categories from 1987–8 to 1990–1, and indeed to 1993–4, are dramatic, particularly in occupations where one would expect a high incidence of poor workers. At the same time, real wages of skilled and unskilled labour have drastically declined.

One would expect an increase in inequality and poverty to accompany high unemployment rates and declining real wages, and that is indeed what occurred. Between 1987–8 and 1990–1, inequality and poverty both increased notably. Apart from unemployment, cuts in subsidies and increases in prices of commodities that are a large component of the consumption pattern of the poor account for this phenomenon. Finally, while the reliance on indirect taxes decreased over 1987–8 to 1990–1, and while the indirect tax structure in Pakistan was mildly progressive in the base year, the incidence of indirect taxes on the poorest tax group increased during this period by 10.4 per cent while that on the richest tax bracket declined by 4.3 per cent.

Our research shows that structural adjustment conditionalities are proving to be detrimental for the socio-economic well-being of the poor.

We recommended that close attention be paid to the effects of these policies on employment and on the consumption pattern of the poor. While policies like the Social Action Plan in Pakistan, which invest in the human capital of the poor, are necessary for the long run, short-run measures such as efficiently directed jobs and nutritional programmes are also called for.

NOTES

1. Paper prepared on behalf of Pakistan Institute of Labour Education and Research, Karachi for PP-21 South Asia Meeting on International Aid, Kathmandu, Nepal, July 1994 by Shahrukh R. Khan and Safiya Aftab. It has been published in *Lahore Journal of Economics*, 2, no. 1, 1997.
2. There has been a ban on recruitment in government offices in Pakistan since June 1990. This has been lifted for short periods from time to time, but has always been reimposed and is still in effect. In late 1997, public sector downsizing began in ernest, but was subsequently aborted, at least temporarily, due to political and popular opposition.
3. The consumer price index drawn from the *Economic Survey 1995–96*, Statistical Appendix (1996, p. 137) was used to deflate 1992–3 nominal values to a 1987–8 base.
4. Bilquese (1992, pp. 4–5) shows that for most public sector employees, 'there was a massive erosion [in real wages] in the late 1980s'.
5. Part of the increase in unemployment rates represents a concession by the Federal Bureau of Statistics that they had been understating the unemployment rates in the past. Even so, the increase in unemployment rates is dramatic.
6. Chaudhry and Chaudhry (1992, pp. 6–8), in a more detailed study of the agricultural sector, show that growth in employment opportunities in the 1984–5 to 1989–90 period at 0.65 per cent came to a virtual standstill compared to earlier periods. They attribute this to a fall in agricultural profitability due to the elimination of input subsidies.
7. According to the *World Development Report 1997* (p. 224), 40 per cent of the children under five were malnourished between 1985 and 1995.
8. Education expenditures by plan period are cited in Table 3 of the SDPI *Citizen's Report* (1995), chapter on education.
9. *Pakistan Economic Survey 1995–96*, Statistical Appendix (1996, pp. 26, 60).
10. See Chapter 10, below.
11. *Economic Survey 1996–97*, Statistical Appendix (1997, p. 125).

REFERENCES

Banuri, T., S. R. Khan and M. Mahmood, eds, 1997, *Just Development: Beyond Adjustment with a Human Face* (Karachi: Oxford University Press).

Bilquese, F., 1992, 'Trends in Intersectoral Wages in Pakistan: 1977–1990', Eighth Annual General Meeting of the Pakistan Society of Development Economists, Pakistan Institute of Development Economics, Islamabad.

Chaudhry, M. G. and G. M. Chaudhry, 1992, 'Trends in Rural Employment and Wages in Pakistan', Eighth Annual General Meeting of the Pakistan Society of Development Economists, Pakistan Institute of Development Economics, Islamabad.

Ender, G., A. Wasay and A. Mahmood, 1992, 'Wheat Price Policies in Pakistan: Should There be a Subsidy?' *The Pakistan Development Review*, 31, no. 4.

Government of Pakistan, Economic Advisors Wing, *Economic Survey*, several years, Islamabad.

Government of Pakistan, Federal Bureau of Statistics, 1987–8, *Household Income and Expenditure Survey*, Karachi.

Government of Pakistan, Federal Bureau of Statistics, 1990–1, *Household Integrated Expenditure Survey*, Islamabad.

Government of Pakistan, Federal Bureau of Statistics, *Labour Force Surveys*, several years, Islamabad.

Gazdar, H., et al., 1994, 'Poverty in Pakistan: Measurement, Trends, and Patterns', prepared for the World Bank, mimeo.

Huntington, S. P., 1993, 'The Clash of Civilizations', *Foreign Affairs*, 72, no. 3, July–Aug.

Kemal, A. R., 1994, 'Structural Adjustment, Employment, Income Distribution and Poverty,' Paper presented at the Tenth Annual General Meeting of the Pakistan Society of Development Economists, Pakistan Institute of Development Economics, Islamabad.

Kemal, A.R. and M. Mahmood, 1997, 'Poverty and Policy in Pakistan', in Banuri et al., eds, *Just Development.*

Khan, S. R., S. Kazmi and Z. Ahmed, 1996, 'Structural Adjustment and Food Security in Pakistan', Proceedings of a Conference on Newer Forms of Insecurities in South Asia, Regional Centre of Strategic Studies, Sri Lanka.

Malik, S. J., et al., n.d., 'Rural Poverty in Pakistan', Paper prepared for the Asian Development Bank, Manila, mimeo.

Malik, S. J., and N. S. Malik, 1992, 'Reporting on the World Nutrition Situation: A Case Study of Pakistan (1976 to 1991)', Report prepared for the Administrative Committee on Coordination/Sub-Committee on Nutrition of the UN.

Sustainable Development Policy Institute, 1995, *Nature, Power, People: Citizen's Report on Sustainable Development* (Islamabad: SDPI).

World Bank, 1997, *World Development Report 1997* (New York: Oxford University Press).

7 Gender and Structural Adjustment[1]

INTRODUCTION

'If men and women were to take turns bearing children and if men were to bear the first, no family would have more than two children.' This is a hard-hitting saying by a down-to-earth woman. One could also say that if men lived the lives of poor rural or urban women for a day, they would quickly endorse a special focus on the condition of women. As things stand, in Pakistan, a special focus on women is often suspected to be driven by a foreign agenda. Even so, one needs to consider the ideological resistance to studying women, and to focus on interventions to improve their social and economic conditions.

Without quoting specific sources, it is possible to present the general view negating a special focus on women. Households are viewed as integrated units to which all contribute as teams. Women are viewed as part of households in their capacity as mothers, wives and daughters, etc. Hence any independent identity for them negates this concept of an integrated household in which women play a central role and for which they are accorded their due respect. This is a comfortable view for men, but it denies the harsh social reality that women confront. Many quotes are possible to represent this harsh social reality, but the following one from the *Report of a Commonwealth Expert Group on Women and Structural Adjustment* (1989, p. 3) sums it up well: 'Women account for half the world's population, perform two-thirds of the hours worked (though are recorded as working only one-third of those hours), receive one-tenth of the world's income, and have one-hundredth of the world's property registered in their name'.[2] Given such statistics, one has to be blind to basic social justice to condemn studies and policies with a special focus on women as inspired by a culturally alien foreign agenda.

The harsh social reality confronted by so many women is an important reason that justifies a special focus on women as a subject of research and as a target group. Another reason for such a special focus is that women may not share men's vision of an integrated household. There is evidence that women have opted for wage work rather than work for their husbands in order to retain control over income (Elson, 1991). This does not negate that women in general work as a team with their husbands to attain household goals. However, it suggests, as is corroborated by evidence, that women's expenditure choices are often different. Various studies have documented that women are likely to spend more on improving the nutrition, health and education of their children than men are (Onimode, 1991). This gives credence to the conceptualization of household decision-making in a cooperation–conflict framework as opposed to the more simplistic framework of new household economics that assumes a benign household head (normally male) acting in the best interests of the family.[3]

We present the conceptual framework used for the data collection in the next section, and following that present and report on the evidence. We end with summary and conclusions.

CONCEPTUAL FRAMEWORK AND METHOD

The *Commonwealth Report* suggested a useful conceptual framework for systematically presenting empirical evidence pertaining to women and structural adjustment. This framework suggests sorting information in terms of the multiple roles women perform, i.e. as producers, household managers, mothers and community organizers.[4] Structural adjustment affects the nature of women's labour force participation, working hours and wage rates and hence their role as producers. It results in household reallocation decisions by affecting consumer prices and subsidies and hence their role as home managers. Finally, it affects the price and availability of social services and hence their role as mothers. A more active community role could be a component of survival strategies that women seek in dealing with the effects of structural adjustment.[5]

This multiple role framework concentrates on women's current situation. In addition, structural adjustment could also affect the future ability of the current generation of girls to perform these multiple roles by more adversely affecting their nutrition, health and education than it does those of boys. Thus, evidence on comparative social statistics of children by gender is relevant to an investigation of woman and structural adjustment. Since the intensive period of structural adjustment reform started in 1988, when possible we will compare the period following 1987/8 to earlier periods.

EVIDENCE

Women as Producers

In most countries, including Pakistan, women's household work is ignored by the national accounts and women's contribution in the informal sector, where the majority of women are employed, is also underestimated. Women supplement the family income by selling home-grown vegetables and craft goods such as embroidered clothes. Alternatively, they are involved in subsistence agriculture and this contribution to the economy is also seldom recognized. Thus inadequate statistics on the contribution of women in various activities serves as a barrier in estimating the true contribution of women to the economy and hence in discerning the impact of structural adjustment policies on women as producers.

The age specific participation for the years 1969–99 and 1988–92 is reported in Table 7.1.

For the 10–14 age group, there is a very notable decline in labour force participation rates for males over the two sub-periods. This suggests a decline in male child labour which is a positive development. However, for the same age group, female labour increased by about 0.8 per cent. This selective increase in female child labour is distressing given that girl enrolment ratios are already much worse than those of boys (section 3c).

Overall, male participation in the most active 15–44 age-group rates declined by about 4 per cent across the two periods while there was a corresponding increase in female participation rates of 3.5 per cent (5.0 per cent in the 45–60 age bracket). Thus it would appear that as men were forced out of the labour force or migrated, more women entered it to compensate for the fall in household income.[6] This is confirmed by looking at the gender composition

Table 7.1 Labour force participation rates by age and gender

Age Group	1969–79 1986–7	1987–8 1994–5
10 years and above		
Male	76.0	70.5
Female	9.1	12.5
10–14		
Male	32.1	19.6
Female	6.0	6.8
15–44		
Male	88.1	83.8
Female	10.3	13.8
45–60+		
Male	87.0	83.2
Female	8.1	13.1

Source: *Economic Survey 1996–97*, Statistical Appendix, pp. 24–5.

of the civilian labour force, which shows almost a tripling of women in the labour force over the structural adjustment period being considered.

Table 7.2, however, also shows a sharp increase in the female unemployment rate from about 1 per cent to 10 per cent. Thus while many more women entered the labour force, many of them were unable to find jobs or were squeezed out by men. It also appears that, over this period, the ability to make ends meet working for oneself sharply declined. There was about a 10 per cent decline in self-employment among males and about a 40 per cent decline in self-employment for females.[7]

Women as Home Managers

While men allocate income for household consumption, managing and budgeting household consumption to meet basic needs is usually the responsibility of women. Inflation makes making ends meet more difficult. Table 7.3 reports inflation from 1977–8 onwards with averages for two sub-periods.

Table 7.2 Selected labour force statistics by gender (percentages)

	1987–8		1993–4	
	Female	Male	Female	Male
Civilian labour force	5.1	94.9	14.6	85.4
Self-employed	20.9	55.7	15.6	46.3
Unemployed	0.9	3.4	10.0	3.9

Source: *Labour Force Survey* 1987–8 (pp. 100, 101, 137) and 1993–4 (pp. 169, 284, 200).

Table 7.3 Annual percentage change in the sensitive (SPI) and general consumer price index (CPI)

Year	SPI (12 months average)	CPI (12 months average)
1977–87	4.6	4.8
1988–95	10.6	9.8

Source: *Annual Report 1994–95*, State Bank of Pakistan, p. 24.
Note: 1980–81 is the base year.
The CPI coverage is confined to 464 items of mass consumption collected from 24 urban centres. The SPI is confined to 46 essential items and 47.6 per cent weight in the basket is given to low income consumers with a monthly income of Rs 1000 or less.

From being slightly lower than general inflation prior to 1987, the SPI became higher in the following period. Thus coping became more difficult for women in poor households. Ironically, eliminating inflation is one of the main areas of concern for structural adjustment policies, and yet many components of structural adjustment induce supply-side shocks result in a spiralling process of cost–price increases which generate self-fulfilling inflationary expectations. These structural adjustment 'shocks' include price increases, from general price de-controls (e.g. raising producer prices for farmers), from devaluation, from the imposition of user charges for various publicly provided services and from the reduction of subsidies, especially on food items. Tables 6.6 and 6.7 evince the changing pattern of government subsidies over the structural adjustment period.

The dramatic decline in subsidies as a percentage of total government expenditure (from a peak of 7.8 in 1988–9 to 1.5 in 1994–5) is evident from the first column of Table 6.6. Of more concern is the decline in subsidy to wheat and edible oil, which constitutes large proportions of the caloric and protein intake for the poorest quarter of the population. Between 1987–8 and 1992–3, the consumption of cereals for the bottom 10 per cent of the population declined by 10 per cent.[8] Such a decline could be expected given the decline in wheat subsidy indicated above, which translated into a more than doubling of the retail price of wheat and wheat flour as reported in Table 7.4.

Between 1980–1 and 1994–5, food and wheat prices increased by 20 per cent more than non-food prices. Thus women as home managers in the lowest income groups have had to confront much higher prices for food in general and for wheat in particular. Our estimates also show that the poorest 25 per cent of the population derived 47 per cent and 75 per cent of their calories and protein from just wheat.[9]

Wages have not kept pace with price increases. Real daily wages of unskilled and skilled labour (depreciated by the food price index) declined

Table 7.4 Average retail price level of wheat and wheat flour

Year	Wheat (Avg. Qlty. Kg.)	Wheat flour (Avg. Qlty. Kg.)
1974–81	1.4	1.5
1988–95	3.6	4.2

Source: *Economic Survey 1996–97*, p. 139.

by 15 per cent and 21 per cent respectively in Karachi, Pakistan's highest paying city.[10] Entitlements and capabilities for the poor have in general declined since the start of the structural adjustment period. This includes a steep rises in the unemployment rates and a sharp fall in household incomes, which can be expected to accompany a rise in unemployment and a fall in real wages.[11]

Based on perceptions about intra-household bargaining power, one might expect the nutritional fallout of a decline in entitlements and capability to be worse for girls and women. Past evidence we were able to muster is reported in Table 7.5, and it does not support such a view.

Table 7.5 shows that the nutritional intake of adult females exceeded that of males and that it improved over time while that of males declined.[12] The numbers for 1985–7 also show that girls' nutritional input was better than that of boys.[13] More recent evidence is unfortunately not available by gender disaggregation.

Women as Mothers

The more the state divests its social sector provision to the private sector, the greater the burden on poor mothers in preparing the young for future survival. Structural adjustment programmes, with their emphasis on budget-cutting, have been severely criticized in the past for the collapse in public social sector expenditure which has imposed a greater burden on the role of women as mothers. Probably in response to this criticism, in which Cornia, Jolly and Stewart (1987) are particularly influential, structural adjustment programme budget-cutting started protecting basic social sector expenditures.

Table 7.5 Percentage under 70 per cent of recommended daily allowance (RDA) of calories by gender

Year	Adult male	Adult female	Boys 6–15 years	Girls 6–15 years	Boys 0–5 years	Girls 0–5 years
1976–7	27	20	n.a.	n.a.	n.a.	n.a.
1985–7	32	18	28	18	34	30

Source: *Micro-Nutrient Survey 1976–77*, p. 40; *National Nutrition Survey Report 1985–87*, p. 103.
Note: The findings of the 1976–7 survey are based on 1,000 households while those of the 1985–7 survey are based on 8,334 households.

In Pakistan, this protection has taken the form of the Social Action Programme (SAP), which is designed to concentrate massive expenditures on basic education, health and sanitation to eradicate gender and rural–urban imbalances in schooling and health.[14] SAP became operational in 1992–3 so one could consider 1991–2 as a benchmark year. Table 7.6 shows how the share of expenditure on education and health has changed since the structural adjustment and the SAP periods. Our interest here is in the total sector allocation with a view to ascertaining if the SAP represented a net reallocation to these sectors or if it induced a sectoral reallocation.

Table 7.6 indicates that for both education and health, SAP has meant a net addition to the sectors because total expenditures since 1991–2, the benchmark year, have increased by 0.4 per cent of GNP by 1996–7.[15] Even so, educational expenditures as a percentage of GNP in 1996–7 barely exceeded the structural adjustment base year of 1987–8, while health expenditure in 1996–7 as a percentage of GNP was still below that in 1987–8. Input in the form of expenditure is important, but progress in any sector must be measured by looking at output data.

Table 7.7 shows the progress in school enrolments over benchmark years and over the SAP time period. There was a sizeable jump in female primary enrollment in 1992–3 compared to 1991–2, the benchmark year. Thus the concerted focus of the SAP on female primary schooling does show up in the numbers. Boys' primary enrolment rates have also shown steady progress. However, the big gains for both girls and boys at

Table 7.6 Expenditure on education and health as a percentage of GDP

Year/ Expenditure	Education expenditure as a percentage of GNP	Health expenditure as a percentage of GNP	Total 1+2
	1	2	3
1987–8	2.4	1.0	3.4
1988–9	2.4	1.0	3.4
1989–90	2.2	0.9	3.1
1990–1	2.1	0.7	2.8
1991–2	2.2	0.7	2.9
1992–3	2.2	0.7	2.9
1993–4	2.2	0.7	2.9
1994–5	2.4	0.6	3.1
1995–6	2.4	0.8	3.3
1996–7	2.6	0.7	3.3

Source: *Economic Survey 1996–97*, Statistical Appendix, p. 7.

Table 7.7 School participation rates by level and gender

Level	Primary		Middle		High	
Year/gender	Female	Male	Female	Male	Female	Male
1987–8	48	80	19	41	10	24
1991–2	49	83	30	59	17	37
1992–3	54	85	30	58	18	38
1993–4	55	86	31	58	19	38
1994–5	55	87	31	58	20	38
1995–6	57	89	32	59	22	42

Sources: For 1987–8, *Seventh Five Year Plan*, Statistical Appendix, pp. 414–15 and for 1991–2 to 1995–6, *Economic Survey*, various years.

both the middle and higher levels between 1987–8 and 1991–2 have tapered off.

Some comparison to other countries puts these enrolment numbers in perspective. Pakistan is still poorly lagging even by South Asian standards. For example, the participation rate at the primary level in 1992 for low income economies was 102 per cent and for India it was 98 per cent.[16] The secondary enrolment for low income countries is reported in the World Bank, *World Development Report 1995* (1995, p. 216) to be 41 per cent, which is almost double the rate cited for Pakistan (21 per cent). Also, between the benchmark year, 1991–2, and 1994–5, the gender gap in absolute terms closed slightly at the primary level but was unchanged at the middle and higher levels.

In any case, enrolments represent only half the battle. Retention, the other important half, is also an area in which Pakistan has not been doing well. While about 77 per cent of boys and girls who ever attended school complete class five, less than half complete the eighth class and less than a third matriculate.[17] Thus while there has been some progress with regards to the support available to mothers in educational provision, it has been slow and the levels attained are poor even by South Asian and low income country standards, despite the Social Action Programme. As in the case of education, we concentrate on children's health output statistics in Table 7.8.

Mortality rates could be viewed as a summary health statistic. Girls' natural advantage of higher survival rates at an early age show up in lower and more rapidly declining neonatal and infant mortality rates. However, this natural advantage is already offset, possibly via intra-household food

Table 7.8 Childhood mortality rates by gender

	1965–79*		1981–91@	
	Boys	Girls	Boys	Girls
Neonatal Mortality (< 1 month)	79	70	60	46
Infant Mortality (0–11 months)	120	117	102	86
Child Mortality (1–5 years)	44	48	22	37

Sources: * Sathar (1985, p. 355).
@ Ahmad, Bhatti and Bicego (1992, p. 118).

allocation, in early childhood, and this shows up in lower and more rapidly declining boy mortality rates relative to those of girls.

Apart from gender differentials, Table 7.8 indicates that children's health, and hence mortality, indicators improved in the period that coincides with the structural adjustment period compared to an earlier period. However, much of the credit for this could be attributed to the Expanded Programme of Immunization (EPI) which was launched in 1979 and accelerated in 1982.[18] While significant improvements have been made, Pakistan lags behind other low income countries even in prominent health indicators. For example, the less than 5-year child mortality rate (per 1,000 live births) of 129 for girls and 142 for boys for the year 1992 is much more than the average of 102 and 114 respectively for low income countries.[19]

The role of women as mothers has been facilitated indirectly by the improvement of children's health and also more directly by the improvement in their own health. This is evident from the decline in the maternal mortality rate (per 100,000) from 500 in the 1980–7 period to 270 in 1988–93.[20] Recent progress in women and children's health has been made despite a decline in health expenditure. However, with this low level of commitment, Pakistan is unlikely to be able to even match, on various indicators, the health standards of the low income countries. We discuss this issue in more detail in the next chapter.

SUMMARY AND CONCLUSIONS

We have reviewed the impact of structural adjustment on the role of women as producers, as home managers and as mothers. In most cases, it is very difficult to isolate the effects of structural adjustment from the effects of other social and economic changes in society. However, in some cases, the chain of causality can be identified, and we have attempted to do so when possible. In other cases, we merely compare the social and economic status of girls and women in an earlier period to the period following 1988, when the intensive bout of structural adjustment got underway in Pakistan.

Overall, female labour force participation in the 1987–95 period was 4.5 per cent higher than in the 1969–87 period, and between 1987–8 and 1993–4 their share in the civilian labour force increased about threefold. Simultaneously, there was a corresponding decline of 6 per cent in the male labour force participation rate over these periods. While there are reasons to applaud a rise in the female labour force participation rate, this statistic in conjunction with two others puts a bleak slant on the socio-economic status of the poor. First, over the 1987–8 to 1993–4 period, there has been a decline of 5.3 per cent in female self-employment. Second, there has been an increase in the female unemployment rate from 0.9 to 10 per cent over this period. Thus, while it seems that women are being forced to enter the labour force to compensate for male unemployment, migration and the subsequent fall in household income, the opportunities for attaining employment are not as readily available. If wage work were to lighten the domestic burden of child and home care, it might be welcome given the increased bargaining power in the household this can accompany. This, however, is unlikely to be the case in Pakistan's current cultural milieu.[21]

Another negative aspect of the labour force participation statistics are that in the 10–14 age group, the female labour force participation ratio increased by 0.8 per cent (from 6.0 to 6.8 per cent). This increase in female child labour occurred across the 1969–87 to 1987–95 time periods, when boys' labour force participation rates in this age group dropped by over one-third from 32.1 to 19.5 per cent. Since boys' school enrolment rates are already much higher than those of girls, this trend for girls is doubly unwelcome.

As home managers, women have had to confront several hardships. The doubling of the sensitive price index from 4.6 to 10.6 per cent between 1977–87 and 1988–95 made it difficult to make ends meet at a time when joblessness was rising. While structural adjustment cannot be blamed directly for this inflation, it could have contributed to the cost–price spiral and rising inflationary expectations via devaluation, user charges, price decontrol, and cuts in consumption subsidies.

Between 1985–6 and 1995–6, consumption subsidies as a per cent of the budget declined from a peak of 7.8 per cent in 1988–9 to 1.5 per cent in 1994–5. The subsidy to wheat and sugar as a per cent of the total declined and the subsidy to edible oil declined by over three-fourths from 22 to 5 per cent. As expected, the retail price of wheat doubled between the 1974–81 and 1988–94 periods. This probably led to a decline in the consumption of wheat by about one-tenth between 1987–8 and 1990–1 for the poorest income group. Research has shown that the poor in Pakistan derive about three-fifths of their calories from wheat, and so this consumption decline is of concern.

Women's role as mothers is facilitated by social sector provision. Structural adjustment faced hostile criticism in the 1980s for inducing budget cuts and letting the burden fall on the social sectors. The philosophy underlying the UNICEF-inspired *Adjustment With a Human Face* seems to have been absorbed by the World Bank, and it is endorsing and partially funding social investments such as in the Social Action Programme (SAP) in Pakistan. SAP has a particular focus on rural women and girls. We looked at expenditure on education and health to investigate if SAP represented an addition or whether it simply reallocated existing social sector expenditure. Data show that compared to 1991–2, the SAP benchmark year, education and health expenditure as a per cent of GNP have increased; but if 1987–8 is used as a benchmark, educational expenditure has increased only slightly while health expenditure has declined.

The SAP reallocation towards rural girls shows up in a 5 per cent increase in rural primary girls' enrolment from 49 to 57 per cent between 1991–2 and 1995–6. These enrolment rates, however, are way below the mean for low income countries and comparable enrolment rates in India. Also, enrolments and gender gaps at the middle and high levels have been virtually static. Overall, there is little positive to report about the socio-economic condition of women during the intensive phase of structural adjustment.

NOTES

1. The chapter has been published as a paper written by Shahrukh R. Khan and Mehnaz Ahmad in *The Lahore Journal of Economics*, 1, no. 1, 1996. Thanks are due to Saba Gul Khattak, Pervez Tahir and Tariq Banuri for comments.
2. Referred to in this paper as the *Commonwealth Report*.
3. See for example Dreze and Sen (1989, pp. 56–9).
4. See also Afshar and Dennis, eds (1992), particularly the contributions of Frances Stewart and Diane Elson, Tanski (1994) and Haddad et al. (1995).

In Pakistan and other developing countries, instead of viewing women as community 'organizers', it may be more appropriate to study the impact of structural adjustment on womens' community 'role'.

5. This conceptual framework is useful for organizing and presenting data in categories, although the originators of this framework are unlikely to assert that these are either exhaustive or non-overlapping.
6. For evidence on a dramatic increase in unemployment rates post 1987–8 in occupations where one could expect a high incidence of the poor, see Chapter 6, Table 6.3, above.
7. Unfortunately, the secondary statistics we are relying on are not reported by household head. The *Household Integrated Economic Surveys*, however, show that the reported female-headed households increased from 6.07 per cent of the total in 1987–8 (p. 51) to 7.86 per cent of the total in 1992–3 (p. 51), a 30 per cent increase.
8. See Chapter 10, Table 10.2, below.
9. Ibid.
10. See Table 6.4.
11. See evidence reported in Chapter 6.
12. As is now well known, the numbers in Table 7.5 are very crude indicators of aggregate nutrition security. Caloric intake is still a very crude approximation for nutrition security for many reasons, including different dietary needs across different individuals at a point in time and across time.
13. Alderman and Garcia (1993, p. 83) also expressed surprise at their finding of gender having no statistically significant impact on nutritional status for children. We conferred with Dr D. S. Akram, who is a nutritional expert at the Dow Medical College and Civil Hospital in Karachi, for a possible answer to this puzzle. Her response was that her own studies, based on patients in the hospital and squatter communities, consistently show the nutritional status of girls to be worse than that of boys. The evidence reported in Table 7.8 also supports the latter view. Informal fieldwork in Afghanistan produced similar results. UN World Food Programme nutritional experts discovered that females are breast fed for much longer. The reason is that the boys were weaned earlier to put them on what was believed to be a healthier diet of tea and biscuits. While UN biscuits were very fortified, this was not true of the local variety families used when UN rations were no longer available. A more conclusive answer will follow from further research.
14. For an official statement see *Economic Survey 1992–93*, pp. 137–44.
15. One could also take the position that SAP should be given credit for preventing a decline in social sector expenditures and for reordering priorities without a powerful indigenous lobby calling for it.
16. *World Development Report 1995* (1995, p. 216). Note that this source cites Pakistan's total primary enrolment rate for 1992 to be 46 per cent.
17. *Pakistan Integrated Household Survey, Final Results* (1992, p. 72).
18. *Economic Survey 1993–94*, p. 110, and Cornia (1997).
19. *World Development Report 1994*, p. 214. Also, the infant mortality rate of 92 (per 1,000 live births) in 1994 for Pakistan was much higher than the corresponding rate of 58 for low income countries (*World Development Report 1996*, p. 198).

20. *Human Development Report 1992*, p. 148, for the 1980–7 number, and *World Development Report 1995*, p. 218, for the 1988–93 number.
21. Thus the term 'triple burden' for women has been coined, indicating labour market, child care and home care responsibilities.

REFERENCES

Alderman, H. and Marito Garcia, 1993, 'Poverty, Household Food Security and Nutrition in Rural Pakistan', Research Report no. 96, International Food Policy Research Institute, Washington, DC.

Afshar, H. and C. Dennis, eds, 1992, *Women and Adjustment Policies in the Third World* (London: Macmillan).

Ahmad, T., M. Bhatti and G. Bicego, 1992, 'Infant and Child Mortality', in *Pakistan Demographic and Health Survey 1990–91* (Islamabad: National Institute of Pakistan Studies).

Commonwealth Secretariat, 1989, *Engendering Adjustment for The 1990s: Report of a Commonwealth Group on Women and Structural Adjustment*, (London: Commonwealth Secretariat).

Cornia, G. A., 1997, 'Accelerating Human Development in Pakistan', in eds T. Banuri, S. R. Khan and M. Mahmood, *Just Development: Beyond Adjustment with a Human Face* (Karachi: Oxford University Press).

Cornia, G. A., R. Jolly and F. Stewart, 1987, *Adjustment with a Human Face: Protecting the Vulnerable and Promoting Growth* (Oxford: Oxford University Press).

Dreze, J. H. and A. Sen, 1989, *Hunger and Public Action* (New York: Oxford University Press).

Elson, D., 1991, 'Male Bias in Macroeconomics: The Case of Structural Adjustment', in ed. D. Elson, *Male Bias in the Development Process* (Manchester: Manchester University Press).

Government of Pakistan, Economic Advisors Wing, Ministry of Finance, *Economic Surveys*, various issues, Islamabad.

Government of Pakistan, *Household Income and Expenditure Survey 1984–85*, Federal Bureau of Statistics, Karachi.

Government of Pakistan, *Household Integrated Economic Survey 1990-91*, Federal Bureau of Statistics, Karachi.

Government of Pakistan, *Labour Force Surveys*, several years, Islamabad.

Government of Pakistan, 1978, *Micro-Nutrient Survey 1976–77*, Nutrition Cell, Planning and Development Division, Islamabad.

Government of Pakistan, 1988, *National Nutrition Survey 1985–87 Report*, National Institute of Health, Islamabad.

Government of Pakistan, 1992, *Pakistan Integrated Household Survey: Final Results*, Federal Bureau of Statistics, Islamabad.

Haddad, L., L. R. Brown, A. Richter and L. Smith, 1995, 'The Gender Dimension of Economic Adjustment Policies: Potential Interactions and Evidence to Date', *World Development*, 23, no. 6, pp. 897–912.

Khan, S. R. and S. Aftab, 'Structural Adjustment, Labour and the Poor', forthcoming in proceedings of a conference organized by the South Asia Forum in Dhulikhel, Nepal, July 9–21, 1994.
Khan, S. R., S. Kazmi and Z. Ahmad, 1996, 'Structural Adjustment and Food Security in Pakistan: An Aggregate Analysis', SDPI, mimeo.
Onimode, B., 1991, 'The Impact of Structural Adjustment on Women in Nigeria', in *Women and Structural Adjustment: Selected Case Studies*, Commissioned for a Commonwealth Group of Experts, Commonwealth Economic Papers.
Sathar, Z. A., 1985, 'Infant and Child Mortality Rates in Pakistan: Some Trends and Differentials', *Journal of Biosocial Science*, 17, pp. 351–9.
Tanski, J. M., 1994, 'The Impact of Crisis, Stabilization and Structural Adjustment on Women in Lima, Peru', *World Development*, 22, no. 11, pp. 1127–642.
Toye, J., 1995, *Structural Adjustment and Employment Policies: Issues and Experience* (Geneva: ILO).
UNDP, *Human Development Report 1992* (New York: Oxford University Press).
World Bank, *World Development Report 1995* (New York: Oxford University Press).

8 Structural Adjustment and Health[1]

INTRODUCTION

A clear statement is contained in the *World Development Report 1993* (Report) on the World Bank's (Bank) view with regards to health sector reform in less-developing countries. As is the case in reading many other Bank documents, this one seems to have drawn on numerous critiques of conventional health practices. Government inefficiency and corruption is criticized. Also, the practice of heavy expenditures on curative medicine and related specialized health training, which subsidizes the rich or the offspring of the rich, is criticized; and restructuring expenditures from tertiary medicine to primary healthcare (PHC) is endorsed. Indeed, in some respects, the Report makes the Bank sound like a 1960s radical. Adopting such a view would, however, be erroneous. While the Bank suggests many sensible reforms, such as the ones mentioned above, there remain important differences in the Bank's approach and that of its radical critics.

The most fundamental difference is one of perspective. Simply put, the Bank wants to restrict the role of goxvernment to the bare classical essentials and enhance the role of private provision and markets. This is consistent with the Bank's ideological underpinnings, which come through in most Bank documents. The Bank acknowledges the following role for government. First, since positive externalities exist in public health, such as in the realm of disease control, a role for government is required for immunization and diet supplement programmes, probably school based, since private providers would provide too little of this public good. Second, the related role of disseminating information for disease control is also viewed as essential.

Third, regulation is considered important for market-based insurance, since a market failure is acknowledged as resulting from moral hazard (incentives for oversupply in the case of third-party insurers). Fourth, regulation is called for in drug supply and the concept of an 'essential drug list' is endorsed. Fifth, since exclusion of the most needy and high risk is likely when insurance is left to the private sector, the Bank does not rule out efficiently provided cost-containing social insurance. Pre-paid private sector insurance provided in a health maintenance 'managed competition' framework is endorsed as an alternative. Finally, the role of government is acknowledged in providing essential clinical services for the poor.

However, many of the above activities require modest expenditures, and so government expenditures are recommended to be pared down by half. This could be done not only by cutting back on subsidies and inessential services, but also by improving efficiency via decentralization, performance-based incentives and management systems development. Costs could be further reduced by engendering competition in supply by enhancing the role of the private sector in delivering health services and in delivering inputs such as drugs, other medical supplies and equipment. Indeed, the Bank recommends a subsidy to private providers delivering services to the poor! Other ways recommended for cutting costs are vouchers for the poor to enhance choice, competition and efficient delivery, while user fees are recommended for recovering costs. The Bank places a great deal of faith in medical technological improvements, the research for which would continue in the richer countries, due to their comparative advantage, and this too requires subsidy.

The reforms mentioned above fit into what the bank calls a three-pronged approach. Macro stabilisation is called for to improve growth. This is necessary for enhancing the incomes of the poor, and in turn increasing their ability to invest in household health.[2] At the same time, government expenditures are viewed as being wasteful due to inefficiency and corruption, and hence should be cut. Thus the other main reforms suggested fit into the categories of improving (restructuring and reducing) government spending on health, and promoting diversity and competition (enhancing the role of the private sector).

Thus, as indicated earlier, while the Bank has absorbed much of the critique of health systems in less-developing countries, its approach to reform is fundamentally one of paring down the size of government and in enhancing the role of the market, even to the extent of subsidizing private sector provision. The Bank's critics, of whom Qadeer (1997) is a very articulate one in the South Asian context, remain unmoved by the Bank's incorporation of many elements of their critique in its own agenda.[3]

Thus Qadeer views the Bank's approach as technocentric and narrowly interventionist in the areas of population control, reproductive and child health and communicable diseases. She also views the Bank's notion of primary healthcare as a very narrow one. Further, she sees the dismantling of the public sector and the cuts in food and basic service subsidies (see Chapter 6) as part of the cut in the public sector's role in healthcare. Juxtaposed to the Bank's approach, Qadeer endorses a much broader concept of comprehensive public sector primary healthcare which includes the provision of basic minimum services such as nutrition, housing, water supply and sanitation, education and livelihoods, along with preventive care which is in touch with the political, cultural and economic realities of the poor. This perspective is fundamentally different from that of the Bank, since it regards alternative solutions such as private or NGO provision as an abdication by the state of its central role as a tax collector and provider of basic human needs.

Pakistan's recently announced new health policy in 1997 reveals the influence of World Bank thinking in several respects.[4] First, the private sector is expected to take on more responsibilities in areas of preventive services, family planning and drugs. Second, selected Basic Health Units and Rural Health Centres are slated to be contracted out to private physicians, NGOs or existing staff to deliver a standard package of services at fixed user charges under the supervision of community-based organizations. Third, autonomy will be given to selected hospitals to be run by Hospital Management Boards under the supervision of District Health Authorities. These hospitals will be authorized to levy user charges.

It is inevitable that the debate on health policy in Pakistan between the Bank and its critics will sharpen. Our perspective is a pragmatic one. In principle we agree that providing comprehensive primary healthcare is the role of the state. However, we feel that public pressure for reform of government to one that is accountable and focuses on efficiently delivering services should continue but that, in the meantime, alternatives, such as grassroots NGO service delivery as well as private initiatives, should be welcomed if they work well.[5] While the debate above is important, the ultimate objective is to improve the well-being of the poor. Thus it seems foolish to hold the ultimate objective hostage to the resolution of the debate. It would be equally foolish to wait until the reform of government is realized to the point where it is capable of engaging in the kind of service delivery that many expect it to provide.

Below we briefly discuss the method we employ for assessing impacts. One would have to wait for the implementation of the new health policy to assess its impact on general health. However, it is possible to assess the changing state of general health over the structural adjustment period, particularly over the period that the Social Action Plan (SAP) has been in place. We present this evidence in terms of health expenditures, outputs and impacts and also present evidence on hypothesis testing with regards to testing the effectiveness of government health expenditures. We end with a summary and conclusion.

METHOD

The approach we used for assessing impacts is a variation of a 'results-based assessment' that some donors are moving towards.[6] First we investigate expenditures as a level of effort or input indicator. Following that, we document outputs which include changing access to various facilities such as doctors, nurses and hospital beds. Finally, we examine how these access or outcome variables translate into impact variables which reflect the health status of the population. These impact variables include the usual indicators such as the infant, child and maternal mortality rates as well as life expectancy at birth and nutritional changes.

In considering access and impact, we review Pakistan's progress using both secondary data and also published data which were specifically generated by the government of Pakistan and the World Bank to assess the progress of the Social Action Plan. Finally, we contrast Pakistan's achievements to date with that of other developing and South Asian countries.

The results-based method described above for assessing impact assumes that government expenditure is of consequence in improving health indicators. However, as pointed out above, in laying out a three-pronged approach to government policies for improving health, the *World Development Report 1993* views government expenditures as being wasteful due to inefficiency and corruption, and asserts that governments should spend about 50 per cent less (p. 7). Instead, it mentions pursuing economic growth policies in the forefront. Evidence is cited to indicate that in countries in which average income rose by more than 1 per cent, child mortality fell by more than twice that of countries for which average income fell. The causation is viewed as going from faster growth to increased household income to more household health expenditures to better health.

These statements suggest testing the following associations:

$$HI = HI\ (PCGDP, GEH, REM) \tag{1}$$

where

HI = Health indicators
PCGDP = Per capita GDP
GEH = Total government expenditures on health
REM = Remittances

PCGDP is a proxy for personal household expenditures on health. Zaidi (1997, p. 7) suggests that improvements in health indicators in Pakistan over the 1980s could have been due to the inflow of remittances of

Pakistani workers abroad. This makes sense since personal household incomes and hence health expenditures can also be influenced by remittance inflows (REM). To justify the Bank's assertion that government health expenditure should be pared back by about a half, the estimation of equation (1) above should show a positive association of HI and PCGDP and REM, and at best an insignificant association between HI and GEH.

FINDINGS

Input or Level of Effort

We are inferring the government's commitment to the health sector or its level of effort from its development and recurring expenditures. Table 8.1 presents evidence on how this commitment has changed over time.

Information in Table 8.1 is reported for three time periods that coincide with those used in the rest of the book. In Table 8.1, both time series and period averages are presented.

Development expenditure on health as a percentage of GDP rose from 0.14 to 0.45 from 1971–2 to 1974–5 and then declined to 0.31 per cent in 1977–8. Recurring expenditures on health as a percentage of GDP rose steadily from 0.29 in 1971–2 to 0.34 in 1977–8. Both these expenditures continued to rise steadily in the 1978–88 period. The 1978–88 period average for development and recurring expenditure as a percentage of GDP was 0.39 and 0.44 respectively, compared to 0.29 and 0.30 in the 1971–8 period. Subsequently, post-1988, both recurring and development expenditures steadily declined.

That development and recurring expenditures declined in the structural adjustment period would not generally be considered surprising. The austerity imposed by structural adjustment programmes to meet the budget deficit targets have traditionally had an adverse impact on social sector expenditures.[7] Also, public sector health expenditure cuts are consistent with the Bank's view on this issue, presented in the introduction to this chapter. However, in Pakistan, so much has been said about protecting the social sectors via allocations to the Social Action Plan (SAP), that the post-1988 reduction does come as a surprise.

Assuming that a healthy population is of high value because it contributes directly to individual well-being and also indirectly by enabling individuals to be more productive, Pakistan can hardly afford reductions in health expenditures, if indeed it can be established that they are effective (see the 'Impact' section below).[8] This argument is reinforced when

Table 8.1 Time series development and recurring health expenditure

Years	Expenditure as a percentage of GDP		Total
	Dev.	Rec.	
1970–1	0.12	0.29	0.40
1971–2	0.14	0.29	0.43
1972–3	0.20	0.28	0.48
1973–4	0.31	0.28	0.59
1974–5	0.45	0.29	0.74
1975–6	0.45	0.31	0.76
1976–7	0.35	0.33	0.68
1977–8	0.31	0.34	0.65
Average 1970–7	0.29	0.30	0.59
1978–9	0.33	0.33	0.66
1979–80	0.35	0.31	0.66
1980–1	0.36	0.32	0.68
1981–2	0.34	0.34	0.68
1982–3	0.37	0.38	0.75
1983–4	0.37	0.40	0.77
1984–5	0.37	0.44	0.81
1985–6	0.44	0.55	0.99
1986–7	0.50	0.64	1.14
1987–8	0.44	0.64	1.08
Average 1978–87	0.39	0.44	0.83
1988–9	0.36	0.59	0.95
1989–90	0.32	0.56	0.88
1990–1	0.25	0.55	0.80
1991–2	0.19	0.56	0.75
1992–3	0.19	0.56	0.75
1993–4	0.21	0.51	0.72
1994–5	0.25	0.52	0.77
Average 1988–94	0.25	0.52	0.77

Source: *Pakistan Economic Survey 1995–96* (p. 239).
Notes: GDP = Gross Domestic Product.
Rec. = Recurring expenditure. It includes salaries, maintenance and other recurring items.
Dev. = Development expenditure; consists of expenditure on infrastructure in the form of buildings and durables.

Pakistan's progress in health is judged in a cross-country perspective (see the section on cross-country perspective, below).

Outputs

The level of effort reflected in the expenditures in Table 8.1 translates into trained medical personnel and facilities. In Table 8.2, we present the

Table 8.2 Access to health facilities and personnel

Years	Population per			
	Hospital Bed	Doctor	Dentist	Nurse
1970	2,061	15,256	155,466	—
1971	1,804	14,343	137,870	—
1972	1,792	13,190	123,953	—
1973	1,848	12,824	120,018	—
1974	1,893	12,164	111,311	73,065
1975	1,852	11,628	107,661	36,332
1976	1,843	11,133	102,153	29,426
1977	1,834	10,278	101,405	23,908
Average	1,866	12,602	119,980	40,682
1978	1,804	9,526	98,079	20,283
1979	1,779	8,695	93,309	17,873
1980	1,716	7,549	87,672	15,712
1981	1,731	6,027	82,357	14,147
1982	1,717	5,033	77,110	13,045
1983	1,708	4,271	72,930	12,504
1984	1,714	3,584	68,110	11,441
1985	1,695	3,153	66,900	9,276
1986	1,692	2,870	62,689	8,382
1987	1,678	2,610	62,552	7,985
Average	1,723	5,331	77,171	13,065
1988	1,610	2,422	58,589	7,638
1989	1,613	2,263	55,808	6,958
1990	1,512	2,127	53,134	6,713
1991	1,501	20,47	51,883	6,463
1992	1,525	1,954	51,496	6,232
1993	1,555	1,919	50,341	6,147
1994	1,510	1,880	48,046	5,976
1995	1,503	1,837	46,498	5,842
Average	1,541	2,056	51,974	6,496

Source: *Pakistan Economic Survey 1995–96* (pp. 238–9).

aggregate level of access of the population to medical personnel and facilities.

The time series data reported in Table 8.2 show a steady and continuous improvement is access to both health personnel, as measured by population per doctors, dentists and nurses, and facilities, as measured by population per hospital bed. Indeed, it appears to be a puzzle why the decline in health expenditures as a percentage of GDP did not translate into a decline in access to medical personnel and facilities per capita. The answer is actually quite straightforward. While development and recurring health expenditures have declined as a percentage of GDP, because of a growing GDP, in absolute real terms they have increased by 11 per cent and 38 per cent respectively between 1988–9 and 1994–5.[9] Thus the real issue is not that access to medical personnel and facilities has declined, but that it has not increased by as much as it should have.

Published data in the 1995–6 *Pakistan Integrated Household Survey* (1997, pp. 44–58) makes possible an assessment of the population's health during the structural adjustment period in which the SAP was underway. Once again, the evidence suggests an across-the-board improvement in access to services and preventive coverage.

Consultation of a medical practitioner for the treatment of diarrhoea in children 5 years or under declined from 90 to 87 per cent in urban areas but rose from 82 to 85 per cent in rural areas. Since ORS is generally recommended, these numbers show an increasing confidence in self-treatment in urban areas. The gender gap in consultation closed from 6 to 4 per cent in urban areas and from 6 to a 1 per cent higher consultation for girls in rural areas. There has been an increase (from 22 to 27 per cent) in rural areas in the percentage of cases in which a government health practitioner was consulted first for diarrhoea treatment.

The percentage of children five years and less that have received at least one immunization increased from 81 to 87 in the urban areas and from 66 to 74 in the rural areas. The percentage of children five years and less that have received full immunization increased from 40 to 61 in the urban areas and from 20 to 51 in the rural areas. These results again show a closing of the regional (urban/rural) gap. The gender gap also once again closed from a 6 and 7 per cent gap in urban and rural areas to a 2 and 1 per cent gap respectively.[10]

Access is one area in which progress seems limited. Of those who did not visit a government facility for treatment of diarrhoea, 51 per cent in urban areas and 47 per cent in rural areas cited distance as the reason for not doing so. For other illnesses and injuries, about a third in urban and rural areas cited distance as the reason for not visiting a government facility and a fifth cited the lack of medicines as the reason. Thus access continues to be perceived as a problem in both urban and rural areas.

This perception can be juxtaposed with actual distances from government facilities in rural areas. Fifteen per cent of the households in the sample had a government hospital within 5 kilometres from their home, a third a government dispensary or rural health centre and about two-fifths a basic health unit by 1995–6. Thus it appears that the perception of a lack of access is grounded in reality.

Impact

We have subdivided this section into three parts. First, we review Pakistan's progress in health by reporting and discussing its conventional health indicators utilizing the period analysis reflected in the earlier Tables based on secondary data, and by reporting on findings of the *Pakistan Integrated Household Survey*. Second, we identify variables that may be responsible for improved health indicators. Finally, we contrast Pakistan's achievement to date with that of other developing and South Asian countries.

1. Pakistan's Health Progress over Time

Table 8.3 below shows that the increase in output of medical personnel and facilities has been effective in that conventional health indices show an improvement corresponding to the output increase.

Table 8.3 shows a steady improvement, including in the structural adjustment period, in all health indices for which data were available. Thus the infant mortality rate has improved by 33 per cent from 1972 to 1994, the maternal mortality rate has more than halved from 1980 to 1988, the child mortality rate has declined by 10 per cent from 1980 to 1994, the life expectancy at birth has increased by 12 years to 61 from 1972 to 1994 and child malnutrition declined by 38 per cent (from 55 per cent underweight in 1977 to 40 per cent underweight in 1990).

The findings reported in the 1996 *Pakistan Integrated Household Survey* show that the percentage of children under 5 suffering from diarrhoea (30 days prior to the time of survey) decreased from 22 to 15 in urban areas and 27 to 19 in rural areas. There was virtually no gender gap in either year, and for 1995–6 no evidence that the incidence of diarrhoea was inversely associated with household income.

The infant mortality rate (IMR – deaths per 1,000 live births) encapsulates summary information about the general state of children's health and is therefore a useful indicator. Between 1987 and 1989, the IMR for boys

Table 8.3 Child survival and other health indicators

Years	IMR	MMR	<5MR	LEAB	CMN<5
1970	142	—	—	48	—
1972	140	—	—	49	—
1977	130	—	—	52	55
1980	—	600	151	—	—
1982	120	—	—	54	—
1985	116	—	—	—	57
1987	104	—	—	57	49
1990	105	—	—	—	40
1993	100	340	137	—	—
1994	98	—	137	62	40
DC*	68	384	101	62	30
SA*	82	583	120	61	52

Sources: *World Development Report*, *Human Development Report*, various issues, and *Human Development in South Asia 1997*.

Notes: IMR = Infant Mortality Rate (per 1,000 live births)
MMR = Maternal Mortality Rate (per 100,000 live births)
<5 MR = Under Five Mortality Rate (per 1,000 live births)
LEAB = Life Expectancy at Birth (years)
CMN<5 = Child Malnutrition Under age 5 (% under weight)
DC = Low Income Countries
SA = South Asia
* – Data are for 1993 or 1994.

in urban areas declined from 123 to 77 and for girls from 100 to 85. The corresponding decline in rural areas was from 152 and 125 to 115 and 101 respectively. While the regional gap for boys is larger, the gender gap in both urban and rural areas narrowed considerably.

2. *Explaining Improvements in the Infant Mortality Rate*

We estimated equation (1) in the method section to identify the determinants of improvements in health indicators. We managed to cobble together a time series for the infant mortality rate (see notes to Table 8.4). This should be expected to respond to government expenditures on health and public health and also to private household expenditures. We regressed

Table 8.4 Determinants of the infant mortality rate (IMR)

	Coefficients	SE
INP	289.77*	(87.75)
T	−5.08*	(0.97)
GDP(−1)	−0.02	(0.02)
WREM(−1)	−0.21**	0.07
HEXP	−0.54*	0.14
R-bar-squared	0.97	
F-Stat.	44.16*	

Sources: *World Development Report 1984* (1984, p. 262) for the 1982 IMR, *Social Indicators of Development 1995* for the IMRs from 1984–92, and 1995. We have extrapolated the IMRs for 1983, 1993 and 1994 as an average of the prior and preceding year IMR. GDP, remittances, expenditures and population were drawn from the *Economic Survey 1996–97*, Statistical Appendix (1997, pp. 30–1, 150–1, 209 and 21 respectively).

Notes: GDP = Real gross domestic product per capita

WREM = Real remittances per capita

HEXP = Real health expenditure per capita

IMR = Infant mortality rate. Measured as the number of deaths per 1,000.

SE = Standard error

The results are corrected for serial correlation by using the Cochran–Orcutt Method. Since not all variables were stationary, we tested for equation cointegration using the Augmented Eagle–Granger (AEG) test which is a Dicky Fuller (DF) test of the stationarity of the residuals. The absolute value of the estimated τ statistic of 4.6362 is greater than the critical value, with trend, of 3.9272 in absolute terms at the 95 per cent level of significance. Thus the residuals μ_t are stationary, and we conclude that the estimated equation is cointegrated and that the associations identified are not spurious.

SE = Standard error

* = Significant at the 1% level

** = Significant at the 5% level

(−1) = One period lag

HEXP lagged one period was not statistically significant

this variable on GDP per capita, public health expenditure per capita, and remittances per capita. The results are reported in Table 8.4.

Contrary to the World Bank view, public sector health expenditures proved to be very effective in reducing the infant mortality rate. The coefficient for the public sector health expenditures are significant at the 1 per cent level and magnitude of the coefficient suggests a ten rupee increase in public health expenditures per capita per annum is associated with a decline in the infant mortality rate of five per thousand.

GDP per capita is not significantly associated with a decline in the infant mortality rate. If income distribution is very uneven and the growth process is neutral to or accentuates inequalities, higher PCGDP cannot be expected to be associated with a generalized improvement in health indicators. Evidence reported in Chapter 6 suggests growing inequalities, and so this result is not surprising.

Ideally, we should use private household expenditures on health, but no such time series was available. Since remittances are an important source of household income, particular for the lower income groups, we have used remittances per capita. This variable proved to be significant at the 5 per cent level and a ten rupee increase in remittances per capita per annum is associated with a decline in the infant mortality rate of two per thousand. Thus public sector health expenditures, which are targeted, are much more effective as should be expected.

However, the significance of remittances is premised on some of the money flowing into households finding its way into better nutrition and increased household expenditure on health. Data [Government of Pakistan, 1995, p. 165] show that the percentage of private household expenditure on health, as a percentage of total household expenditure, did increase from 1.9 per cent in 1970–1 to 2.9 per cent in 1990–1. This increase in private health expenditures could be reflecting a greater household priority on health, or an increase in private health expenditures induced by increased user charges and less public subsidies.

One way to get a handle on increased user charges is by reviewing how government receipts in the health sector have changed over time. The data available are reported in Table 8.5.

It is quite clear from the table below that, over time, there has been a substantial increase in government receipts for health and public health services across all provinces. Thus, user charges have not merely appeared in policy documents but are actually being implemented. It appears then that the increased private household expenditures are at least partly induced by public sector fees for service delivery. One would, however, expect better and more effective services to be demanded when user fees are paid.

Table 8.5 Provincial government receipts from health services (Rs, million, real)

Province	1970–1	1994–5
Balochistan	1.19	5.25
NWFP	2.19	19.75
Punjab	11.10	39.94*
Sindh	15.45#	24.78*

Source: Govt. of Balochistan, Finance Department, *Statements of Receipts 1971–92* (1971–2, pp. 40–2, 1995–6, pp. 35–7); Govt. of NWFP (1971–2, pp. 53–5, 1995–6, pp. 66–70); Govt. of Punjab (1971–2, pp. 49–52, 1992–3, pp. 48–51); Govt. of Sind (1989–90, pp. 35–41, 1992–3, pp. 37–43).
Notes: Receipts included those collected from general and public health services provided. 1980 has been used as the base year and the price index was drawn from *Economic Survey 1996–97*, Statistical Appendix (1997, p. 21).
* Data used are for 1991–2.
# Data used are for 1988–9.

3. Pakistan's Health Progress in a Cross-country Perspective

Table 8.3 also reports the mean outcome variables for South Asia and less-developed countries. While the outcomes for Pakistan are encouraging when viewed over time, they are much less so when viewed in a cross-country perspective at least with regard to child survival statistics. Pakistan's infant mortality rate and less than five mortality and malnutrition rates are higher than the averages for developing countries and South Asia. Pakistan's life expectancy at birth matches the average of South Asia and developing countries, but its maternal mortality rate is lower than these cross-country averages.

SUMMARY AND CONCLUSION

A review of the background statistics for Pakistan's health sector shows that while some progress has been made, much more is needed. Data on government expenditure on health show that, true to form, the structural adjustment period is associated with declines in development and recurring expenditures as a percentage of GDP. In absolute real terms, expenditures did increase, and these have translated into better access over time to medical personnel and facilities. Also, health impacts, as gauged by conventional health indicators, including maternal mortality, infant and child survival statistics, nutrition and life expectancy, were positive.

Survey data also show improvements in basic health with regards to access to services, preventive coverage and incidence of ailments. Also, gender and rural gaps in this regard and in immunization and infant mortality rates closed between 1991 and 1996. Closing such gaps is a stated objective of the Social Action Plan.

However, access continues to be perceived as a problem in both rural and urban areas, and data on actual distances from government facilities suggest these perceptions are grounded in reality. Also, compared to the average of developing countries and South Asia, Pakistan lags in all the child survival statistics. Thus there is little justification in allowing health expenditures as a percentage of GDP to slip as recommended by the World Bank.

This is particularly the case since evidence shows that government expenditure on health has a significant and sizeable association with the decline in the infant mortality rate in Pakistan. Also, contrary to the Bank's view, the growth in GDP per capita was not significantly associated with a decline in the infant mortality rate.

NOTES

1. Paper prepared for the Sustainable Development Policy Institute Working Paper Series by Shahrukh Rafi Khan and Sajid Kazmi. Thanks are due for comments to Mozaffar Qazilbash and Haris Gazdar.
2. The Report does point out that this association would be much stronger if economic policies are pursued which would increase the income of those in poverty. However, the Report does not acknowledge that there could be conflict between the macro stabilisation policies it endorses and pro-poor policies (see Chapter 6).
3. Many progressive writers resent the Bank's proclivity towards absorbing their concepts, due to its vast research and dissemination capacity, but in not fundamentally altering its orientation. A case in point is the concept of 'participation', which the Bank is viewed as having appropriated. While some researchers in the Bank are aware that this concept was originally about empowerment of the poor, for others in the Bank it is about a more efficient way of engendering service delivery.

4. 'Salient Features of New Health Policy,' *The News International*, 18 Dec. 1997, p. 8.
5. We deliberately avoid mentioning 'good governance'. While we endorse much that that is mentioned in the package of good governance reforms, we feel that the choice of the word governance is a very unfortunate one. In so far as language is important, the emphasis should be on providing 'good service' rather than on governing well. Civil society elects political representatives and pays for civil and military bureaucracies via taxes, to be served rather than to be ruled or governed.
6. For example, the Canadian International Development Agency (CIDA) has instituted a 'results-based matrix' to assess the work of institutions whose funding it contributes to.
7. Cornia, Jolly and Stewart (1987).
8. This view is influenced by Chambers (1995). Also see Dreze and Sen (1995, pp. 14–15).
9. Real development and recurring health expenditures increased from Rs 1.46 and Rs 2.41 billion to Rs 1.63 and Rs 3.34 billion respectively. The development expenditures were deflated by the building materials price index and the recurring expenditures by the general price index, both drawn from the *Economic Survey 1995–96*, p. 146. In each case, the base was 1980–1.
10. These improvements are probably the result of the acclaimed UNICEF expanded programme of immunization. See Cornia (1997).

REFERENCES

Cornia, G. A., 1997, 'Accelerating Human Development in Pakistan', in eds T. Banuri, S. R. Khan and M. Mahmood, *Just Development: Beyond Adjustment with a Human Face* (Karachi: Oxford University Press).

Cornia, G. A., R. Jolly and F. Stewart, 1987, *Adjustment with a Human Face: Protecting the Vulnerable and Promoting Growth* (Oxford: Clarendon Press).

Chambers, R., 1995, 'Poverty and Livelihoods: Whose Reality Counts?' New York, United Nations Development Programme.

Dreze, J. and A. K. Sen, 1995, *India Economic Development and Social Opportunity* (New York: Clarendon Press).

Government of Pakistan, 1996, *Pakistan Integrated Household Survey, Round 1: 1995–96*, Federal Bureau of Statistics, Islamabad.

Government of Pakistan, 1997, *Economic Survey 1995–96*, Economic Advisors Wing, Ministry of Finance, Islamabad.

Government of Pakistan, 1997, *Pakistan Integrated Household Survey*, Federal Bureau of Statistics, Islamabad.

Government of Pakistan, 1997, *Social Indicators of Development*, Federal Bureau of Statistics, Islamabad.

Human Development Centre, 1997, *Human Development in South Asia 1997* (Karachi: Oxford University Press).

Pakistan Integrated Household Survey, 1996, *Annual Report 1995–96*, State Bank of Pakistan, Karachi.

Qadeer, I., 1997, 'Impact of SAP on Concepts in Public Health', Paper presented at conference on the Impact of Structural Adjustment Programmes on Health, Jawaharlal Nehru University, New Delhi, Sept.

UNDP, *Human Development Report* (New York: Oxford University Press), various years.

World Bank, *World Development Report* (New York: Oxford University Press), various years.

Zaidi, S. A., 1997, 'Health Well-being and Adjustment: The Case of Pakistan', Paper presented at conference on the Impact of Structural Adjustment Programmes on Health, Jawaharlal Nehru University, New Delhi, Sept.

9 Trade Liberalization and the Environment[1]

INTRODUCTION

Trade liberalization is viewed as damaging to the environment for several reasons. Trade is considered to be a magnifier, and if the correct environmental policies are not in place, enhanced production that accompanies enhanced trade could exacerbate the pressure on natural resources and increase industrial pollution.[2] In addition, the social costs of liberalization that results in unrestricted import of dirty second-hand manufacturing technologies and hazardous agricultural inputs may outweigh the social benefits.

In this chapter we review various issues pertaining to trade liberalization and the environment. This is done from a southern perspective with a focus on issues on which there is some empirical evidence. We look at the trade–environment link from the export and import side, and, within these categories, look at manufacturing and agriculture separately. Our major concern from a Pakistani perspective is with the imports of environmentally unfriendly agricultural inputs. Since environmentalists are often accused of being one-sided by neo-liberal economists, we look at both sides of these issues. While we did not have data to do a rigorous cost–benefit analysis, we have engaged in a 'suggestive' cost–benefit analysis.

Below we review the issues with regard to trade liberalization and the environment; briefly state our view of the cost–benefit approach; and then provide a suggestive cost–benefit analysis of the imports of pesticides and fertilizers into Pakistan.

A REVIEW OF ISSUES AND EVIDENCE

Environmentally Motivated Trade Restrictions

Tariffs have been proposed for attaining a cleaner environment in several situations. If environmental regulations vary across countries, the country with the more stringent regulations may feel justified in imposing a tariff on imports from countries with less stringent regulations. The argument is that the less stringent regulations represent unfair competition. It has been pointed out that this may not be an issue in North–North trade for two reasons. First, most of the richer industrialized countries adopted environmental regulations at roughly the same time.[3] Second, even if the stringency of the regulations varies across countries, the abatement cost is such a small proportion of the total costs that arguing for protection is not called for. The latter reason also removes the justification for protection against imports from poorer countries.

Even if abatement costs were high, neo-liberal economists argue against protection on efficiency grounds. First, they argue that the social tolerance for pollution may vary and so imposition of a common standard is not called for. Second, countries may differ in their pollution absorption capacity and should be free to exploit their comparative advantage. Finally, pollution results from firms not being made to absorb the full social costs, and so the answer to the problem lies at home and not in trade policy.[4]

The logic above is persuasive but involves a double standard in the North's treatment of social issues under the WTO. Suppose we acknowledge a market failure to justify a boycott of products made by child labour to prevent child abuse; then why should this benign concern not extend further? Why not also extend the boycott to products that entail a high social cost from untreated effluent pumped into open spaces to mix at will with the water supply? Children are most vulnerable to the resulting health problems (evidence reported later). If governments are viewed as incapable of preventing child abuse, should they be deemed capable of preventing environmental abuse? Selective application of free trade principles by the North only leads to cynicism in the South. It is probably best to let the South deal with its own social and environmental problems.[5] Material and technical assistance is likely to be welcomed by all.

The North may have more tolerance for imports into the South of goods produced from environmentally 'dirty' manufacturing processes that do not dislocate competing Northern industries. However, as French (1993, p. 34) points out, lower prices for such goods in the North are at the expense of ecological damage somewhere else.[6]

Liberalization, Exports and the Environment

Prior logic once again suggests that export promotion in the manufacturing sector should help the cause of the environment. Birdsall and Wheeler (1992) point out that competition would induce the drive towards the latest manufacturing technologies, and since these are likely to be procured from the North they are likely to be much cleaner. Further, Western importers may require cleaner processes to ensure greener products.[7] They present evidence from their own cross-country analysis showing greater openness to be associated with less pollution-intensive industrialization.[8] Cross-country evidence can at best be viewed as suggestive, and so more evidence on this issue, based on country industry case studies, is needed.

French (1993, p. 16) cites evidence suggesting that primary export promotion can have adverse environmental effects because a rise in cash crop production can encourage deforestation. A rise in Costa Rican beef exports to the US resulted in deforestation, while beef exports from Botswana to Europe resulted in soil erosion and land degradation due to overgrazing. Somalia also abandoned ecologically sensitive livestock grazing in its attempt to boost beef exports.

A World Wildlife Fund report (1994) analysed the impact of the WTO liberalization on US and EC agriculture and concluded that environmental benefits of direct and export subsidy cuts and land set-asides in the North will be minimal if any.[9] WTO-resistant direct payments to large farms will continue, and environmentally destructive intensive-farming-induced productivity increases will continue to put downward pressure on world food prices. To deal with food dumping and to protect their farming systems, the South would have to adopt similarly environmentally destructive intensive agriculture.[10] We consider issues pertaining to structural adjustment and food security in the next chapter.

Liberalization, Imports and the Environment

Much less attention has been given in the literature to the issue of the environmental impact of imports into the LDCs. There are several mechanisms via which import liberalization could be damaging to the environment in the importing country. First, there could be a scramble for dirty plants that are being phased out in the North.[11] Second, the import of hazardous chemicals and pesticides could increase because of the lower import duty. That there are benefits accruing from the use of these chemicals and pesticides is not in dispute. However, whether the benefits outweigh the environmental and other costs needs to be explored. While we did not have the data to do a rigorous cost–benefit analysis, we provide some arguments and evidence relevant for a review of trade policy in Pakistan.

METHOD

To get consensus on an appropriate methodology for cost–benefit analysis would be virtually impossible. Quantifying the benefits side is, in principle, relatively straightforward. One approach could be magnifying the results of farm studies using reasonable assumptions. Using a production function approach, it should be possible to isolate the contribution of pesticides and fertilizers in enhancing output of different crops in varying agro-ecological zones. While clear in principle, this approach still requires a large number of careful studies. An alternative approach, which we adopted, is to get a ball-park valuation based on estimates of crop saving due to pesticide and crop enhancement due to fertilizer use.

One method of quantifying the costs would be to identify the direct medical costs and the costs of forgone earnings due to a losses in work, labour and land productivity. However, many would object to such quantification since it is much too narrow an approach to measuring the decrease in the quality of life resulting from the negative effects of pesticide or fertilizer use, and ignores many other damaging environmental effects.

We agree with the latter view, but had data been available on work and productivity loss and on the direct medical cost resulting from the adverse medical effects of pesticide or fertilizers, we would none the less proceed with generating a cost estimate. We would concede that this would represent an understatement of the true social cost, but none the less, such estimates can inform policy. One could argue that even one life is worth more than all the crop gain from synthetic pesticide and fertilizer use. However, crop gains reduce food prices, could avert malnutrition and famine, and hence save lives.

BENEFITS AND COSTS OF AGRICULTURAL INPUT IMPORTS[12]

Pesticide Trade Liberalization

As documented in Chapter 5, second section, Pakistan began to liberalize its trade policy in earnest in 1991–2.[13] Although maximum tariff rates have been on the decline since then, the tariff rate on pesticides was actually doubled in 1993–4.[14] In spite of this increase in the tariff rate, there has been no substantial decrease in the imports of pesticides or in the value of domestic production, as is obvious from Table 9.1.[15]

Table 9.1 shows that the duty on pesticides increased in 1994–5, ostensibly bucking the liberalization trend. Also, the additional duty of 30 per cent applied to the imports of packaged brands of insecticide appears to be restricting imports. However, the former policy did not discourage pesticide consumption as the increase in tariff rate was preceded by the liberalization of imports of pesticides under generic names in 1992. The regulatory duty

Table 9.1 Pesticide tariff, import and domestic production

Years	Tariff rates@	Imports (Mtons)	Production (Mtons)	Total availability
1990–1	10	6157	14056	20213
1991–2	10	6691	16748	23439
1992–3	10	6128	14151	20279
1993–4	20	10692	14176	24868

Source: Department of Plant Protection, Ministry of Food and Agriculture, *Agricultural Statistics of Pakistan 1993–94* (1995, p. 160).
Note: @ Since 1991, a regulatory duty of 30 per cent has been imposed on the import of insecticides in retail packaging.

was also imposed to discourage the more expensive-brand packaged imports in favour of the cheaper domestically packaged generics. Information made available by the Ministry of Food and Agriculture reveals that generics are between about 50 to 70 per cent cheaper than the brands. The immediate effect of this policy was a sharp increase in the total quantity of pesticides imports (see the third column in Table 9.1).[16] Local dealers took the opportunity to import pesticide chemicals in bulk for supply to the local markets in local packaging.

In March 1995, however, the import of generic pesticides by local companies was discontinued. Local importers claim that this trade policy change has been instigated by multinational corporations who are in cahoots with the bureaucracy. Cotton experts argue that local importers were engaged in adulterating pesticides and that this was responsible for immunities that developed among pests, which then became resistant even to much stronger doses of pesticides (reported in the English-language Pakistani newspaper *Dawn*, 'Pesticide importers perturbed over ban', 14 March 1995).

Another trade policy decision that the government has taken to make pesticides more readily available was announced in the 1995–6 Trade Policy. The government has decided to discontinue its policy of the 1971 Pesticide Ordinance which required pesticides to be registered and in use in the exporting country. Thus, despite the seemingly higher duty of 1994–5, the objective of trade policy has been to make pesticides more readily available at cheaper prices.

Benefits

Jabbar and Mallick (1994, p. 4) claim that crop saving due to pesticide use is estimated to be 15 to 25 per cent of the total value of the crop.

Table 9.2 Estimated value of major crop saving in Pakistan from pesticide use (1991–2)

Crop	Production (000 tons)*	Price per ton@	Value (mill. Rs)
Cotton	1682	16206	27258
Wheat	15405	3288	50652
Sugarcane	39335	422	16599
Rice	3404	3588	12214
Total			106723
Crop saving value (15 per cent of total)			16008

Source: *Economic Survey 1994–95*, Statistical Appendix pp. 47, 60–1.
Notes: * All figures are averages for 1990–1 to 1993–4.
@ Prices used are averages for wheat and sugarcane, and prices for IRRI-6 and Desi cotton lint for rice and cotton respectively.

No source was available for this claim, and so we are unable to critically assess it. However, these numbers are consistent with numbers cited elsewhere. For example, Gianessi (1993) cites a Texas A&M University study claiming that if currently available non-chemical methods were substituted for synthetic chemicals, production of soybean would decrease by 37 per cent, of wheat by 24 per cent, of cotton by 39 per cent, of rice by 57 per cent, of peanuts by 78 per cent and of corn by 32 per cent. Assuming crop saving due to pesticide use in Pakistan is 15 per cent of the total value of the crop, the values of crop saving for the four major crops are as shown in Table 9.2.

As estimated in Table 9.2, the benefits from the use of pesticides amount to a value of around Rs 16 billion. Sandhu (1993, p. 22) reports that the crop losses have been estimated at 35 per cent, and if so, the loss would translate to about Rs 37 billion. This in fact is a conservative estimate given that, where applicable, we have used prices for the inferior varieties of the crops and we have calculated losses for only the major crops.

Costs

The costs are by now well documented and hence not difficult to classify. Carson's *Silent Spring* (1962) started the questioning and concern, and many writers have since written about the negative effects of pesticides, particularly with regard to their use in developing countries.[17] Weir and Schapiro in The *Circle of Poison* (1981, p. 11) pointed out that pesticide poisoning in LDCs was thirteen times greater than in the USA, due to the lower level of education, despite the much greater use in the US. Drifting pesticide sprays, leaky applicators and overuse result in run-offs into water and soil.

Residues in soil and food and unsafe contact result in various medical problems including enzyme imbalances, skin and allergic reactions, delayed neurotoxicity, behavioural changes, lesions, changes in the central nervous system, peripheral neurities, carcinogenic and oncogenic diseases, sterility, cataracts, lung proliferation, memory loss and damage to the immune system. Colburn (1994, p. 89) points out that most of the past testing focused on individuals directly exposed and not on the functionality of their offspring. He points out that studies reveal that 'as a result of [pesticide] exposure in the womb of mammals including human – the endocrine, immune and nervous systems of embryos do not develop normally.'

Sandhu (1993, p. 23) cited an FAO study claiming that only 5 per cent of the insecticide fell on target plants; the rest pollutes the environment.[18] The adverse impact on the land base includes a reduction in the natural fertility of the soil, harm to the soil structure and soil aeration, reduction of the water holding capacity of the soil making it more prone to soil erosion by water and wind, and lower drought tolerance of crops. Finally, pesticides are viewed as indiscriminately killing useful insects, microorganisms and insect predator species, breeding more virulent and resistant species of insects and vectors and reducing the genetic diversity of plant species.[19]

Jabbar and Mallick (1994, p. 15) reviewed the scanty evidence on this issue in Pakistan and based on that reported the existence of residues in water, soil, food and people.[20] This evidence also indicated the existence of the above-mentioned maladies resulting from pesticides.

As things stand, what can we say about Pakistan's pesticide import policy? We have a rough quantification of the benefits but none of the costs, beyond a documentation of the nature of the costs. Given this gap in information, we recommend caution. Manifold suggestions of the potentially serious social costs of pesticides, and a lack of hard evidence disputing them, suggest that the government's trade liberalization policies are uncalled for. This is particularly so since knowledge about alternatives, often included as part of an integrated pest management (IPM) strategy, are now widespread.[21] As early as 1987, the Office of Technical Assessment estimated that 'this approach could reduce pesticide use in the USA by 75 per cent on some crops, reduce pre-harvest losses by 50 per cent and result in significant pest control savings.'[22]

Fertilizer Trade Liberalization

Table 9.3 shows the import, domestic production and subsidization of fertilizers in Pakistan.[23]

Imports decreased from about two-fifths of total fertilizer consumption in 1990–1 to 35 per cent in 1993–4. At the same time, fertilizer subsidies have declined steadily from 10.5 per cent of total subsidies to just 0.9 per cent in the 1994–5 budget estimates.[24] All of this subsidy is now for imported fertilizers.

Benefits

Once again, the benefits are, in principle, easier to quantify than the costs. We have adopted a similar back-of-the-envelope approach to quantifying the benefits of fertilizer use as in the case of pesticides. Estimates were available from a total of 435 farm experiments conducted from 1980–1 to 1982–3 in Saleem et al. (1989, p. 29) of the incremental yield from the use of a combination of nitrogen, phosphorus and potassium fertilizers. Although these estimates are not recent, we assume that they provide an approximate indication of the effects of fertilizer on yields of the major crops.[25] These yield figures were converted into production equivalent data using a four-step method: First we used the above yield estimates to

Table 9.3 Import, production and subsidization of fertilizers in Pakistan*

Years	Imports	Domestic production	Subsidies		
			Amount	Domestic (%)	Imported (%)
1990–1	5911	8954	1386	15	85
1991–2	6367	8692	1224	22	78
1992–3	6438	11252	810	14	86
1993–4	8018	14888	805	0	100
1994–5	3954	12469	79	—	—

Sources: *Economic Survey 1994–95* (1995, pp. 74, 133, 167–8) and *Annual Fertilizer Review 1993–94* (1994, p. 48).
Notes: * = All figures are in millions of rupees if not otherwise indicated.
— = Not available.

calculate what the yield would be without fertilizers using the following equation:

$$YWOF = YWF/(1 + r)$$

Where

YWOF = Yield without fertilizer
YWF = Yield with fertilizer
r = Estimate of yield increase

Second, having estimated YWOF, we estimated what production would be without fertilizer use by multiplying this estimated yield by crop acreage under cultivation using average acreage data from 1990–1 to 1993–4. Third, the loss in production from not using fertilizer is the actual production minus the estimated production without fertilizer use. Fourth, this production loss was then multiplied by the average price for the corresponding time span to get the value of the aggregate production loss.[26] These calculations are detailed in Table 9.4.

As shown in Table 9.4, the benefits from the use of pesticides amount to approximately Rs 61 billion.

Table 9.4 Benefits of fertilizer use

Crop yield (Kg/ha)	Yield increase attributed to fertilizer use (%)	Average production without fertilizer	Average production with fertilizer	Average price per ton	Loss in value (mill. Rs)
Wheat	127	5934	15405	3288	31141
Rice	51	2129	3404	3588	4575
Cotton	97	699	1682	16206	15930
Sugarcane	106	15635	39335	422	10001
Total loss in value					61647

Notes: Column 2, based on Saleem et al. (1989, p. 28).
Column 3, as explained in text.
Columns 4 and 5, *Economic Survey 1994–95*, pp. 47, 60–1.
Column 6 = (Column 4 − Column 3) × Column 5.

Costs

Qutab (1994, p. 16) documents the costs of fertilizers to human health and the environment. Excess nitrate and nitrite in water and foods can result in methemoglobinemia in infants, are viewed as carcinogenic, and can result in respiratory illnesses.[27] Run-off can result in eutrophication via enhanced algae growth and hence hurt fish stocks and also humans via algae toxins. Soil erosion could result from volatilization and denitrification. Finally, nitrates contribute to soil-pan formation and nitrogeneous gasses can contribute to the green house effect.[28]

Fertilizer use in Pakistan has steadily increased from 20 kgs per hectare in 1971–2 to 91 kgs per hectare in 1991–2. This exceeds fertilizer use in India and interestingly the United States, where fertilizer use has declined and in 1991–2 was 71 kgs per hectare. Use is much more intensive in Europe and Japan with the Netherlands applying the most (599 kgs per hectare) in 1991–2.[29] Evidence on the negative environmental impact of fertilizers in Pakistan is once again very limited. Ali and Jabbar (1992, p. 92) tested soils in Faisalabad in a pilot study and concluded that nitrates are present in subsurface soils in considerable quantities.

As in the case of pesticides, alternatives have started being explored. In an ESCAP document (1993, p. 9), Integrated Plant Nutrient Systems (IPNS) is presented as a method which entails the judicious and efficient use of mineral fertilizers, organic matter, green manuring, biological nitrogen fixation and other inoculants. Further, minor modifications of existing practices could lead to a cut in fertilizer use by about one-third (p. 53).[30]

SUMMARY

Much of the literature on trade and the environment is concerned with the use of the environment as a protective device. Environmentalists see potential benefit in such a policy while neo-liberal economists argue that domestic measures, such as the polluter pay principle, is the better way of dealing with environmental externalities. The major reservation the latter have concerning the harmonization of environmental standards is that countries differ in their social and physical tolerance of pollution and should benefit from their comparative advantage. Much of this literature also concerns North–North trade, and so further arguments cited against 'environmental protectionism' are that environmental standards are quite similar in the North and, furthermore, that abatement costs are an insignificant portion of total costs anyway. The latter argument rules out Northern environmental protection against competing Southern products.

A priori reasoning and some evidence suggests that manufacturing export promotion could result in the use of cleaner technologies in the

South. However, evidence also suggests that primary export promotion could have environmentally detrimental effects such as deforestation and soil degradation. The Uruguay Round concessions to the South appear to be illusory. It appears that the North is continuing to give WTO-resistant direct support to its agriculture and is likely to continue flooding international markets with the cheap products of its intensive agriculture. This would leave the South with little choice but to pursue intensive agriculture.

Pakistan's trade policy is very much geared to the promotion of intensive agriculture even though it may have serious environmentally detrimental effects. Using rough calculations, we can quantify the potential low-end benefits from the use of pesticides and fertilizers. Even these are not negligible by any means (about Rs 100 billion). However, the list of the social costs to humans and the environment from the use of these chemicals and synthetic minerals seem endless. Given that the costs in Pakistan have not been quantified as yet, we recommend that as the first order of business. However, without awaiting results from these cost quantification exercises, we also recommend that the government extension service should start exploring and promoting strategies such as integrated pest management (IPM) and integrated plant nutrient systems (IPNS) to radically cut down use of these agricultural inputs. These alternatives are being demonstrated as not only environmentally friendly but also more productive.

In view of the above, Pakistan needs to reconsider its trade policy with regard to agricultural inputs. Succumbing to pressure from the Bretton Woods institutions, it fully discontinued subsidies to domestically produced fertilizers in 1994. It is still subsidizing fertilizer imports which are duty free. There is, similarly, an unusual recent history of a very liberal trade regime with regards to pesticides. In 1992 Pakistan allowed the import of generic pesticides to make them available at lower prices. While allegations of adulteration and long-term damage via the development of pest resistance resulted in the discontinuation of this policy in March 1995, a more dangerous form of liberalization has been adopted. In June 1995, as part of its new Trade Policy, Pakistan repealed the 1971 Agricultural Pesticide Ordinance, and is now allowing the import of pesticides that are not registered and in use in the exporting country.

Until results of cost quantification exercises become available, Pakistan should at a minimum reintroduce the repealed clause of the 1971 Agricultural Pesticide Ordinance. Further, it should stop subsidizing fertilizer imports. This would be entirely consistent with the neo-liberal economic philosophy underlying structural adjustment.

NOTES

1. This chapter was written by Shahrukh R. Khan as a paper for the SDPI Green Economics Conference, 12–14 Sept. 1995, and has been published in the conference proceedings SDPI (1997). Many thanks are due to Safiya Aftab for invaluable assistance.
2. GATT (1992, p. 20; 1994, p. 10).
3. See the survey article by Cropper and Oates (1992). This article reports evidence that pollution control measures have not exerted a systematic effect on trade and estimates abatement costs at between 1 and 1.5 per cent of total costs. These views are supported in another survey article by Dean (1992).
4. Braga (1992) makes this point with regard to trade policy and deforestation.
5. Environmental problems with cross-broader implications are not addressed in this chapter.
6. Leather tanneries are a case in point.
7. They cite as evidence German imports of fish meal and paper products from Chile which required treatment of effluent to ensure reduced bacteriological contamination of products (p. 160).
8. Wheeler and Martin (1992) present evidence of greater openness leading to cleaner technologies due to competitive pressures in the case of wood pulp production.
9. The report concludes (p. 25) that appropriate environmental management and production control is not in use, and various regulations and payment practices associated with the set-aside policy limit its environmental benefits.
10. Some of the negative environmental effects of intensive agriculture are increased chemical use, contamination of groundwater, eutrophication of surface water, loss of natural and semi-natural habitats and loss in bio-diversity from limiting the seed bank (pp. 9–10).
11. A good example of this is the agreement in 1994 between a Danish firm and Ravi Alkalis of Pakistan to import a plant into Pakistan that environmental regulation made redundant in Denmark.
12. Pesticides include insecticides, fungicides, herbicides/weedicides, acaricides, rodenticide, nematicides and fumigants.
13. See *Economic Survey, 1991–92*, section on Economic Reforms.
14. There are some selective exemptions, e.g. the rate of duty on weedicides was still 10 per cent at the time this chapter was revised.
15. Domestic production here refers for the most part to domestic formulation by multinational corporations based on the import of the active ingredient and the other inputs.
16. We were told by a Ministry of Food and Agriculture official that the fall in the total availability from 1991–2 to 1992–3 represented the adjustment to excess imports due to the introduction of the generic scheme. Imports subsequently picked up again, as is evident from the jump between 1992–3 and 1993–4.
17. Not all were persuaded by *Silent Spring* and the literature it spawned. Avery (1994, p. 89) argues that such argumentation roots from 'an almost mystical belief that manmade chemicals are more dangerous than 'natural' chemicals'. The latter, such as caffeic acid, limonene and hydrazines, are in various

foods and ingested in much larger quantities than pesticide residue. Also, natural chemicals test out to be as dangerous as the synthetic variety in rats. By implication, he argues, the human body is capable of handling the 'small carcinogenic insults' resulting from pest residues.

18. This is more likely to be the case for aerial spraying. Since 1981–2, the maximum aerial spraying has been 1.6 per cent of total cropped area in 1992–3. Ground plant protection in 1991–2, the latest year for which data were available, was about 20 per cent of total cropped area. *Agricultural Statistics of Pakistan 1993–94* (1995, pp. 154–8).
19. See Carr-Harris and Dudani (1992, pp. 10, 14).
20. Most dramatic is an account of 194 cases of endrin poisoning in Talagang, Attock. Seventy per cent of the cases were among minors between one and nine years and in all 19 people died. Carr-Harris and Dudani (1992, pp. 9–11) document pesticide poisoning cases in India and report that 3,029 known deaths occurred in 1990–1. Sandhu (1993, p. 22) cites a WHO study claiming about half a million people in the world are poisoned each year and about 5,000 of these people die.
21. Harte et al. (1991, pp. 132–7) review alternatives to the use of chemical pesticides.
22. Jensen (1987, p. 17).
23. The manufacture of urea in the country has suffered a severe loss since gas supply to the industry was diverted to producing electricity starting in January 1995 (Ikram Hoti, 'Fertilizer Industry Facing Crisis', *The News*, 3 Sept. 1995, p. 12.)
24. *Pakistan Economic Survey 1994–95*, Statistical section, p. 133.
25. Saleem et al. (1989, p. 23) claim that the four major crops and maize account for 90 per cent of fertilizer use.
26. For wheat and sugarcane, the average price was used, whereas for cotton and rice prices used were for the varieties Desi cotton lint and IRRI-6 respectively.
27. Conway and Pretty (1991, pp. 232–57) cite evidence indicating that the link between nitrate uptake and the incidence of various kinds of cancers is not unambiguous.
28. For details on the human and environmental effects of fertilizer use see Conway and Pretty (1991, pp. 157–271).
29. *Agricultural Statistics of Pakistan 1993–94* (1995, p. 142).
30. Also see Conway and Pretty (1991, pp. 581–612) for improved fertilizer application and alternatives.

REFERENCES

Ali, M. and A. Jabbar, 1992, *Effect of Pesticide and Fertilizer on Shallow Groundwater Quality*, Pakistan Council of Research in Water Resources, Islamabad.

Avery, T. D., 1994, 'Do Pesticides Accumulate in the Environment, Posing a Growing Risk of Cancer and Other Diseases?' *C. Q. Register*, 4, no. 4.

Birdsall, N. and D. Wheeler, 1992, 'Trade Policy and Industrial Pollution in Latin America: Where are the Pollution Havens?' in ed. Patrick Low, *International Trade and the Environment*, World Bank Discussion Papers no. 159.

Braga, C. A., 1992, 'Tropical Forests and Trade Policy: The Cases of Indonesia and Brazil', in ed. Patrick Low, *International Trade and the Environment*, World Bank Discussion Papers no. 159.

Carr-Harris, J. and A. T. Dudani, 1992, *Agriculture and People: Eco-Health Hazards of Chemical Based Agriculture and Proposed Techniques for Sustainable Farming* (New Delhi: South-South Solidarity).

Carson, R., 1962, *Silent Spring* (Boston: Houghton Mifflin).

Colburn, T., 1994, 'Do Pesticides Accumulate in the Environment, Posing a Growing Risk of Cancer and Other Diseases?' *C. Q. Register*, 4, no. 4.

Conway, G. R. and J. N. Pretty, 1991, *Unwelcome Harvest: Agriculture and Pollution* (London: Earthscan).

Cropper, M. L. and W. E. Oates, 1992, 'Environmental Economics: A Survey', *Journal of Economic Literature*, 30, no. 2.

Dean, J. M. , 1992, 'Trade and the Environment: A Survey of the Literature', in ed. Patrick Low, *International Trade and the Environment*, World Bank Discussion Papers no. 159.

ESCAP (Economic and Social Commission for Asia and the Pacific), 1993, 'Proceedings of the Regional FNDINAP Seminar on Fertilizers and the Environment', Chiang Mai, Thailand, Sept. 1992.

French, H. R., 1993, *Costly Trade-offs: Reconciling Trade and the Environment*, World Watch Paper 113, World Watch Institute, Washington, DC.

GATT, 1992, 'Trade and the Environment', in *GATT and International Trade 1990–91*, Vol. 1, Geneva.

GATT, 1994, 'Trade and the Environment', *News and Views from GATT*, Symposium on Trade Environment and Sustainable Development, TE 008.

Gianessi, L., 1993, 'Why Chemical Free Farming Won't Work', *Consumer Research*, 76, no. 12.

Government of Pakistan, *Economic Survey*, Economic Advisors Wing, Ministry of Finance, several years, Islamabad.

Government of Pakistan, 1994, *Annual Fertilizer Review 1993–94*, Planning and Development Division, National Fertilizer Development Centre, Islamabad.

Government of Pakistan, 1995, *Agricultural Statistics of Pakistan 1993–94*, Ministry of Food Agriculture and Livestock, Economic Wing, Islamabad.

Harte, J., C. Holdren, R. Schneider and C. Shirley, 1991, *Toxics A to Z: A Guide to Everyday Pollution Hazards* (Berkeley: University of California Press).

Jabbar, A. and S. Mallick, 1994, 'Pesticides and Environment Situation in Pakistan', Sustainable Development Policy Institute Working Paper Series no. 18.

Jensen, J. K., 1987, 'Sustainable Agricultural Crop Rotation through Integrated Pest Management', *Development Environment and Agriculture*, 5, no. 1.

Qutab, S. A., 1994, 'The Divergence Between Private and Environmental Costs and Benefits: A Case Study of Chemical and Organic Fertilizer in Pakistan', Tenth Annual General meeting of the Pakistan Society of Development Economists, Islamabad.

Saleem, M. T., J. G. Davide, H. Nabhan and A. Hamid, 1989, 'Soil Fertility and Fertilizer Use in Pakistan with Special Reference to Potash', in *Potassium and Fertilizer Use Efficiency* (Islamabad: National Fertilizer Development Centre).

Sandhu, G. R., 1993, *Sustainable Agriculture*, A Pakistan National Conservative Strategy Sector Paper, International Union for the Conservation of Nature, and Environment and Urban Affairs Division, Karachi.

SDPI, 1997, *Green Economics* (Islamabad: Sustainable Development Policy Institute).

Weir, D. and M. Schapiro, 1981, *Circle of Poison* (San Francisco: Institute of Food and Development Policy).

Wheeler, D. and P. Martin, 1992, 'Cross-Country Projection of Pollution Intensity: A Test on Technology Mix in Wood Pulp', World Bank, Washington, DC, mimeo.

World Wildlife Fund, 1994, 'Agriculture in the Uruguay Round: Implications for Sustainable Development in Developing Countries'.

10 Structural Adjustment and Food Security[1]

INTRODUCTION

It is difficult to think of a more important issue than ensuring an adequate diet for a population.[2] Food security is the subject of this chapter.[3] Our focus is on aggregate food security in that we investigate Pakistan's overall past, present and future capability of feeding its population. We also explore how national food availability translates into food security on an aggregate level and what bearing structural adjustment may have on food security.

Availability may be neither a necessary nor a sufficient condition for food security for all on a national level. This issue has been extensively written about and probably the most influential work is that of Dreze and Sen (1989). A comprehensive strategy for food security includes sustainable increase in production capacity, which is a necessary supply-side condition if a country cannot rely on imports.[4] However, on the demand side, two sufficient conditions need to be satisfied. First, all households must have access to food, but beyond that, have entitlements to jobs, decent wages and access to basic social services that ensure nutritional security. These include access to basic education, health and clean water supply and sanitation. Second, if due to the lack of sustainable livelihood, assets and other entitlements, households do not have adequate claim to healthy food, then a comprehensive public social security system needs to be in place.

Both the necessary and sufficient conditions for food security need to be investigated. The possible necessary condition that looks at the supply side is more straightforward, and a reasonably comprehensive picture can be drawn by relying on readily available secondary statistics. Such aggregative analysis can at places probe deeper, as we will indicate later, but the story will remain one-sided unless such analysis is complemented by micro studies exploring household entitlements, their change over time and household survival strategies to cope with income/food shortages.

In this chapter, we concentrate mainly on the aggregative supply-side issues. We discuss the case for and present evidence on food self-sufficiency in Pakistan. Then we explore aggregate food and nutrition security and investigate entitlements and the resulting capabilities. Finally, we look at the likely impact of structural adjustment on small-farmer cultivation and on capabilities. We end with a summary section.

FOOD SELF-SUFFICIENCY

When examining food security at the aggregate level, the area devoted to food crops and cash crops and how these numbers have changed over time would seem to be of primary interest. One could adopt a neo-liberal position suggesting that this is not an interesting issue from a food security perspective, since cash crop exports could pay for food imports, so the distribution of land by crop categories is irrelevant. This may be a dangerous position to assume for several reasons. First, most South Asian countries, including Pakistan, suffer from a chronic trade deficit. Second, given the deficit, food imports would have to compete with other imports and, in this struggle, even if the political urge to have adequate food at hand exists, it may lose out to more powerful political interests such as those backing military or industrial purchases. Third, even if it were sensible for one Southern country to follow its comparative advantage, it may not be sensible for them to do so as a collective. Northern countries like the US already dominate the food market and greater dominance would mean higher food prices for essential crops such as wheat.[5]

This is also one reason why market prices need not be considered sacrosanct. Even neo-liberal economists would concede, if challenged, that market prices would only bear paying attention to under competitive conditions. However, this qualification is seldom made in macro policy documents and sector studies that advocate relying on market prices. Beyond this, even if competitive conditions did hold, it is well known that market prices on the demand side are determined by those with purchasing power. Since, by definition, the poor have much less purchasing power, they have much less say in what gets produced. This would be a good reason to encourage the domestic production of food crops if prevailing market prices were not providing adequate incentives to induce self-sufficiency. However, as we explain later, food self-sufficiency in and of itself does not ensure food security.

We show in Table 10.1 the state of self-reliance in producing major food items in Pakistan.

Table 10.1 reports imports of wheat, pulses, edible oils and milk as a percentage of total domestic production. It is clear from Table 10.1 that in the first three of these four major food consumption items, Pakistan is relying more on imports in the more open trade regime period since 1987–8 compared to the earlier period. Milk is an exception, and the

Table 10.1 Major food imports as a percentage of total domestic production

Year	Wheat	Pulses	Edible oil	Milk
1980–1	0.2	—	188.3	14.82
1981–2	1.2	22.2	243.8	12.09
1982–3	—	17.5	232.7	21.10
1983–4[&]	—	6.0	349.8	4.40
1984–5	5.0	5.8	221.0	1.31
1985–6	13.3	8.5	243.0	1.20
1986–7	—	11.9	205.7	0.98
Average (1980–1/ 1986–7)	4.9	12.0	240.6	7.99
1987–8	—	11.5	288.0	0.86
1988–9	13.9	20.5	262.7	0.74
1989–90	11.1	7.4	284.8	0.51
1990–1	4.4	9.8	284.0	0.59
1991–2	11.3	16.1	215.2	0.52
1992–3	15.0	33.5	353.7	0.29
1993–4	8.7	46.1	356.8	0.39
Average (1987–8/ 1993–4)	10.7	20.7	292.2	0.56

Sources: *Agricultural Statistics of Pakistan*, various years (pp. 269–71 for 1993–4), *Annual Report*, State Bank, various years (for 1993–4, pp. 116, 118, 131).
Notes: [&] Major crop imports are estimates.
— Not specified in source or information not available. Averages are thus over years for which there were positive imports.

remarkable increase in domestic production of milk suggests that important reversals are possible. Thus in the 1980–1 to 1986–7 period, an average of 8 per cent of total milk consumed domestically was imported (mostly in powder form) and the 1987–8/1993–4 period the average was under 1 per cent.

Some justification is needed for the selection of these four items. As Table 10.2 shows, these four items account on average for about four-fifths of total caloric intake and nine-tenths of total protein intake for the lower income group in 1992–3.

One reason for the lack of self-reliance in the basic food items could be the lack of incentive for producing food crops. Before addressing that issue,

Table 10.2 Percentage daily expenditure, caloric and protein intake from major food items for the lower income group, 1992–3

Food items	E	C	P
Wheat	9.99	55.43	69.84
Edible oil	4.18	10.68	—
Milk	12.46	8.90	13.60
Pulses	1.92	4.37	7.22
Total	28.55	79.38	90.66

Sources: *Household Integrated Economic Survey 1992–93* (1996, p. 438).
Notes: E = Food expenditures
C = Caloric intake
P = Protein intake
The lower income group here accounts for 25.4 per cent of households. Actual food consumption was converted into caloric and protein intake using conversion factors in the food tables provided by the Nutrition Cell of the National Institute of Health.

in Table 10.3 and Table 10.4 we present the area devoted to and production of food crops relative to cash crops, and follow this with a discussion of the prevailing incentive structure and wheat policy in Pakistan. Table 10.3 shows the area devoted to various crop categories and how this has changed over time.

By 1993–4, these four categories covered 82 per cent of the total area under cultivation, which is a sizeable increase over 72 per cent in 1975–6. The area devoted to food crops (wheat, rice, maize, jowar, bajra and barley) in 1975–6 was almost four times the amount devoted to cash crops (mainly cotton, sugarcane and tobacco), and this ratio declined to about three to one in 1993–4. This occurred because the area devoted to food crops has gone up by 22 per cent over two decades, whereas the area devoted to cash crops increased by almost double that (47 per cent). The area devoted to pulses stayed virtually unchanged while the area under edible oilseeds declined by 10 per cent.[6] Table 10.4 shows production and the change over time by major crop categories.

Despite the smaller increase in land area, aggregate food production growth of about 63 per cent over two decades has matched that of the cash crop category of 75 per cent. Also, edible oilseed production increased by 128 per cent despite a decline in acreage devoted to it, while production of pulses declined by 22 per cent.

Table 10.3 Area under major crop categories as a percentage of total area under cultivation

Year	Food crops	Cash crops	Pulses	Edible oilseeds
1975–6	0.49	0.13	0.07	0.03
1976–7	0.51	0.14	0.08	0.03
Average	0.50	0.13	0.08	0.03
1977–8	0.51	0.19	0.08	0.02
1978–9	0.53	0.14	0.08	0.03
1979–80	0.53	0.14	0.08	0.02
1980–1	0.53	0.15	0.06	0.03
1981–2	0.54	0.16	0.06	0.02
1982–3	0.55	0.16	0.07	0.03
1983–4	0.55	0.16	0.06	0.02
1984–5	0.55	0.16	0.07	0.02
1985–6	0.54	0.15	0.07	0.02
1986–7	0.56	0.16	0.07	0.02
1987–8	0.53	0.17	0.06	0.02
Average	0.54	0.16	0.07	0.02
1988–9	0.56	0.17	0.07	0.02
1989–90	0.57	0.17	0.07	0.02
1990–1	0.57	0.17	0.07	0.02
1991–2	0.55	0.18	0.07	0.02
1992–3	0.57	0.18	0.07	0.02
1993–4	0.55	0.18	0.07	0.02
Average	0.56	0.17	0.07	0.02

Source: Computed from *Agricultural Statistics of Pakistan, 1993–94*, p. 2.
Notes: Food crops include wheat, rice, maize, jowar, bajra and barley.
Cash crops include sugarcane, cotton, tobacco, jute and sugarbeet.
Pulses include gram, mung, masoor, mash, mattar, other kharif and other rabi pulses.
Edible oilseeds include R&M seed, sesamum, groundnut, soybean, sunflower, safflower and cotton seed.
Area is given as percentage of total cultivable area.

INCENTIVE STRUCTURE AND WHEAT POLICY IN PAKISTAN

As indicated earlier, cropping patterns respond to economic incentives. A World Bank Study (1994, pp. 39–40) showed that domestic prices for wheat and rice have consistently been below world market prices. Also, the effective rate of protection for 1991–2 in selected districts was also negative for these crops. In fact sugarcane, probably due to the clout of

Table 10.4 Production under major crop categories (thousand tons)

	Food crops	Cash crops	Pulses	Edible oils
1975–6	12830	26392	784	1368
1976–7	13341	30420	844	1243
Average	13086	28406	814	1306
1977–8	12861	31054	812	1472
1978–9	14720	28203	736	1261
1979–80	15592	28644	510	1775
1980–1	16188	33595	526	1764
1981–2	16319	37758	488	1835
1982–3	17492	33630	694	2014
1983–4	15853	35041	710	1321
1984–5	16692	33340	726	2355
1985–6	18462	29287	797	2785
1986–7	17216	31635	791	2981
1987–8	17471	35024	556	3244
Average	16261	32474	668	2073
1988–9	19395	38818	642	3224
1989–90	19313	37360	768	3267
1990–1	19587	38021	732	3650
1991–2	20634	41458	706	4791
1992–3	21050	39934	547	3487
1993–4	20916	46138	614	3115
Average	20149	40288	668	3589

Source and *Notes*: As for Table 10.3.

sugar barons, is the only crop that has a positive effective rate of protection. Not surprisingly, the same study shows, citing domestic resource costs, that wheat and basmati rice (and coarse rice marginally so) are among the most efficient for Pakistan, and sugarcane the least (p. 12).

Wheat policy in Pakistan is critical given that it accounts for about 55 per cent of the caloric intake and 70 per cent of the protein intake of the bottom quartile of the population (see Table 10.2). There is also a market case to encourage the production of wheat by removing the negative protection. Higher producer prices help both the large and small farmers but hurt the poor (landless) rural and urban consumers. Even so, we would not necessarily advocate suppressing producer prices since this can discourage production, encourage smuggling, result in scarcity and provide a blanket subsidy to those who don't need it. Ryan and Khan (1993) have shown that the subsidy involved in keeping the release price to mills lower than the world price is absorbed by the millers as producer surplus or dissipated as excess capacity. It does not result, as intended, in lower consumer prices. Their recommendation, and that of others writing on wheat policy such as Ender, Wasay and Mahmood (1992), is that a more direct targeting of subsidy to those who need it would be more sensible.

Rationing is administratively expensive, and rife with leakages. In any case, it was not successful in Pakistan and hence discontinued in 1987. Other approaches to providing food entitlements, such as 'food for work', which involve an exchange of labour for food and hence maintain the dignity of the receiver, have been successfully used.[7]

Even if domestic production were adequate, it is obvious that, due to inequitable distribution, this would not necessarily result in food security for all. In the next section we show how, on an aggregate level, food production translates into per capita food availability and nutrition security.

FOOD AND NUTRITION SECURITY

To get a crude sense of the ability of a country to deliver food security, one can see how food production plus imports translate into per capita availability, and how this has changed over time. These numbers are reported in Table 10.5.

The *Agricultural Statistics of Pakistan* adopts a standard method for computing per capita availability. For example, for wheat they start with the production base, exclude exports, add imports, and deduct 10 per cent for seed, feed and wastage. Private sector availability is then added to offtake from government stocks.

Our concern in presenting availability statistics is to show how these have changed over time. For this purpose, computation method flaws cancel out and reasonable change patterns can be identified. Except for pulses, per capita availability of all food items has increased over time.[8]

There are three important issues to consider. First, can present availability levels be sustained? Second, how does availability translate into consumption patterns? And third, how do consumption patterns translate into average food, calorie and protein intake by population groupings? Appendix 10.2, Tables 10.9 and 10.10 address these issues.

In Appendix 10.1 we estimate a Cobb–Douglas agricultural production function to identify the factors critical to ensuring continued growth in per capita availability of both food grains as a whole and wheat in particular.

Table 10.5 Per capita availability of major foods (kgs per annum)

Year	Food[@] crops	Wheat	Pulses	Edible oil	Veg. oil	Fruit	Meat	Milk	Fish*
1971–2	175.6	—	11.2	—	30.7	26.2	—	—	—
1972–3	178.5	—	11.4	—	32.8	27.4	—	—	—
1973–4	181.9	—	12.3	—	33.7	28.4	—	—	
1974–5	175.3	—	10.2	—	31.9	29.4	—	—	1.02
1975–6	183.3	112.57	10.9	4.86	29.4	29.3	8.95	63.71	1.03
1976–7	173.5	113.03	11.4	5.54	27.3	28.8	9.19	55.47	1.14
Average	178.0	112.80	11.2	5.20	30.9	28.3	9.07	59.59	1.06
1977–8	170.2	119.59	10.6	5.70	27.2	27.3	9.38	56.33	—
1978–9	201.9	—	9.3	—	29.3	27.9	—	—	—
1979–80	185.7	—	6.3	—	27.3	29.3	—	—	1.82
1980–1	181.9	118.96	6.3	7.37	28.6	30.2	10.53	53.04	1.58
1981–2	182.0	113.77	5.6	7.77	28.4	34.0	10.83	52.09	1.99
1982–3	190.6	115.08	7.8	7.93	28.4	35.6	10.73	53.34	1.80
1983–4	161.9	116.91	7.7	7.92	28.4	35.6	11.01	52.24	1.60
1984–5	179.0	116.45	7.7	—	27.0	36.0	—	—	1.80
1985–6	195.1	114.00	8.2	—	28.9	37.0	—	—	1.80
1986–7	162.6	112.11	7.9	9.02	33.4	36.1	12.15	56.86	1.80
1987–8	162.4	105.83	5.4	11.20	34.1	34.5	12.67	57.84	1.80
Average	178.8	114.74	7.5	8.13	29.3	33.3	11.04	54.53	1.78
1988–9	193.5	127.38	6.0	9.97	33.8	35.4	13.12	58.89	1.80
1989–90	186.8	128.97	7.0	10.35	35.6	35.2	13.63	59.81	1.67
1990–1	170.1	115.18	6.4	9.99	33.7	34.8	13.90	60.93	1.70
1991–2	180.2	125.48	6.0	13.07	34.5	34.0	14.38	61.69	1.80
1992–3	189.4	127.90	4.5	12.50	34.6	34.0	15.48	62.63	1.82
1993–4	175.4	131.91	4.9	10.50	35.7	39.0	15.84	64.12	1.85
Average	182.4	126.14	5.8	11.06	34.7	35.4	14.39	61.35	1.77

Sources: Food availability is directly taken from various issues of *Agricultural Statistics of Pakistan* when available, and computed using this source and various issues of *Economic Surveys* otherwise.

Notes: — = not available.

@ = Food crops include wheat, rice, maize, jowar, bajra and barley.

* = The per capita data is for actual years rather than fiscal years. For example, 1.02 kgs of fish per capita was available during the year 1974.

Our results suggest that land is the most critical factor, followed by fertilizer, in delivering continued increases in production. Since increases in cultivated area are less and less likely to be forthcoming, Pakistan will find it increasingly difficult to deliver continued increases in per capita availability relying on this source.[9]

The numbers in Appendix 10.2, Tables 10.9 and 10.10 are very crude indicators of aggregate nutrition security since they make no allowance for age or gender. However, even if they did, caloric and protein intake is still a very crude approximation for nutrition security for many reasons, including different dietary needs across different individuals at a point in time and across time.[10] Even so, our intention was to get a sense of nutrition intake for the lower income group and of how this has changed over time. Being much below the recommended daily allowance by some acceptable standard would be cause for policy concern.

Given the qualifications above, the findings in Appendix 10.2, Tables 10.9 and 10.10 appear to be very encouraging. This is because they show that the caloric and protein intakes improved across the board between 1987–8 and 1992–3, and the most improvement was evident for the lowest income groups accounting for about the bottom 40 per cent of the population. Moreover, the protein and calorie intakes for these groups in 1992–3 is very close to or above the FAO recommended daily allowance of 2,187 calories and 53 gms.[11] Closer examination suggests that these results are suspect for two reasons. First, they suggest that caloric and protein intake does not vary positively with income. Second, the caloric and protein intake for the lowest income groups constituting 8.9 and 9.5 per cent of the population in 1987–8 and 1992–3 is second only to the intake of the top 10.5 and 13.4 per cent of the population. Finally, what these numbers suggest about capabilities is diametrically opposed to all the other indicators of what happened to entitlements and resulting capabilities for the poor between 1987–8 and 1992–3. We turn to this third point in the next section.

STRUCTURAL ADJUSTMENT, CAPABILITIES AND FOOD SECURITY

Capabilities and Survival Strategies

In Chapter 6, we show that the period of intensive structural adjustment is associated with (though not necessarily the cause of) a rise in unemployment, a decline in real wages and a sharp decline in average household income. One would expect a concentration of the poor in the clerical, sales, services, agricultural, production and related categories. In all of these, the unemployment rate rose dramatically between 1987–8 and 1993–4.[12] Accompanying the rise in unemployment is the fall in real wages for skilled and unskilled workers. In Karachi, real wages for unskilled workers declined by about 1 per cent in the 1980–1 to 1986–7 period, and about 25 per cent in the 1987–8 to 1994–5 period. Between 1980–1 and 1986–7 real wages for masons declined by 16.5 per cent and 7.0 per cent, while during the 1987–8 to 1994–5 period they declined by 18.0 and 19.2 per cent in Peshawar and Karachi respectively.

Given the rise in unemployment and the fall in real wages one would expect a fall in average monthly household real income. This has indeed been the case and real household income declined across the board between 1987–8 and 1992–3. For the lower two income groups, comprising about 40 per cent of the population, this decline was about 55 per cent and 42 per cent of the 1987–8 income.[13]

Remittances have been an important complement to household income for the poor in Pakistan. However, this is not a source households can continue to count on indefinitely. The average per capita real remittance dropped from Rs 510.7 in 1983 to Rs 201.6 in 1993.[14] All this information above suggests that over the intensive phase of structural adjustment for which we have information, entitlements and hence capabilities to ensure food security have eroded.

Adding to the erosion of household entitlements and capabilities is the higher inflation rate for food prices relative to non-food prices, as indicated in Table 10.6.

Some interesting findings are apparent from the table 10.6. First, inflation in the structural adjustment period (1988–95) is about three times more than the 1981–8 period for the food and non-food groups and over five times more for wheat. Second, over the whole period (1980–1/1994–5), there has been 26 per cent and 12 per cent higher inflation in food and wheat prices than in non-food prices respectively.

Most of the results reported above are on an aggregate level. So far, there has been a dearth of research investigating entitlements on a micro level. An exception is the research of Alderman and Garcia (1996) who analysed data of a micro survey of poverty, household food security and nutrition in five districts of rural Pakistan. They found that consumption risks are partially mitigated by sharing through family networks and income risks by diversification of income sources. Interestingly, they found that income fluctuations did not result in calorie intake fluctuations since consumption smoothing occurred via saving and credit. In three of the five districts they found female primary or post-primary education positively influenced food consumption. A simulation showed that education of mothers to the primary level would reduce wasting by about a half. While this is an interesting study with important findings, much more work still remains to be done.

Table 10.6 Inflation rates for food, non-food and wheat

Year	Food	Non-food	Wheat
1981–2	111.30	102.38	117.41
1982–3	116.90	106.80	122.55
1983–4	125.20	120.80	128.72
1984–5	135.43	123.25	141.04
1985–6	140.15	130.82	149.59
1986–7	146.69	137.46	148.09
1987–8	160.17	155.46	148.45
Increase (1981–8)	48.87	53.08	31.04
1988–9	175.77	170.54	162.81
1989–90	187.55	185.31	180.22
1990–1	204.50	207.15	205.23
1991–2	226.23	223.15	241.36
1992–3	249.32	231.66	254.36
1993–4	284.45	271.98	275.26
1994–5	337.39	311.93	323.90
Increase (1988–95)	161.62	141.39	161.09

Source: *Economic Survey 1995–96*, Statistical Appendix, pp. 146, 154.
Notes: Non-Food Index is a summation of indices of raw materials, fuel lighting and lubricants, man ufactures and building materials. 1980–1 is the base period.

Structural Adjustment, Agriculture and Food Security

Structural adjustments in agriculture are fairly recent. In due course, micro studies would be the most effective way to ascertain their impact on food security and the small farmer. However, it is possible to infer the likely impact of reforms that have been completed and those that are anticipated.[15] Some advocated reforms like agricultural tax, tenancy protection, targeting development expenditure to marginal farmers, and eliminating capital subsidies make eminent sense. However, other advocated and completed reforms may have negative short- and long-run effects on the poor and on small farmers.

The wheat procurement price was raised and eventually all output prices including wheat are to be liberalized. Tying wheat price increases to its border price might initiate a severe political reaction. As earlier indicated, a blanket subsidy is wasteful and not the first best food policy. However, in the absence of more directly addressing the food security needs of the poor, eliminating this subsidy will be very damaging given that the rural poor derive over half their calories and over two-thirds of their protein intake from wheat.[16]

There has been a general liberalization and privatization, and a move towards market-determined prices for both outputs and inputs. Edible oil export has been liberalized since 1991–2, and quotas removed in the distribution of edible oil to public and private mills. Ninety per cent of production is now controlled by the private sector. The fertilizer industry was completely liberalized with regard to import and marketing by 1994 and all subsidies eliminated by October 1995. An effort is underway to encourage the participation of the private sector in the seed industry and to encourage certification and patent protection for seed varieties. All directed credit is to be eliminated along with the subsidy on electricity. The process of decentralizing irrigation water supply has begun and provinces have started raising water rates. These have increased 40 per cent for Sind and 75 per cent for NWFP between 1992/3 and 1995/6. Further use of Water User Associations and a market in water rights is being encouraged and is on the agenda. Farmer extension is to be streamlined, cut back, and directed towards farming systems and the larger farmers on a commercial basis.

This deregulation, liberalization and privatization, and the market determined prices for outputs and inputs are in keeping with neo-liberal philosophy, and not necessarily bad. However, the implicit assumption is that of the existence of a free market with no dominance of multinationals in the input markets of fertilizers, insecticides and seed, and that there is no dominance by large farmers in drawing inputs such as credit and water. Both these assumptions seem heroic. Evidence of the dominance of multinationals was pointed to earlier in note 5. Credit allocation provides an example of the domestic dominance of large farmers in input access. The Agricultural Development Bank of Pakistan credit, drawn by the smallest farm size category (< 12.5 acres), decreased from 41.2 per cent in 1987–8 to 16.5 per cent in 1993–4, while that drawn by the largest farm size category (> 100 acres) increased over the same period from 4.6 to 29.5 per cent, even though small farmers (< 10 acres) represent 93 per cent of total farms (see Table 10.7 for the size distribution of farms).[17]

The issue of concern here is the likely impact of structural adjustment on the ability of small farmers to survive the liberalization drive. Their marginalization would accentuate a concentration in land ownership.

Table 10.7 Change in land ownership and cultivated area by farm size

Farm size (acres)	1980		1990	
	% of farms	% of cult. area	% of farms	% of cult. area
<5	74	38	81	43
5–10	17	26	12	23
10–20	6	17	5	15
20–60	3	16	2	12
>60	—	3	—	7

Sources: *Economic Survey 1992–93*, Statistical Supplement, p. 77 for the 1980 numbers, and *Economic Survey 1995–96*, Statistical Appendix, p. 53 for the 1990 numbers.
Note: 1 acre = 0.4047 hectares.

There are some signs that this is happening.[18] Table 10.7 presents the size distribution of farm holdings and this highlights the same point.

Several points are noteworthy. First, due to inheritance laws, an increasingly larger area is being cultivated by the smallest farm category of less than five acres. While about three-fifths of all farms fit into this very small farm category in 1980, over four-fifths of all farms fit into this category in 1990. There is a corresponding increase in the total area cultivated. Second, while small farms in 1990 accounted for 81 per cent of all farms, they cultivated only 43 per cent of the total land. Third, perhaps due to the corporatization of agriculture accompanying structural adjustment, large farms accounted for a negligible number of total farms in both 1980 and 1990, but the area they cultivated more than doubled from 3 to 7 per cent. Finally, it is evident from Table 10.7 that the middle farm size categories are thinning out and land concentration is increasing.

Given the growing numbers of small farmers in Pakistani agriculture evident from Table 10.7, there is an urgent need for micro farm profit studies to explore how small farmers are faring now compared to a 1987–8 benchmark and what the implications are for rural food security. The 1996 *Pakistan Household Integrated Survey* and the planned *Household Integrated Economic Surveys* should provide researchers with the information needed, and this could be complemented with micro case studies.

Most major World Bank reports now address poverty, gender and the environment when relevant. It is not clear how much energy will actually be put into such reforms, since they are much harder to attain than price liberalization and privatization. For example, while the World Bank rural poverty strategy recommends removing capital subsidies, the last government (1993–6) had an extensive 'yellow tractor scheme' underway. While development expenditures are recommended to be directed to the poor, these are hijacked by the people's representatives even under the Social Action Plan. While participatory development based on community organizations is recommended, such organizations are increasingly being viewed as a political threat and are being served notices and shut down. While enforcing tenancy protection is recommended, all assemblies are dominated by the large landlords. Thus the poverty policy is not really a policy other than saying the 'right things' that under current political conditions have little chance of getting implemented without serious arm-twisting.

The environment policy is similarly ineffectual. There is the usual mention of the participatory organizations which are now the convenient panacea for all woes. Pricing water at cost is recommended without mention or concern about the likely regressive impact. Incentives for integrated pest management and pesticide regulation are good, but the government liberalized pesticide imports in 1995.[19] The recommendation for phasing out sapling subsidies, to encourage private sector participation in the sapling industry, is puzzling, since Pakistan has a forest cover of less than 5 per cent. While better management of the subsidy could be urged, its elimination seems as ideologically driven as the other recommendations.

SUMMARY AND CONCLUSION

Our objective in this chapter was primarily to focus on the supply side and investigate Pakistan's ability to deliver food security, as well as how structural adjustment is likely to affect such capability. Of course, even if Pakistan were able to deliver food security that does not mean it is doing so or will do so. What needs to be done to ensure food security has been well articulated by many, including the UNDP's (1994) *Agenda for Food-Secure Asia-Pacific Region by 2010* and the 'Report of the Regional NGO Consultation for Asia and the Pacific on the World Food Summit' (1996). Our focus is more limited and restricted to Pakistan's supply-side strengths and shortcoming. On an aggregate level, we explore issues of nutritional security, entitlements and resulting capabilities by income group, and the association of structural adjustment with food capabilities and its likely impact on the small farmer.

We make a case for self-sufficiency in food production and show that over the period of the liberal trade regime that structural adjustment has ushered in, Pakistan has started relying more on imports for wheat, edible oils and pulses (milk is an exception). These four food items accounted on average for about four-fifths and nine-tenths of total caloric and protein intake for the lower income group in 1992–3. Wheat by itself accounts for about 55 per cent of the caloric intake and 70 per cent of protein intake, and is thus central to food policy in Pakistan.

The area committed to food crops has increased over two decades (mid-seventies to mid-nineties) by 22 per cent, and that devoted to cash crops has increased by over double that (47 per cent). However, the increase in production of food crops of 63 per cent has lagged less behind that of cash crops of 75 per cent. The economic incentives in terms of the effective rate of protection favour sugarcane, while the domestic resource costs indicate that wheat and cotton have a comparative advantage. Confronting the sugar barons to rationalize the incentive structure will not be easy, but is necessary.

The increase in food production has translated into a steady increase in the per capita availability of most food crops including wheat. This is an encouraging finding, as is the increase between 1987–8 and 1992–3 in the caloric and protein intake for all including the lower income group. However, the latter finding may be suspect because this and other research shows that capabilities over the structural adjustment period have deteriorated. There has been a major decline in real wages for skilled and unskilled labour, a more rapid increase in food prices relative to non-food prices, a decline in average household income and an increase in unemployment. Furthermore, remittances that where an important addition to household income have declined sharply in real per capita terms from their peak in 1983.

The liberalization and deregularization policies of structural adjustment may also make coping harder for the small farmer and, as small farmers are marginalized, result in an increasing concentration of land holdings. There is already evidence of an increasing concentration of land holdings over the 1980s. Policies of liberalizing the prices of inputs and outputs are well underway, the seed sector is to be privatized with certification and patent protection provided, a market created in water rights, and credit allocation discontinued. One effect may have been the decline in state and commercial credit allocations to small farmers. In view of the decline in capabilities and the liberalized macroeconomic environment, it is clear that micro case studies to ascertain the change in household food security and survival strategies and the profitability of small farmer agriculture are now essential. This is particularly the case since about four-fifths of the farms in 1990 were less than five acres. It also appears that the neo-liberal prescriptions for agriculture are not based on serious thinking about what is politically possible and necessary for food security.

NOTES

1. This chapter was initially prepared by Shahrukh R. Khan with the assistance of Sajid Kazmi and Zahid Ahmed for presentation at a South Asian Consultation in Delhi (1–2 Aug. 1996) preparatory to the World Food Summit. It was revised and subsequently presented in an international seminar on Newer Sources of National Insecurity in South Asia, Paro, Bhutan, 7–11 Nov. 1996, organized by RCSS, Sri Lanka.
2. The Report of the Regional NGO consultation for Asia and the Pacific on the World Food Summit (1996) refers to food as 'a human right that supersedes property rights, free trade and the dictates of the domestic market'.
3. Food security has been defined in many related ways. The World Nutrition Declaration at the International Conference on Nutrition (1992) (as cited in UNDP, 1994) defined it as 'access by all people at all times to the food needed for a healthy life'. Thus food would only include what is nutritious and safe.
4. UNDP (1994), Alderman and Garcia (1993).
5. According to Dawkins (1996), fewer than five companies control 90 per cent of the export market for wheat, corn, coffee, tea, pineapples, cotton, tobacco, jute and forest products. Multinational companies are also the force behind the move to protect their perceived intellectual property rights, which is viewed as a threat to bio-diversity and food security. See Shiva (1996).
6. *Agricultural Statistics of Pakistan 1993–94*, p. 2.
7. Dreze and Sen (1989) point out why the issue of food pricing is more complex than it appears, and also various approaches, with empirical documentation, to attaining food security.
8. Wheat stocks in Pakistan have declined sharply from a peak of 2,525 thousand tons in 1987–8 to 350 thousand tons in 1994–5 (*Economic Survey 1995–6*, Statistical Appendix, p. 62). According to information in the *Household Income and Expenditure Survey 1990–91*, we computed the per capita annual consumption of wheat in 1990–1 to be 121.2 kgs. Stocks available in 1994–5 were sufficient to meet a whole year's need of 2.89 million people. This seems like a comforting statistic but stocks, looked at another way, were adequate to meet only about 8.3 days' requirement for the whole population. To get more perspective on Pakistan's wheat stocks, one should consider that an estimated 0.65 million tonnes of wheat annually find their way from Pakistan to Afghanistan. Thus while the 0.35 million 1994–5 stocks seems adequate to contend with a localized crisis, they appear precipitously low to cope with a national crisis such as a wheat shortage, real or contrived, or a famine that might result from it.

9. The data suggest that land availability may well have peaked (*Economic Survey 1996–97*, Statistical Supplement, p. 49). This problem is compounded by serious water-logging, salinity and soil erosion.
10. See Dreze and Sen (1989, p. 37) for a discussion and references.
11. National Institute of Health (1988, p. 103).
12. Chapter 6, Table 6.3.
13. Ibid., Table 6.1.
14. Data for these calculations is taken from the World Bank *World Tables*.
15. ADB (1996, pp. 34–9) and World Bank (1994, pp. ix–xii) .
16. An extensive report on social safety nets and social networks by Beall et al. indicates that the delivery capacity to directly address the food security needs of the poor in Pakistan does not exist at the moment.
17. *Agricultural Statistics 1993–94*, p. 168. Note that since large farmers may often use small farmers for syphoning loans to themselves, the inequality in credit access is understated. The same source shows that there was a similar decline of credit drawn by small farmers from commercial banks over this period, but in 1993–4 small farmers still drew 60 per cent of the commercially available credit while the large farmers drew 9 per cent (p. 177).
18. M. H. Khan (fourth coming, Table 9) calculated, using the findings of the 1980 and 1990 Censuses of Agriculture, that the gini coefficient increased from 0.53 to 0.57 per cent.
19. See Chapter 9 below on pesticide import liberalization, and the concomitant negative impact of enhanced pesticide use on the environment.

REFERENCES

Asian Development Bank, 1996, 'Program Completion Report on the Agriculture Program Loan', mimeo.

Alderman, H. and M. Garcia, 1996, 'Poverty, Household Food Security and Nutrition in Rural Pakistan', Research Report no. 96, International Food Policy Research Institute, Washington, DC.

Beall, J., N. Kanji, F. Faruqi, C. M. Hussain and M. Mirani, n.d., 'Social Safety Nets and Social Networks: Their Role in Poverty Alleviation in Pakistan', World Bank, UCL-DPU, Washington, DC, mimeo.

Dawkins, K., 1996, 'US Agricultural Policy and the Uruguay Round', paper presented at a conference titled Globalization, Food Security and Sustainable Agriculture, New Delhi, 30–1 July.

Dreze, Jean and A. K. Sen, 1989, *Hunger and Public Action* (Oxford: Clarendon Press).

Ender, G., A. Wassy and A. Mahmood, 1992, 'Wheat Price Policies in Pakistan: Should There be a Subsidy?' *Pakistan Development Review*, 31, no. 4, pp. 1157–71.

Government of Pakistan, Economic Advisors Wing, Ministry of Finance, *Economic Survey*, various issues, Islamabad.

Government of Pakistan, Ministry of Food, Agriculture and Livestock, *Agricultural Statistics of Pakistan*, various issues, Islamabad.

Government of Pakistan, 1988, *National Nutrition Survey 1985–87*, Nutrition Division, National Institute of Health, Islamabad.
Government of Pakistan, State Bank of Pakistan, *Annual Report*, various issues, Karachi.
Khan, M. H., 1994, 'The Structural Adjustment Process and Agricultural Change in Pakistan in the 1980s and 1990s', paper presented at the Tenth Annual General Meeting of the Pakistan Society of Development Economics, Pakistan Institute of Development Economics, Islamabad.
Khan, M. H., forthcoming, 'Agricultural Development and Changes in the Land Tenure and Land Revenue System in Pakistan', in ed. S. R. Khan, *Fifty Years of Pakistan's Economy* (Karachi: Oxford University Press).
'Report of the Regional NGO Consultation for Asia and the Pacific on the World Food Summit', 1996, Bankok, Thailand, 29–30 April, mimeo.
Ryan, J. and S. R. Khan, 1993, 'The Impact of GOP's Wheat Pricing Policy on Flour Prices', *Pakistan Development Review*, 32, no. 4, pp. 823–32.
Shiva, V., 1996, *Future of Our Seeds, Future of Our Farmers: Agricultural Biodiversity, Intellectual Property Rights and Farmer's Rights* (New Delhi: Research Foundation for Science, Technology and Natural Resource Policy).
UNDP, 1994, 'Agenda for a Food Secure Asia-Pacific Region by 2010 AD', UNDP / RAS / 060, New York.
World Bank, 1994, 'A Strategy for Sustainable Agricultural Growth', Agricultural Operation Division, South Asia Region, Islamabad.

Appendix 10.1

The question we wanted to explore is Pakistan's continued ability to deliver increases in per capita availability at the rate it has been doing so in the past. Our expectation was that water and land would prove to be binding constraints. The results reported in Table 10.8 based on time series data from 1959–60 to 1995–6, suggest that this is the case for land.

Table 10.8 Cobb–Douglas agricultural productions functions

	Total food grain	Wheat
Constant	5.1195*	3.3264*
	(7.01)	(2.80)
Cultivated area	0.6834*	0.8297***
	(2.91)	(0.080)
Credit disbursed[@]	−0.0513***	−0.0632
	(1.76)	(1.50)
Tractors	0.0095	0.0015
	(0.38)	(0.04)
Fertilizer off-take	0.2939*	0.3033*
	(5.08)	(4.87)
Water availability	0.1104	0.3372
	(0.59)	(1.16)
R-bar-square	0.98	0.97
F-Stat	312.29*	167.39*
DW	1.86	2.12
n	29	29

Source: All data were taken from *Economic Survey 1995–96*, Statistical Supplement, pp. 43–4.
Notes: Several variables were non-stationary and so we performed the Eagle–Granger unit-root test on the residuals to establish if the equations were cointegrated. On the bases of this test, but not the augmented Eagle–Granger test, both equations are found to be cointegrated.
All variables are in log form so that the coefficients are elasticities.
* = Significant at least at the 1 per cent level.
*** = Significant at least at the 10 per cent level.
[@] = Measured in real terms.

Appendix 10.2

Table 10.9 Daily per capita caloric intake by income group

	I		II		III		IV		V	
	1987–8	1992–3	1987–8	1992–3	1987–8	1992–3	1987–8	1992–3	1987–8	1992–3
Cereals	1433.01	1359.46	1369.81	1357.17	1372.11	1318.09	1338.78	1349.12	1323.84	1353.72
Pulses	64.65	108.52	61.19	81.97	57.72	70.42	61.19	75.04	64.65	76.19
Milk and Milk Prod.	142.20	195.39	155.89	174.49	175.64	185.39	201.45	219.88	221.20	251.48
Edible Oils	198.00	225.00	204.00	243.00	186.00	291.00	201.00	267.00	219.00	273.00
Meat and Fish	16.21	24.32	20.77	24.83	24.83	23.81	32.43	28.37	45.09	43.07
Poultry	0.73	1.82	1.82	1.82	1.45	1.82	2.91	2.54	4.72	5.45
Fruits	4.81	7.70	5.97	10.59	6.35	10.01	8.47	13.67	12.51	23.10
Vegetables	41.81	61.96	37.05	62.58	37.68	67.84	40.80	65.59	43.93	74.98
Condiments and Spices	18.79	3.21	16.04	3.21	14.21	3.21	13.75	3.21	13.29	3.21
Gur and Sugar	152.30	238.21	149.69	197.85	152.30	212.17	165.31	167.92	180.93	182.23
Total	2072.51	2225.51	2022.23	2157.51	2028.29	2183.76	2066.09	2192.34	2129.16	2280.43

Source: *Household Income and Expenditure Survey 1987–88*, p. 399, *Household Integrated Economic Survey 1992–93*, p. 438.
Notes: The income groups across the two years respectively represent 8.9, 36.7, 20.5, 23.4, 10.5 per cent and 9.5, 31.9, 23.1, 22.1 and 13.4 per cent of the population. Actual food consumption was converted into caloric intake using conversion factors in the food tables provided by the Nutrition Cell of the National Institute of Health, Islamabad.

Table 10.10 Daily per capita protein intake by income group (gms)

	I		II		III		IV		V	
	1987–8	1992–3	1987–8	1992–3	1987–8	1992–3	1987–8	1992–3	1987–8	1992–3
Cereals	40.44	38.37	38.66	38.30	38.78	37.20	37.79	38.08	37.36	38.21
Pulses	4.39	7.37	4.16	5.57	3.92	4.78	4.16	5.10	4.39	5.18
Milk and Milk Prod.	6.26	8.61	6.87	7.82	7.74	8.17	8.37	9.69	9.74	11.07
Edible Oils	—	—	—	—	—	—	—	—	—	—
Meat and Fish	2.67	4.00	3.42	4.08	4.08	3.92	5.33	4.67	7.42	7.08
Poultry	0.17	0.43	0.43	0.43	0.35	0.43	0.59	0.60	1.12	1.30
Fruits	0.07	0.10	0.08	0.14	0.09	0.44	0.11	0.19	0.17	0.31
Vegetables	1.70	2.53	1.51	2.55	1.54	2.76	1.56	2.67	1.79	3.05
Condiments and Spices	1.29	0.22	1.10	0.22	0.97	0.22	0.94	0.22	0.91	0.22
Gur and Sugar	0.01	0.15	0.10	0.13	0.10	0.14	0.11	0.11	0.12	0.12
Total	57.09	61.78	56.33	59.24	57.52	58.06	59.56	61.33	63.02	66.46

Source: *Household Income and Expenditure Survey 1987–88*, p. 399, *Household Integrated Economic Survey 1992–93*, p. 438.

Notes: The income groups across the two years respectively represent 8.9, 36.7, 20.5, 23.4, 10.5 per cent, and 9.5, 31.9, 23.1, 22.1 and 13.4 percent of the population. Actual food consumption was converted into protein intake using conversion factors in the food tables provided by the Nutrition Cell of the National Institute of Health, Islamabad.

Summary and Conclusion

The main purpose of this book is to rely on evidence and to go beyond rhetoric, ideology and anecdotes in assessing structural adjustment (SA) in Pakistan. In a much-cited article, Huntington (1993, p. 39) stated that 'Through the IMF and other international economic institutions, the West promotes its economic interests and imposes on other nations the economic policies it thinks appropriate.' Such statements are enough to make even the most level headed of Third World thinkers paranoid.

Why would industrialized countries want to enforce structural adjustment (SA) policies on poor countries? The worst possible motive is that for various economic reasons they want to see poor countries shaped in their own image. The best motive is that they are persuaded that SA is in the interest of the economies they lend to. We assume no *a priori* position on this issue for Pakistan and rely instead on the evidence.

However, looking at the evidence is not as straightforward as it sounds since there can be different perspectives from which it could be viewed. As prudent bankers, the IMF and the World Bank worry about repayments, and so they naturally adopt a lender's perspective. Nevertheless, lenders and borrowers may have conflicting interests, and so it is important to assess structural adjustment from a national perspective also. Further, since SA policies vary in their impact of different social groups, it is important to delve deeper and identify who gains and who loses, and in what way, from such policies. We refer to the latter as a political economic perspective.

Much of the evidence cited in the context of structural adjustment has been of a cross-country nature. Country case studies, however, have now become more readily available. To date, the evidence has not conclusively demonstrated that countries that have tried to reform their economies according to IMF/World Bank-prompted structural adjustment prescriptions (in exchange for loans) have succeeded, judged either from the perspective of the donors or borrowers. There are some success stories and many failures.

Establishing success empirically is difficult, since often counter-factuals are needed but not available, i.e., what would have been the condition of the country without structural adjustment? Even when enough time has passed to assess reforms, it is difficult to isolate the impact of structural reforms from everything else going on in the economy. Failures sometimes stare one in the face in the form of the riots that have often followed structural adjustment programmes in the Third World.

Even so, SA and the neo-liberal paradigm that underlies it is now the dominant economics paradigm practised by developing countries and has been so since the early 1980s. The reasons for this probably include the endorsement of such economic reforms by the G-7 governments and hence its propagation by the IMF, the World Bank, as well as many Western bilateral aid agencies such as USAID. There is also predominant support for such a reform programme in academia as well as in prominent advisory or consulting bodies.

On most critical economic issues, SA-initiated reforms embody an internally consistent set of hypotheses. These can be viewed as the orthodoxy, since neo-liberal economic theory has been dominant for about two decades. In Part I of the book, we tested the neo-liberal hypotheses on various critical economic issues such as devaluation, financial sector reform, privatization, trade policy and industrialization. In Part II, we assessed the overall impact of structural adjustment on labour and the poor, as well as the gender, health, environmental and food security impact. While we adopt a national and political economic perspective when assessing SA reforms, we are completely open to accepting whatever results emerge. We summarize now the major findings reported in detail in the Chapters 1–10.

Chapter 1 has the overarching objectives of first, examining the terms on which Pakistan receives aid, and second, examining the impact of aid and debt on economic growth. There is little encouraging that can be said about how the terms on which Pakistan receives aid over time have changed. Concessional aid as a percentage of the total has declined, the average interest rate has increased, the maturity period has decreased and the grant element has decreased. Thus Pakistan's debt in absolute real terms, the debt/GDP ratio and the debt/export ratio have increased, particularly since 1988, when the more intensive phase of the structural adjustment period started. Given the changing terms under which Pakistan is receiving aid, there is every likelihood that the debt/GDP ratio will continue to rise. This is particularly the case since our research shows that aid has a negative (Granger) causal impact on GDP, and has a negative and significant impact on economic growth. The latter finding holds up when subjected to a test for robustness after controlling for supply-side shocks. We provide various reasons for the negative aid–growth association in a discussion at the end of Chapter 1.

Following Chapter 1, we test specific structural adjustment hypotheses at the sectoral level. In Chapter 2, we investigate the impact of devaluation, which is frequently recommended as part of structural adjustment programmes, on the balance of trade. Estimating export and import demand functions is the conventional method of evaluating the likely effect of a devaluation on the external balance. In Chapter 2, we address an important critique of the conventional method of estimating export demand functions and make a case for using real effective exchange rates rather than relative prices in the demand functions. We also demonstrate that high income elasticities in the conventional export demand functions need not be cause for concern. Using quarterly data, we find a modified version of a Marshall–Lerner condition barely satisfied for Pakistan, suggesting little or no positive effect on the external balance due to a devaluation. This finding is reinforced by estimating disaggregate export demand functions.

In Chapter 3, we explore the neo-liberal case for financial liberalization. This is premised on a positive association of real and financial saving, productivity and growth with the real term deposit rate. Such evidence has been presented by some researchers for Pakistan, which has embarked on a series of financial sector reforms including interest rate liberalization. On the one hand, using appropriate time series analysis, we reexamine the evidence, and find mild support at best for the neo-liberal hypotheses. On the other hand, a case is made on political economic grounds for avoiding or postponing interest rate liberalization. We do find support for privatization of commercial banks based on efficiency gains post-privatization, and also based on the better performance of privatized banks compared to the nationalized banks.

In Chapter 4, we compare the pre- and post-privatization experience of five firms in three industries in which employee buy-outs and conventional privatization occurred. We do not find evidence to support the hypothesis that labour productivity is higher in employee-owned firms. We find that private sector firms are more successful than employee buy-outs in raising profit rates. In general, private ownership seems to lead to less labour retrenchment, although in one case the complete replacement of the labour force lends credence to employee concerns about privatization and job insecurity.

In Chapter 5, we explore whether trade liberalization has ushered in the large-scale de-industrialization that is feared by some to follow in its wake and whether it has been successful in enhancing export promotion. We rely on several different kinds of evidence and find that the evidence with regards to industrial and export growth in the structural adjustment period is mixed. The performance of the consumer goods sector in promoting exports and displacing imports has been robust. Other evidence also points to an improvement in export performance, although Pakistan is still not meeting its export potential or matching the mean performance of even low income countries. However, there is evidence of imports displacing domestic production in the intermediate goods sector, average annual growth in industry declining, and industry growth falling further behind potential in the period of economic liberalization compared to the earlier period. We are not able to establish, possibly due to the paucity of time series observations, that either industry or exports generated positive externalities for or used resources more productively than the rest of the economy.

In Chapter 6, we cite evidence regarding the likely impact of IMF/World Bank policies on labour and the poor in Pakistan. Our findings show that since the 1988 bout of structural adjustment, public sector employment has decreased while wages have been frozen. Also, overall unemployment in occupations with a high incidence of the poor has dramatically increased and real wages of skilled and unskilled labour has sharply declined. In addition, subsidies that were critical to the consumption pattern of the poor have been cut while the burden of indirect taxes on the poorest income group has increased. Not surprisingly, there has been an increase in poverty and inequality, particularly in the rural areas.

In Chapter 7, we review the change in the socio-economic condition of women during the intensive period of structural adjustment, and its effects on their roles as producers, as home managers and as mothers. In their role as producers, overall female labour force participation increased such that their share in the labour force virtually tripled. However, over this period there was a dramatic decline in female self-employment and a more dramatic rise in the female unemployment rate. In their role as home managers, women confronted a more than doubling of the sensitive price index and a cut in consumption subsidies as a per cent of the budget by about two-thirds. The price of wheat, from which the poor derive about 55 per cent of their caloric intake and about 70 per cent of their protein intake, also more than doubled. The numbers show that compared to 1987–8, education expenditure as a per cent of GNP has been constant while that of health has actually declined. This could have had an adverse impact on women in their role as mothers.

In Chapter 8, we show that government health expenditures as a percentage of GDP have declined in Pakistan, though not in absolute real terms, over the structural adjustment period. Progress over this period is evident on a number of health indicators, such as the infant, child and maternal mortality rates, as well as life expectancy. However, Pakistan still lags far behind the mean rates of low income and South Asian countries in all child survival statistics. In view of this, and since the evidence shows a significant and sizeable association of public sector health expenditures and the decline in infant mortality rates, there is little justification in halving public sector health expenditures as recommended by the World Bank.

In Chapter 9, we start with a survey of the issues on trade and the environment from a Southern perspective and with a focus on the available evidence. There is reason to believe, and a little evidence confirming, that manufacturing export promotion would result in the use of cleaner technologies than producing for a protected domestic market. Evidence suggests that primary export promotion may be environmentally detrimental. Much less has been written about the environmental impact of the import liberalization that is required to accompany export promotion. There is a danger that unregulated import liberalization may result in the dumping of second-hand dirty Northern machinery and hazardous agricultural inputs. We focus on the agriculture sector and show that Pakistan is pursuing a very open regime with regards to the import of pesticides and fertilizers. We conduct a suggestive cost-benefit exercise to highlight potential environmental costs and the relevant policy issues.

In Chapter 10, we explore issues of food security, entitlement and resulting capabilities on an aggregate level. The positive finding is that even though the area being devoted to cash crops is rising much more rapidly than the area devoted to food crops, the increase in food production is keeping pace with the increase in cash crop production. This appears to have translated into a steady increase in per capita availability in the important food crops and also in an average increase in caloric and protein intake for all income groups. However, we find that capabilities of the poor have eroded over the structural adjustment period, with real wages sharply falling, inflation in food prices exceeding non-food prices, unemployment rising, and average household income falling. We also explain how privatization, liberalization and deregulation in the agricultural sector may make coping more difficult for the small farmer.

Notwithstanding the findings regarding the adverse social impact of SA, the agenda of this book is not to build a case for completely rejecting neo-liberal economic reform. Instead, it is to build a case for eclecticism, pragmatism and social justice. With regard to the latter, detailed recommendations that endorse social sector investments, decentralization and community participation are presented in Chapters 6 and 7 of *Just Development* (1997).

REFERENCES

Banuri, T., S. R. Khan and M. Mahmood, eds, 1997, *Just Development: Protecting the Vulnerable and Promoting Growth* (Karachi: Oxford University Press).

Huntington, S. P., 1993, 'The Clash of Civilizations', *Foreign Affairs*, 72, no. 3, July–Aug.

Index